Religion and Nation in Modern Ukraine

Religion and Nation
in Modern Ukraine

Serhii Plokhy and Frank E. Sysyn

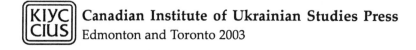
Canadian Institute of Ukrainian Studies Press
Edmonton and Toronto 2003

Canadian Institute of Ukrainian Studies Press

University of Alberta
Edmonton, Alberta
Canada T6G 2E8

University of Toronto
Toronto, Ontario
Canada M5S 2J5

National Library of Canada Cataloguing in Publication Data

Plokhy, Serhii, 1957-
    Religion and Nation in Modern Ukraine

Includes bibliographical references and index.
    ISBN 1-895571-45-6 (bound). — ISBN 1-895571-36-7 (pbk.)

1. Ukraine—Church history.
2. Orthodox Eastern Church—Ukraine—History.
3. Catholic Church—Byzantine rite, Ukrainian—History.
4. Nationalism—Ukraine—Religious aspects—Christianity.

I. Sysyn, Frank E. II. Title.
BR937.U4P56 2001   274.77   C2001-930215-0

Publication of this book was made possible by the generosity of
The Skop Family, in memory of Konstantyn Hordienko,
The Canadian Foundation for Ukrainian Studies,
The Ukrainian Self-Reliance League of Edmonton, and
The SUS Foundation of Canada.

Printed in Canada.

To our parents
Mykola and Lidiia Plokhii,
and Frank and Hattie Sysyn

Table of Contents

List of Acronyms

CARC	Council for the Affairs of Religious Cults
CAROC	Council for the Affairs of the Russian Orthodox Church
CPU	Communist Party of Ukraine
CRA	Council for Religious Affairs
KGB	Committee for State Security (Komitet gosudarstvennoi bezopasnosti)
NKGB	People's Commissariat for State Security (Narodnyi komissariat gosudarstvennoi bezopasnosti)
ROC	Russian Orthodox Church
SSR	Soviet Socialist Republic
UAOC	Ukrainian Autocephalous Orthodox Church
UGCC	Ukrainian Greek Catholic Church
UGOC	Ukrainian Greek Orthodox Church
UNR	Ukrainian People's Republic (Ukraïns'ka Narodnia Respublika)
UOC	Ukrainian Orthodox Church
UOC-KP	Ukrainian Orthodox Church-Kyiv Patriarchate
UOC-MP	Ukrainian Orthodox Church-Moscow Patriarchate
USSR	Union of Soviet Socialist Republics
ZUNR	Western Ukrainian People's Republic (Zakhidn'o-Ukraïns'ka Narodnia Respublika)

Introduction

The last two decades of the twentieth century redirected scholars' attention to the topics of nation and religion in the contemporary world, which had received little focus in the 1960s and 1970s. The re-emergence of national issues and movements in the developed world—from Quebec through the Celtic fringe of Britain to the German question—occurred even before globalization and internationalization undermined the sovereignty of the state and its role in determining identity, thereby increasing the importance of both supra-state identities and sub-state loyalties. At the same time, the high visibility of John Paul II and his assertion of a worldview that challenged both the Marxist East and the capitalist, secular West also stimulated growing attention to religion. Increasingly, religious loyalties were looked to as defining civilizations, providing alternative value systems to global capitalism, and mobilizing political challenges to the liberal secular establishment, above all in the United States.

By the 1960s, Sovietologists in the West had generally eschewed national questions. They saw these questions as resolved or at least managed in the Soviet system, and in a way they thus accepted Soviet ideology. In contrast to East European studies, which had traditionally focussed on the national question, Russian studies and its progeny, Soviet studies, followed the general lack of attention to nationality questions that has characterized much of the Russian intelligentsia's thinking. Therefore even questions of Russian identity, the relationship between Russia and the Soviet Union, and the evolution of the Russian national community were little examined by Soviet specialists. "Nationality studies" were marginalized and left largely in the hands of émigré scholars who had fled to the West from the Soviet Union. Thus, just as specialists in German studies were little prepared for the re-emergence of the German question, Soviet specialists in the West had problems integrating the national factor during the break-up of the USSR and the emergence of the new post-Soviet states.

Although most specialists were at least aware of the national question in a historical context, they were almost totally unprepared for dealing with the importance of religion in the former USSR at the end of the twentieth century. This should not be surprising.

After all, in the 1980s many Western political scientists found it difficult to deal with the question of religion during the Solidarity period in Poland, despite the manifest importance of the Catholic Church and the "Polish pope" in that country. The first focus of Sovietological studies of religion was the issue of Islam in Central Asia, though demography and the problems the Western powers have had with the Muslim world better explain this issue than the careful study of religion in the Soviet Union.

In some ways, the study of the national and religious questions in Ukraine was more advanced than it was for other areas of the former Soviet Union. A considerable body of literature on national and dissident issues in Ukraine was produced in the West, and, unlike in Russian studies, the national question was always assumed to be central to Ukrainian studies. Religious issues were dealt with partly because of the manifest importance of the Ukrainian Greek Catholic Church (UGCC) in pre-Soviet Galician political life and international religious affairs in the twentieth century. It was also fortuitous that the most important student of Soviet religious policies from the 1960s until the late 1990s, the late Bohdan R. Bociurkiw, focussed his attention on Ukraine.[1] Nevertheless, in Western scholarly literature Ukrainian studies and religious affairs in Ukraine did not receive the attention that their significance warranted.

For students of how state building, nation building, and religion interact, Ukraine constitutes one of the most important case studies at the dawn of the twenty-first century. With forty-nine million inhabitants, Ukraine is the second-most populous state to have emerged from the break-up of the former Soviet bloc. Until 1991 the thirty-seven million ethnic Ukrainians in Ukraine and eight million to ten million people of Ukrainian descent in the West and in the "eastern diaspora" made up the largest European people without a national state. With a population predominantly of Orthodox background, Ukraine contains one of the largest Orthodox communities in the world, surpassing Russia in the number of parishes—more than thirteen thousand. Alongside them are more than three thousand UGCC parishes organized in the world's largest Eastern Christian Church united with Rome.[2]

---

1. See, in particular, his magnum opus, *The Ukrainian Greek Catholic Church and the Soviet State (1939–1950)* (Edmonton and Toronto: Canadian Institute of Ukrainian Studies Press, 1996).

2. See A. Krindač, "Kirchenlandschaft Ukraine-Probleme, Kämpfe, Entwicklungen," *Osteuropa* 47, no. 10–11 (1997): 1067; and B. Salmon, "Die ukrainischen orthodoxen Kirchen, 1997," *Aktuelle Analysen: Bundesinstitut für ostwissenschaftliche und internationale Studien*, 10 August 1997. Krindač points

While the outside world focussed primarily on the dynamic political and ethno-cultural situation in Soviet Ukraine during the Gorbachev years, the religious situation underwent just as rapid a change. In the late 1980s Mikhail Gorbachev's policy of glasnost and perestroika permitted the freer exercise of religion and allowed the Russian Orthodox Church (ROC) in particular to rebuild its institutional base. Yet, between 1989 and 1992 the religious monopoly of the ROC over Eastern Christians in Ukraine was broken by the establishment of three Ukrainian Orthodox Churches—only one of which remained in the structure of the Moscow Patriarchate—and the re-emergence of the UGCC. The religious situation has both been influenced by, and had a considerable impact on, state-building processes and relations among national groups in independent Ukraine.

Many Ukrainian citizens assume that the Orthodox Church is intrinsically the state and national church in Ukraine and that the Orthodox situation is therefore quite different from that of other religious groups. This assumption is challenged in Galicia by the UGCC, which already had the characteristics of a unifying national institution there before the Second World War. At the root of these views are the long-term interrelations among state, nation, and church that extend back a thousand years to the conversion of Rus' to Christianity and, in some ways, earlier still to the first centuries of Christianity and the conversion of Constantine the Great. The three elements of the state-nation-church equation possess specific ongoing traditions that have evolved over the centuries. During the nineteenth and twentieth centuries their interrelations changed greatly owing to the onset of secularization, urbanization, and mass literacy, to the rise of nationalism, socialism, and atheism, and in twentieth-century Ukraine, to the prevalence of totalitarianism and terror.

The dynasties, empires, kingdoms, and republics of the past that are often grouped together under the category of states had very

---

out (pp. 1073–4) that up to 1991 the ROC had more parishes in Ukraine (5,000) than in Russia (3,500) and that in 1996 the Moscow Patriarchate still had almost as many communities in Ukraine (6,500) as in Russia (6,700), despite the establishment of two other Ukrainian Orthodox Churches with over 3,000 parishes. For more recent statistics on Ukrainian religious communities, see "Relihiini orhanizatsii v Ukraïni stanom na 1 sichnia 2000 roku," *Liudyna i svit*, 2000, no. 1: 26–33. As of 1 January 2001, there were 12,884 Orthodox communities in Ukraine, according to unpublished tables compiled by A. Zaiarniuk and Y. Komar. The UGCC, which has also been referred to as the Uniate Church, is known in the West as the Ukrainian Catholic Church.

different structures and functions. But they almost always paid great attention to religious affairs. The Ukrainian state that was established in 1991 can draw from a long tradition in which various political structures shaped religious and national life in Ukraine. In accepting Christianity from Constantinople, the polity and dynasty of Kyivan Rus' chose a religious and cultural tradition that shaped all of subsequent Ukrainian history. Since the age of the medieval Kyivan state and Principality of Galicia-Volhynia, there have been only relatively short periods that Ukrainian states or autonomous entities existed. Of these, the Kyiv Principality of the Grand Duchy of Lithuania and later the Cossack Hetmanate of the seventeenth and eighteenth centuries functioned with Orthodoxy as the state religion, while the Ukrainian national governments of 1917–1920 viewed the resolution of the ecclesiastical affiliation of their Orthodox believers as essential to the establishment of statehood. Although it was hostile to religion, even Soviet Ukraine in the 1920s, which had a quasi-state structure, pursued a differentiated policy toward the various Orthodox Churches of the period.

Just as important as examples for the new Ukrainian state and for explaining the religious situation in Ukraine are the non-Ukrainian states that ruled Ukraine in the past. From the seventeenth century, the Russian states of Muscovy and the Russian Empire and the Russian-dominated USSR controlled much of Ukrainian territory. The espousal of Orthodoxy as the state religion of these states until 1917 and, in a limited way, after Stalin's accommodation with the ROC during the Second World War had a tremendous impact on the religious development of Ukraine. Meanwhile, from the fourteenth to the eighteenth centuries, Catholic states—the Grand Duchy of Lithuania, the Kingdom of Poland, and the Polish-Lithuanian Commonwealth— controlled most of Ukrainian territory, while the Catholic Habsburgs greatly expanded their Ukrainian-populated lands in the late eighteenth century, adding Galicia and Bukovyna to Hungarian-ruled Transcarpathia. Roman Catholicism also functioned as the privileged church in the western Ukrainian territories that were part of interwar Poland, but not in those Ukrainian lands that became part of interwar Czechoslovakia and Romania. All of these states reshaped the religious map of Ukraine and influenced national relations.

Of the three elements in the state-nation-church equation, "nation" has posed the greatest difficulty in terms of definition and study. At times the English word is used as a synonym for "state" or to refer to the inhabitants of a sovereign political entity. The term has also been used to designate ethno-cultural communities that consider themselves historical collectivities, regardless of their political allegiance. As Anthony Smith and John Armstrong have shown, these ethno-national communities have long histories in Europe and have often served in modern times as the core of mobilized national communities either based on political entities or in conflict with them.[3] From pre-secular, often agrarian, peoples who conservatively maintained traditional dialects and customs, highly conscious national communities with standard literary languages have emerged. Many of the strongest and most enduring of such communities have professed confessions that, in a given context, have united them internally and differentiated them from other communities. Not all traditional ethno-national communities, however, have made the transition or retained most of their potential constituency.

In the Ukrainians' case, the evolution of a modern national community has been particularly difficult, in part because the linguistically close Russians and Poles have usually insisted that Ukrainians are part of their nations, and in modern times the Russian and Polish peoples have often been politically and socially dominant. Repressive state measures were used in the Russian Empire, interwar Poland, and the Soviet Union to halt or distort the development of a Ukrainian national community. In addition, the Soviet war against traditional peasant culture undermined the great potential pool of adherents of Ukrainian nationhood and the dissemination of Ukrainian spiritual culture. In a similar fashion, the Soviet state attacked Russian peasant culture, though most of Russia did not have to endure the Soviet-engineered genocidal famine of 1932–33. In addition, in the 1930s the Soviet political system began propagating the concept of a Russian-based proletarian culture and promoting the Russification of the urbanized peasantry in Ukraine.

Outside the Russian Empire, in nineteenth- and early twentieth-century Galicia, the dominant Poles also generally sought to retard Ukrainian cultural and national development, as did the Hungarian ruling groups in Transcarpathia. In contrast, the Habsburg authorities and the institutions of Cisleithania provided at least a neutral and, at times, positive environment for Ukrainian nation building. Of the successor states that came into being after the First

3. See Anthony D. Smith, *The Ethnic Origins of Nations* (Oxford, 1986); and John Armstrong, *Nations before Nationalism* (Chapel Hill, 1982).

World War, the interwar Polish and Romanian states carried on discriminatory and assimilatory policies against their Ukrainian population. Only interwar Czechoslovakia pursued a more even-handed policy.

In the nineteenth and twentieth centuries, the shared ROC and liturgical Slavonic language of the Russians and most Ukrainians also retarded the evolution of a Ukrainian national community. The ROC functioned as a vehicle of Russification and a propagator of "pan-Russian" Orthodox or Pan-Slavic views. In contrast, the Greek Catholic Church in Habsburg-ruled Galicia was a virtually exclusive "Ruthenian" institution that differentiated the Galician Ukrainians from the Roman Catholic Poles. In the nineteenth and early twentieth centuries Polish political and Roman Catholic circles sought to mould the relationship between that church and Ukrainian national affairs. Nevertheless, by the twentieth century the UGCC had emerged as a bulwark of modern Ukrainian identity and national sentiment. The mostly Orthodox Ukrainian population of Bukovyna and the Greek Catholic Ukrainian population of the Kingdom of Hungary were subjected to active government intervention in the relationship between the church and national and cultural affairs—an intervention that even extended to the language of the liturgy. This resulted in still other patterns in the evolution of the national movement vis-à-vis religious institutions.

At times religious confessions have turned to the state and the nation as sources of support and fulfilment; at other times they have struggled against them. Certain states have imposed and ensured religious uniformity, and national solidarity has been employed to strengthen ties with certain churches.

The Orthodox Church evolved on the basis of the assumption that the state and the church would develop a harmonious relationship and that the civil authority should uphold the faith in a Christian Empire. The decline of Byzantium, the conversion of distant peoples, and the final fall of Constantinople made this model far from a reality, but it underlay Orthodox thought. Unlike the Latin West, which had developed a uniformity of rites, a single liturgical language, and a centralized administrative structure, the Eastern church had a multiplicity of rites, a number of liturgical languages, numerous religious centres, and four patriarchates, with Rome constituting the fifth. This collectivity evolved into a community of autocephalous churches, which, in modern times, have often reflected political structures and national communities, particularly when and where the liturgical language, e.g., Church

Slavonic in the case of the Slavs, has been closely related to the vernacular. The process by which autocephaly could be obtained was never clearly defined, nor was the relationship between political and ecclesiastical structures. In many cases the churches reflected ethno-national characteristics because of their liturgical languages, the evolution of distinct artistic and architectural styles, and the existence of ecclesiastical institutions associated with a national tradition. In particular, as Orthodox states failed in the late Middle Ages and Orthodox peoples came under the control of non-Orthodox and frequently non-Christian rulers, the Orthodox Churches developed into bearers of historical and national traditions. At the same time, they maintained pan-Orthodox views that transcended national and state differences.

In contrast, the centralization of power in Western Christianity led to the development of a very different tradition in the Catholic Church. The papacy was able to assert its rights in relations with the Western Empire and the rulers who rose to power there. Rome was also able to ensure a uniformity in ritual and language that was challenged only by the Reformation. But even then the Catholic response merely reinforced centralization and uniformity. These tendencies made reconciliation with Eastern Christianity difficult, even when Rome sought to accommodate liturgical and linguistic practices.

Orthodoxy and Catholicism came into competition in the Ukrainian lands. In that interaction, states and national communities played important and, at times, decisive roles. For the modern period, the Union of Brest of 1596, which unified a large group of Eastern Christians with Rome, and the removal of the Kyiv Metropolitanate from the jurisdiction of Constantinople in 1686 and its later dismantling delineated the basic structures for subsequent Orthodox-Catholic interrelations, as well as the engagement of these two confessions with the modern states and national communities in Ukraine.

This interaction of religion, state, and nation in contemporary Ukraine is a theme that runs through the essays collected in this volume. Much of the analysis deals with the responses of Ukraine's Eastern Christians to the challenge of the national idea from the late nineteenth century until the first years of independent post-Soviet Ukraine. These essays place the history and current status of Ukraine's Orthodox and Greek Catholic communities in the context of the modern Ukrainian national revival of the late nineteenth and early twentieth centuries and the resurgence of Ukrainian national consciousness in the late 1980s and early 1990s. They also deal with Russian and Polish national and nationalist agendas and states as they have related to religious groups in Ukraine. Throughout, the states that ruled Ukraine figure as arbiters and objects of religious and national movements.

With one exception, all the essays in this volume were written between 1990 and 2000, a decade during which religious life in Ukraine revived as Soviet rule crumbled and an independent state emerged. Although they do not represent everything that the authors have written about religious life in modern Ukraine, they help to explain the nature and principal characteristics of its contemporary religious developments.

This work does not discuss some important issues of relations between church, nation, and state in modern and contemporary Ukraine. Such omissions are almost inevitable in any collection of essays written at various times and on different occasions. The extensive literature cited in the footnotes should assist the reader who wishes to explore additional questions, especially those that pertain to the UGCC, which is under-represented in this volume but for which a substantial literature exists. Ten of the eleven essays were previously published; one appears here for the first time.

The authors began their research in this field at a time when the East and the West were still divided by the Iron Curtain. Frank E. Sysyn was then resident of the United States, and Serhii Plokhy was still in Ukraine. The collapse of the USSR, the rise of independent Ukraine, and growing co-operation among scholars in the West and the former Soviet bloc are among the factors that transformed the field and made the publication of this volume possible.

Both authors are now residents of Canada. They bring to the volume their own perspectives and interpretations of the history of Eastern Christianity in Ukraine. They hope that the resulting diversity of views will serve to enrich this collection and make it more interesting to the reader. They also hope that this work will shed new light on Eastern Christianity in Ukraine and further Western understanding of its history, current status, and future challenges.

The publication of this volume was made possible by the support of the Ukrainian Church Studies Program at the Canadian Institute of Ukrainian Studies, University of Alberta. Many people helped with the editing of this collection. The authors especially thank Myroslav Yurkevich, Marta D. Olynyk, Roman Senkus, and Bohdan Nebesio.

Frank E. Sysyn

The Formation of Modern Ukrainian Religious Culture: The Sixteenth and Seventeenth Centuries[*]

Few institutions lend themselves as well as the church to examination of its millennium-long history. Religious institutions and traditions change more slowly than their secular counterparts. For example, it was only in the twentieth century that the Orthodox in Ukraine first replaced the Church Slavonic language with Ukrainian in the liturgy and that the Uniates (Ukrainian Greek Catholics) introduced mandatory celibacy in some eparchies. The conservatism of the churches makes it possible to speak of millennial aspects of Ukrainian Christianity. Nevertheless, modification and change have indeed occurred at various rates in different times. The sixteenth and seventeenth centuries—the age of Reformation and Counter-Reformation, Cossack revolts and Polish, Muscovite and Ottoman intervention, the introduction of printing, and the formation of an Eastern Christian higher educational institution in Kyiv—were a period of especially rapid change. The great Orthodox scholar Georges Florovsky labelled this age "The Encounter with the West" and viewed it as an unstable and dangerous time, which bore only sterile progeny.[1] Other scholars have seen it as a period of great accomplishments that arose from challenges to the Ukrainian religious genius.[2]

---

[*]   This article originally appeared in *Church, Nation and State in Russia and Ukraine,* ed. Geoffrey A. Hosking (Edmonton, 1990), 1–22. It has been revised.

1.   Florovsky's *Puti russkago bogosloviia* (Paris, 1937) has been translated into English as *The Ways of Russian Theology,* part 1, ed. Richard S. Haigh, vol. 5 of *The Collected Works of Georges Florovsky* (Belmont, Mass., 1979). See my discussion of his views in my review article "Peter Mohyla and the Kiev Academy in Recent Western Works: Divergent Views on Seventeenth- Century Ukrainian Culture," *Harvard Ukrainian Studies* 8, nos. 1–2 (June 1984): 156–87.

2.   The standard positive evaluation of this period is found in vols. 1–2 of Ivan Vlasovs'kyi, *Narys istoriï Ukraïns'koï Pravoslavnoï Tserkvy,* 4 vols. in 5 bks. (New York and South Bound Brook, N.J., 1955–66). Vols. 1–2 cover

It should suffice to list a number of firsts in the early part of this period to see the beginnings of modern church life in the Kyiv Metropolitanate. In the early sixteenth century the Belarusian printer Frantsishak Skaryna published the first liturgical books on Ruthenian territories. In the 1560s the Peresopnytsia Gospel was translated into the Ruthenian vernacular. In 1562–63 Szymon Budny published the first works for Protestant believers in Ruthenian. In 1574, in Lviv, Cyrillic printing finally began in the Ukrainian territories with a primer that was the first of numerous books to teach literacy. In the late 1570s, in Ostroh, Prince Kostiantyn Ostroz'kyi established the first Orthodox higher educational institution. In 1580–81 the Ostroh circle published the first complete Slavonic Bible. In the 1580s the burghers of Lviv strengthened their communal life by organizing a brotherhood or confraternity centred at the newly rebuilt Church of the Dormition. Receiving stauropegial rights that subordinated the brotherhood directly to the patriarch of Constantinople, the brotherhood challenged the authority of the local bishop. In the 1590s Orthodox bishops began meeting regularly at synods to discuss church reforms. In 1595 the bishop of Volodymyr, Ipatii Potii, and the bishop of Lutsk, Kyrylo Terlets'kyi, travelled to Rome to negotiate a church union, which was proclaimed the next year by the metropolitan and five bishops at a synod at Brest. An opposing synod attended by two bishops met in the same city and rejected the union. In 1596 Lavrentii Zyzanii published the first Slavonic-Latin-Greek lexicon. In the last years of the sixteenth century opposing sides polemicized in print in Ruthenian and Polish about the Union of Brest. Alarmed by the Orthodox counter-offensive, the Uniates began to shoring up their institution, establishing a seminary in Vilnius in 1601 and creating a Basilian monastic order along west European lines in 1613. In 1615 the burghers of Kyiv and the inhabitants of the surrounding region formed a brotherhood and later a school. Combined with the printing press at the Kyivan Cave Monastery, these institutions made Kyiv the centre of religious and cultural activities. In 1618 Meletii Smotryts'kyi published a Church Slavonic grammar that established the norms of the language. In 1632 Petro Mohyla, as metropolitan and archimandrite of the Cave Monastery, formed a collegium in Kyiv. By 1642 he had compiled a

the church's history until the end of the seventeenth century; they have appeared in an abridged English translation as Iwan Wlasowsky, *Outline History of the Ukrainian Orthodox Church*, 2 vols. (New York and South Bound Brook, N.J., 1974, 1979).

confession of the Orthodox faith, which was later accepted by other Orthodox Churches.[3]

From the late sixteenth to the mid-seventeenth century the Eastern Christian believers of Ukraine and Belarus, with their activist hierarchs and churches, their numerous schools and monasteries, their scores of new book titles in Slavonic, Ruthenian, and Polish, their numerous innovations in institutions—church brotherhoods, synods of the clergy and the laity, and western Christian-patterned religious orders—and their elaborate debates on church history, structure, and beliefs had entered a new age. Generations of historians have examined the events and the achievements of the period. However this age is evaluated, there is agreement that from the mid-sixteenth century to the end of the seventeenth-century church life was fundamentally transformed in Ukraine. With this transformation the foundation was laid for Ukrainian religious traditions that have endured into the modern age. More recent ecclesiastical movements find their precedents in this formative period. In acts such as establishing the Orthodox society named in honour of Metropolitan Petro Mohyla in Volhynia in the 1930s and calling on the Soviet government to recognize the legality of the Uniate or Ukrainian Greek Catholic Church, twentieth-century Ukrainian churchmen and believers have frequently used the symbols, rhetoric, and institutions that evolved about four hundred years ago.[4] This essay merely aims to suggest some of the major traditions or themes that have had an enduring impact on Ukrainian religious culture.

This discussion will concentrate on religious traditions among Ukrainian Eastern Christian believers. While in many respects Ukrainians shared with Belarusians a common "Ruthenian" religious culture of the Kyiv Metropolitanate, it was in the sixteenth century

---

3.   The best general treatment of the cultural achievements of this period is Mykhailo Hrushevs'kyi, *Kul'turno-natsional'nyi rukh na Ukraïni XVI–XVII st.*, 2d ed. (n.p., 1919). For the literary production of the period, see *Ukraïns'ki pys'mennyky: Bio-bibliohrafichnyi slovnyk*, vol. 1, *Davnia ukraïns'ka literatura (XI–XVII st. st.)*, comp. L[eonid] Ie. Makhnovets' (Kyiv, 1960).

4.   For interpretations of Ukrainian religious traditions, see V'iacheslav Lypyns'kyi, *Relihiia i Tserkva v istoriï Ukraïny* (Philadelphia, 1925); Dmytro Doroshenko, *Pravoslavna Tserkva v mynulomu i suchasnomu zhytti ukraïns'koho narodu* (Berlin, 1940); Nataliia Polons'ka-Vasylenko, *Istorychni pidvalyny UAPTs* (Rome, 1964); and Volodymyr Ianiv, ed., *Relihiia v zhytti ukraïns'koho narodu: Zbirnyk materiialiv naukovoi konferentsiï u Rokka di Papa (18–20.X.1963)*, vol. 181 of *Zapysky Naukovoho tovarystva im. Shevchenka* (Munich, Rome, and Paris, 1966).

that Ukrainian and Belarusian political, cultural, and religious
history began to diverge more significantly. The Union of Lublin of
1569 divided most of the central and eastern Ukrainian territories,
formerly part of the Grand Duchy of Lithuania, from the Belarusian
territories and united them with the western Ukrainian lands in the
Kingdom of Poland. The Cossack Host developed primarily in the
Ukrainian lands and, in time, created a political and social elite that
was lacking in Belarus. By the same token, economic and
demographic advances supported a greater vitality in cultural and
religious activities in the Ukrainian territories. In religious affairs,
the Ukrainian territories became relatively more important in the life
of the Kyiv Metropolitanate at the end of the sixteenth century, in
part because the elites in Belarus were less resistant to conversion to
Roman Catholicism and Protestantism. The return of the
metropolitans to their titular city of Kyiv in the 1590s symbolized
this change. In the first half of the seventeenth century the religious
cultures of Ukraine and Belarus diverged further because the
Orthodox dominated in the Ukrainian lands, while the Uniates had
more success in the Belarusian territories. Finally, the formation of
an Orthodox Cossack Hetmanate stimulated a development of
specific Ukrainian religious traditions in Kyiv and Left-Bank
Ukraine. Despite these differences, the religious culture of the
seventeenth century may be viewed as a Ruthenian inheritance from
which interacting Ukrainian and Belarusian variants took shape.
Therefore, the traditions outlined here are often also pertinent to
Belarusian religious culture, although they have evolved differently
in Belarus in the modern period.

My discussion of Ukrainian religious culture will be confined to
the Eastern Christians, the adherents of the traditional Rus' church.
However, the distinctiveness of the Ruthenian Eastern Christian
religious culture arose in part because of religious pluralism. Jews,
Muslims, Armenian Gregorians, Latin-rite Catholics, and Protestants
all inhabited the Ukrainian and Belarusian territories alongside the
Orthodox and, after 1596, also Uniate Ruthenian Christians. These
groups both interacted with the Eastern Christians and represented
"other" religious and cultural traditions. For example, the
identification of Roman Catholicism as the *liakh* (Polish) faith in the
Ukrainian lands made religious adherence coincide with
cultural-national identification, and conversion implied a change in
cultural affiliation. The Protestant Reformation emerged from the
Western Christian community but made converts throughout Ukraine,
including among the Orthodox. While the Calvinists, Antitrinitarians,

and Lutherans did not constitute religious bodies that descended directly from the Rus' tradition, they were influenced by their Eastern Christian surroundings. The Counter-Reformation arose to meet the Protestant challenge, but it too directed its efforts to converting Eastern Christians. Latin-rite Catholics, Protestants, and other groups challenged and stimulated the Ruthenian Eastern Christians.[5]

The major significance of the period for Ukrainian and Belarusian Eastern Christians was their division in 1596 into Orthodox and Uniate believers and churches. Before the late sixteenth century, attempts at uniting Ukrainian and Belarusian believers with Rome had been episodic and had not divided the larger religious community. From 1596 Ukrainian and Belarusian believers have been permanently divided into two churches—one that rejects the church union and holds to Orthodoxy, and another that accepts the union and adheres to Catholicism. Both claim to be the true continuation of the church that was formed when Rus' was Christianized in 988.[6]

Modern Ukrainian religious culture emerged in the Kyiv Metropolitanate in the sixteenth century.[7] From the conversion of

---

5. The most comprehensive work on the Roman Catholic Church in the Polish-Lithuanian Commonwealth is *Kościół w Polsce*, vol. 2, ed. Jerzy Kłóczowski ([Cracow], 1969). The most recent study on Protestants in Ukraine in this period is George H. Williams, "Protestants in the Ukraine in the Period of the Polish-Lithuanian Commonwealth," *Harvard Ukrainian Studies* 2, no. 1 (March 1978): 41-72 and no. 2 (June 1978): 184–210. See also Mykhailo Hrushevs'kyi, *Z istoriï relihiinoï dumky na Ukraïni* (Lviv, 1925).

6. On the Union of Brest, see the standard work by Edward Likowski, *Unia Brzeska (1596)* (Poznan, 1896), available in German and Ukrainian translations. See also Oscar Halecki, *From Florence to Brest (1439–1596)*, 2d ed. (Hamden, Conn., 1968) for the period before the union. Josef Macha's *Ecclesiastical Unification: A Theoretical Framework Together with Case Studies from the History of Latin-Byzantine Relations* (Rome, 1974), vol. 198 of *Orientalia Christiana Analecta*, is an excellent discussion of church life in the sixteenth and seventeenth centuries.

7. Fortunately, there is a bibliography for the large literature on Ukrainian church history of this period: Isydor I. Patrylo, OSBM, *Dzherela i bibliohrafiia istoriï Ukraïns'koï Tserkvy* (Rome, 1975), ser. 2, sec. 1, vol. 33 of *Analecta OSBM*; and his addendum in *Analecta OSBM* 10 (1979): 406–87. In this article only a few general works are included in the notes, as are items not included in Patrylo's bibliography, primarily because they are too recent. The basic works on Ukrainian church history are Vlasovs'kyi, *Narys*; Atanasii Hryhorii Velykyi, OSBM, *Z litopysu khrystyians'koï Ukraïny*, vols. 4–6 (Rome, 1971–3); Michaele Harasiewicz [Mykhailo Harasevych], *Annales Ecclesiae Ruthenae* (Lviv, 1862); Hryhor Luzhnyts'kyi, *Ukraïns'ka Tserkva mizh*

988 until the early fourteenth century, one Metropolitanate of Kyiv and all Rus' had encompassed all East Slavic territories. By the twelfth century Kyiv no longer possessed the paramount political influence in Rus', and the Mongol conquest hastened the disintegration of political unity of the vast Kyiv Metropolitanate. In the early fourteenth century Prince Iurii L'vovych, the Orthodox ruler of Galicia-Volhynia, convinced the Constantinople Patriarchate to establish a temporary Little Rus' Metropolitanate for the eparchies of Peremyshl, Halych, Volodymyr, Lutsk, Turiv, and Kholm. More lasting was the migration of the Kyiv metropolitans in the early fourteenth century to the Suzdal Land, where they later took up residence in Moscow. Until 1458 growing centrifugal forces made the retention of a united Kyiv Metropolitanate seem difficult. The Galician or "Little Rus'" Metropolitanate was temporarily revived in 1370 on the insistence of Casimir the Great, the Polish ruler who annexed Galicia to his kingdom. The grand dukes of Lithuania, whose domains reached to Kyiv by 1362, sought to have their candidates appointed metropolitan of Kyiv and reside in their state. When they could not do so, they strove to have separate metropolitanates established for their numerous Ruthenian subjects. In general, the patriarchs of Constantinople preferred to retain the unity of the Kyiv Metropolitanate and entrust its headquarters to the steadfastly Orthodox princes of Moscow rather than to the Catholic kings of Poland or to the pagan and, after 1386, Catholic rulers of Lithuania.[8]

The Constantinople Patriarchate brought about the final division of the Kyiv Metropolitanate by its own wavering in adherence to Orthodoxy. Muscovy refused to accept the Union of Florence of 1439 or Isidore, the Greek metropolitan of Kyiv. Consequently, it rejected the authority of the patriarchs of Constantinople and declared autocephaly by electing its own metropolitan in 1448. In the Ukrainian and Belarusian lands that were controlled by Catholic

---

Skhodom i Zakhodom: Narys istoriï Ukraïns'koï Tserkvy (Philadelphia, 1954); and Ludomir Bieńkowski, "Organizacja Kosciola Wschodniego w Polsce," in *Kościół w Polsce*, 733–1050. Important works in East Slavic church history are Albert Maria Ammann, *Abriss der Ostslavischen Kirchengeschichte* (Vienna, 1950); Anton V. Kartashev, *Ocherki po istorii Russkoi Tserkvi*, 2 vols. (Paris, 1959); and Metropolitan Makarii (Bulgakov), *Istoriia Russkoi Tserkvi*, 12 vols. (St. Petersburg, 1864–86).

8.   J. Meyendorff examines ecclesiastical affairs in his *Byzantium and the Rise of Russia: A Study of Byzantino-Russian Relations in the Fourteenth Century* (Cambridge, 1981).

rulers, no such rejection of Constantinople's authority or Metropolitan Isidore occurred. Therefore, in 1458, when a new metropolitan of "Kyiv and all Rus'" was elected for the lands of the Grand Duchy of Lithuania and the Kingdom of Poland, a permanent break ensued between the two parts of the Kyivan metropolitan see. The change of the title of the metropolitan in Moscow from "metropolitan of Kyiv and all Rus'" to "metropolitan of Moscow and all Rus'" brought titulature in line with reality. Although the Union of Florence failed to take hold in both Constantinople and in the Kingdom of Poland and the Grand Duchy of Lithuania, the division of the old Kyiv Metropolitanate into Ruthenian and Muscovite churches endured.

For both metropolitanates the events of the mid-fifteenth century speeded the indigenization, indeed the nationalization, of the church. In earlier centuries metropolitans had frequently been Greeks, and in the fourteenth and fifteenth centuries foreigners still figured prominently (e.g., Gregory Tsamblak and Isidore). At the same time, the cultural distinctness of Russians and Ruthenians, whose vernacular and administrative languages differed and who lived under markedly different political and social systems, made a metropolitan from Muscovy or one from the Grand Duchy of Lithuania more and more alien in the other territory. From 1448 to the declaration of Moscow as a patriarchate in 1589, all metropolitans of Moscow were native Russians, while from 1458 to the subordination of Kyiv to Moscow in 1686 most metropolitans of Kyiv and bishops of the Kyiv Metropolitanate were native Ruthenians. The final division of the Ruthenian and Muscovite churches and their different experiences from the fifteenth to the seventeenth centuries furthered the evolution of distinct religious traditions.

For the Kyiv Metropolitanate the major problems of the fifteenth century were dealing with the consequences of the Union of Florence and finding a place for itself in Catholic states.[9] As Constantinople renounced the Union of Florence, the daughter church of Kyiv reasserted its Orthodox allegiance. Nevertheless, in the first century after the fall of Constantinople the patriarchs displayed little initiative in guiding their distant daughter church, and the church became increasingly dependent on Catholic rulers and Orthodox lay lords. Throughout the fifteenth and early sixteenth centuries the Polish and Lithuanian governments enacted legislation

---

9.   Kazimierz Chodynicki deals with church-state relations in his *Kościół Prawosławny a Rzeczpospolita Polska, 1370–1632: Zarys historyczny* (Warsaw, 1934).

that placed the church and its believers in a disadvantageous position in comparison with the Catholic Church. Although the Protestant Reformation weakened the privileged position of the Catholic Church, the Protestant believers and their Catholic opponents engaged in an intellectual battle in which the Orthodox Church was unprepared to take part. Western Christian political dominance and intellectual and organizational superiority combined to challenge a Kyiv Metropolitanate that could not depend for support on Orthodox rulers, domestic or foreign, and that found its Slavonic cultural inheritance deficient in answering the new challenges. Faced with the increasing defections to the Protestants and Catholics, particularly from among the Orthodox nobles, the Kyiv Metropolitanate was endangered by dissolution in the sixteenth century. The response to the challenges brought about numerous innovations in religious culture. One of the responses, however—the acceptance of union with Rome by the metropolitan and most of the bishops—brought about an institutional division in the metropolitanate. After 1596 the Orthodox Church had to compete with a Uniate Kyiv Metropolitanate.

From 1596 to 1620 the Orthodox Church had no metropolitan and was viewed as illegal by the Polish-Lithuanian Commonwealth. In 1620 Patriarch Theophanes of Jerusalem consecrated Metropolitan Iov Borets'kyi and five bishops. The government viewed the election of Borets'kyi and his successor, Isaia Kopyns'kyi, as illegitimate. Bowing to pressure from the Orthodox nobility and the Zaporozhian Cossacks, the newly elected King Władysław IV and the Polish-Lithuanian Diet recognized the Orthodox Church as legal in 1632, but assigned only half of the eparchies of the metropolitanate to the Orthodox and required the election of a new hierarchy to replace the one ordained in 1620.

From 1632 to 1647 Metropolitan Petro Mohyla strove to strengthen the Orthodox metropolitanate's institutional structure throughout the Commonwealth, including in the eparchies assigned to the Uniates. Mohyla used his wealth and influence with the government to carry out a far-reaching programme of developing education and printing, as well as of the reform of church practices. He entertained the possibility of a union with Rome on better terms than the Union of Brest, but never made a final commitment.[10]

---

10. Thanks to Stepan T. Golubev's *Kievskii mitropolit Petr Mogila i ego spodvizhniki (Opyt tserkovno-istoricheskago issledovaniia)*, 2 vols. (Kyiv, 1883, 1889), this is one of the best-studied periods in Ukrainian church history. See also *Harvard Ukrainian Studies* 8, nos. 1–2 (June 1984), a special issue on the Kyiv Mohyla Academy; in particular, see there Ihor Ševčenko, "The Many

Mohyla's successor as the Orthodox metropolitan of Kyiv, Syl'vestr Kosiv (1647–57), led the church in more turbulent times. The Cossack revolt that developed into an Ukrainian uprising improved the position of the Orthodox metropolitanate on a number of occasions. In 1649 King John Casimir of Poland promised to abolish the church union, and the church gained advantages, even though the commitment was never carried out fully. In the territories controlled by Hetman Bohdan Khmelnyts'kyi, both Latin-rite and Uniate institutions and lands were handed over to the Orthodox. There were, however, negative consequences of the revolt and the establishment of the Cossack Hetmanate for the Kyiv Metropolitanate. The Pereiaslav Agreement (1654) placed the status of the metropolitanate in question. Its leadership feared correctly that ties with Muscovy would result in Russian interference in church affairs and the eventual transfer of the metropolitanate from the jurisdiction of the patriarch of Constantinople to the patriarch of Moscow.[11]

Already in Metropolitan Kosiv's time the Muscovites insisted that the metropolitan limit his traditional title of "Kyiv, Halych, and all Rus'" to "Kyiv, Halych, and all Little Rus'." In addition, victorious Muscovite armies in the Grand Duchy of Lithuania sought to detach Belarusian areas from the Kyiv Metropolitanate and annex them to the Moscow Patriarchate. Kosiv died in April 1657, four months before Hetman Khmelnyts'kyi. At this critical political moment for Ukraine the clergy of the Kyiv Metropolitanate, with the authorization of the new hetman, Ivan Vyhovs'kyi, elected Dionysii Balaban as metropolitan with the blessing of the patriarch of Constantinople. Balaban supported Vyhovs'kyi in his break with Moscow and his negotiation of the Union of Hadiach (8 September 1658), through which he sought to reintegrate the central Ukrainian lands into the Commonwealth as a Rus' duchy, guarantee places in the Polish-Lithuanian Senate for the Orthodox metropolitan and bishops, and abolish the Union of Brest. The failures of Vyhovs'kyi and the Hadiach policy forced the metropolitan to abandon Kyiv and take up residence in the territories controlled by the

---

Worlds of Peter Mohyla" (9–40), reprinted in his *Ukraine between East and West: Essays on Cultural History to the Early Eighteenth Century* (Edmonton and Toronto, 1996), 164–86. On government policy, see Jan Dzięgielewski, *Polityka wyznaniowa Władysława IV* (Warsaw, 1985).

11. For the history of the Orthodox Church in the late seventeenth century, see Natala Carynnyk-Sinclair, *Die Unterstellung der Kiever Metropolie unter das Moskauer Patriarchat* (Munich, 1970).

Commonwealth. Until his death in 1663, Metropolitan Balaban could not exercise control over the Ukrainian territories on the left bank of the Dnipro River. The Muscovite authorities appointed Bishop Lazar Baranovych of Chernihiv as administrator in these territories in 1659, thereby beginning the division of the Kyiv Metropolitanate along political boundaries.

Political events rapidly eroded the unity and autonomy of the Kyivan metropolitan see in the second half of the seventeenth century. In 1685–86, during the election of Metropolitan Gedeon Chetvertyns'kyi, the Muscovite government arranged, by means of pressure and bribes, the transfer of the see from the jurisdiction of the patriarch of Constantinople to that of the patriarch of Moscow. Nevertheless, the particular cultural and religious traditions of the late sixteenth- and seventeenth-century metropolitanate and the unique position of Kyiv endured well into the eighteenth century. It served as a model for twentieth-century movements supporting the formation of autonomous and autocephalous churches in Ukraine and Belarus.

The Uniate heir to the Kyivan metropolitan see was not able to win a mass following in the Ukrainian lands until the late seventeenth century, but it did produce dedicated followers and important traditions. The mediocre metropolitan Mykhailo Rahoza, who acceded to the church union, was followed by the energetic Ipatii Potii (1601–13) and Iosyf Ruts'kyi (1613–37) as metropolitans of "Kyiv, Halych, and all Rus'". They weathered numerous setbacks. The disappointment that two bishops and a large body of the clergy and the laity would not accede to the church union was followed by the blows of the Polish-Lithuanian Senate's refusal to grant seats to the Uniate bishops, the Diet's concessions of benefices to the Orthodox, the government's unwillingness to move decisively against the "illegal" Orthodox metropolitan and hierarchy consecrated in 1620, and the recognition of the Orthodox metropolitanate as an equal competitor to the Uniate one in 1632. In the first fifty years the Uniate Church was more successful in attracting followers in the Belarusian territories of the Grand Duchy of Lithuania than it was in the Ukrainian territories of the Kingdom of Poland, except for the Kholm region. The great Cossack revolt of 1648 placed the very existence of the Uniate Church in doubt. Nevertheless, in the second half of the seventeenth century the Uniate Kyiv Metropolitanate began to take shape, assisted by support from Rome and some zealous Catholics in the Commonwealth. The retention of all Belarus, Galicia, and Right-Bank

Ukraine by the Polish-Lithuanian Commonwealth after 1667 ensured the victory of the church union in these lands by the early eighteenth century. Reaching its greatest extent in the eighteenth century, the Uniate Church took on its own stable ecclesiastical form at the Synod of Zamość in 1720. The triumph of the Russian Empire over the Commonwealth was to devastate the Uniate Church, so that it would only survive in the Galician lands annexed by the Habsburgs, the very territories that had been so anti-Uniate before 1700. Still, the Galician metropolitan see that was established in 1807 continued the traditions of the Uniate Kyiv Metropolitanate. Despite changes in titulature and legal rights, today the Ukrainian Greek Catholic Church asserts its direct claims to the heritage of the Metropolitanate of Kyiv, Halych, and All-Rus'.[12]

The major tradition of this period, for both Orthodox and Uniates, was the emergence of new religious forms that represented an absorption and adaptation of influences from Latin Christianity, which had accompanied the control of the Ukrainian lands by Western Christian powers in the fourteenth century. At the core of Ruthenian culture was a deeply rooted Byzantine-Slavonic tradition embodied in a church that maintained an institutional structure permeating the thousands of settlements in the Ukrainian and Belarusian lands. As an institution of the Rus' faith, the church functioned in a conserving role for a local culture while, at the same time, connecting it to a Byzantine past, a larger Orthodox community, and a supranational Slavonic culture. Latin Christian political domination was accompanied by the placement of the Orthodox Church in an inferior position and with restrictions on the Orthodox and their worship. Consequently the Rus' church in Ukraine experienced the perils that religious pluralism poses for a church in a subservient position. As Latin Christian culture evolved and flourished, the Orthodox of Ukraine found themselves representatives of an increasingly isolated and inadequate cultural tradition.

This threat ultimately proved to be a stimulus that produced so many of the achievements outlined earlier. Although the Orthodox of Ukraine had faced the Western challenge without the protection of an Orthodox ruler or even the neutrality of a Muslim ruler, they were able to accommodate to Western practices and influences over

---

12.   Although Velykyi's *Litopys* is a publication of his radio lectures, it is based on his extensive study and editing of sources for the Basilian Fathers' *Analecta*. Until a more scholarly history of the Greek Catholic Church is written, it remains the best comprehensive account.

a long period of time. Both the decision of Polish kings in the fourteenth century to tolerate Orthodoxy and even grant the Orthodox elite noble status and the manifest numerical and political strength of the Orthodox Ruthenians in the Grand Duchy of Lithuania, which negated discriminatory legislation, had permitted the Orthodox Church to adjust gradually to Western Christian rule. Even in the cities, where Orthodox Christians were subject to harsh discrimination and numerous restrictions, they were able to maintain some religious and communal institutions. By the sixteenth century religious divisions among Western Christians and the weak powers of central administration, in contrast to the extensive liberties of individual nobles, mitigated the pressures on the Orthodox.[13]

The process of Ruthenian contact with Western Christian culture has still to be studied satisfactorily. Complex cultural changes and adaptation occurred from the fifteenth century, when Iurii of Drohobych presumably converted and became rector of the University of Bologna, to the seventeenth century, when an Orthodox university was established in Kyiv. The Orthodox Church and the Byzantine-Slavonic-Ruthenian culture long seemed inert and unattuned to the challenges of the Latin West. Their eventual response demonstrated how serious the challenge was. In adapting the thought and forms of the Latin West, the Kyiv Metropolitanate proved that it possessed the inner resources to reform rather than disintegrate. Latin philosophical texts, Church Slavonic grammars, and Polish-language polemical works were components of this response. Although Latin accretions and internal inconsistencies were part of the religious culture of the period, Ukrainian or Ruthenian religious practice, both Orthodox and Uniate, represented more a synthesis of the long contact of the Kyiv Metropolitanate with the West than it did a collection of disparate and contradictory religious practices. From the heights of Kyivan theology to the popular Christmas carols, the Ukrainians accepted outside influences without losing their religious and cultural heritage. In Ukraine there were no religious divisions, such as the great schism in Russia, over the introduction of new forms. Even those who objected to Western influences, for example, the polemicist Ivan Vyshens'kyi or the Trans-Dnipro monks, were usually too familiar with the "other" to be able to expurgate it from their own thought or to avoid it in

---

13.   On toleration in the Polish-Lithuanian Commonwealth, see Janusz Tazbir, *A State without Stakes: Polish Religious Toleration in the Sixteenth and Seventeenth Centuries* (Warsaw, 1973).

totality. The division within the Ukrainian community arose over a more substantive issue—union with Rome and a change of faith. Although both Orthodox and Uniate Ukrainians have undergone periodic movements to diminish Latin and Western Christian influence on their religious culture, the Westernization of the sixteenth and seventeenth centuries is so deeply embedded in their religious tradition that it cannot be uprooted.[14]

Most Eastern Christians have followed the models pioneered in Ukraine. Kyivan learning served as the model for the entire eighteenth-century Russian imperial church. Ukrainian music and art, through its importation to Russia, later spread throughout the Orthodox world. Experiments in employing the vernacular in sixteenth-century Ukraine and Belarus were later to be repeated among other Orthodox peoples. Even when other Orthodox and Eastern Christian peoples did not directly import elements of the Ukrainian synthesis, they frequently underwent analogous processes later.[15]

The active role of the laity constitutes a second enduring tradition in Ukrainian church life. Laymen became involved in church affairs and spiritual life and new institutions emerged. The form that the Uniate Church took at the end of the seventeenth century and the remaking of the Orthodox Church in Ukraine in the eighteenth and nineteenth centuries undermined this role of the laity and lay organizations, but new circumstances have frequently caused a revival of earlier traditions and institutions.

Laymen were essential to the administration and preservation of the Orthodox Kyiv Metropolitanate. In the sixteenth century the endangered church turned to great patrons, such as Prince Kostiantyn Ostroz'kyi, to ensure its protection. Nobles, endowed with the sweeping rights of the nobiliary Commonwealth, not only served as patrons and protectors of local churches, but also spoke in the name of the church at Diets and took part in the synods of the Orthodox Church in the early seventeenth century. Burghers had organized their own reform of church and community activities, even exercising the right to dismiss their clergymen. Zaporozhian Cossacks had not only assumed protection over the new Orthodox hierarchy, but also intervened in church councils. The urban

---

14. On the convergence of cultural traditions, see Eduard Winter, *Byzanz und Rom im Kampf um die Ukraine, 955–1939* (Leipzig, 1942).

15. This question has been little explored in recent times, and Konstantin V. Kharlampovich's *Malorossiiskoe vliianie na velikorusskuiu tserkovnuiu zhizn'* (Kazan, 1914) remains the basic study in the field.

Orthodox brotherhoods, or *bratstva*, enrolling burghers as well as nobles and Cossacks, constituted the most creative response to religious and cultural problems in Ukraine and Belarus. They also signified how greatly Ruthenian religious culture had diverged from other Eastern Christian communities. This can be seen by the need of the Lviv burghers to explain what a church brotherhood was to seventeenth-century Russians.[16]

Clergymen resented some lay interventions in religious affairs as being contrary to traditional canons and undermining the position of the clergy.[17] Some were attracted to the church union as a way of restoring full clerical control of the church. The defection of the metropolitan and five bishops increased the importance of the laity, who came to realize that they, not the hierarchs, remained steadfast in preserving the church. Twenty years of church life without a complete hierarchy (1596–1620) were followed by twelve years of governance by hierarchs who often could not take up residence in their sees and depended on the Orthodox nobles, Cossacks, and burghers to support their positions against a government that viewed them as illegal. Even after 1632 Metropolitan Mohyla, who sought to reassert clerical leadership in church affairs, had to depend on the noble laity. After 1648 the higher clergymen might find the Cossacks to be troublesome protectors, but they could not deny the benefits that Cossack successes had brought for the church, and they could not avoid adaptation to a new order in which priests and Cossack administrators not only represented dual powers, but were often members of the same families.

In the early seventeenth century, the need to compete for supporters also influenced the Uniate Church to pay heed to the laity. However, as it lost the support of the great nobles, major church brotherhoods, and the Cossacks, the Uniate Church, influenced by Roman practices, reduced the role of the laity. Ultimately it turned to laymen who were not its members—Latin-rite Catholic nobles—to strengthen its position.

A third element of the religious experience of the age was the "nationalization" of the church and the articulation of a subjective

---

16. On the brotherhoods, see Iaroslav D. Isaievych, *Bratstva ta ïkh rol' v rozvytku ukraïns'koï kul'tury XVI–XVIII st.* (Kyiv, 1966).

17. For an argument that the role of the laity in this period was a complete innovation resisted by the clergy, see Viacheslav Zaikin, *Uchastie svetskogo elementa v tserkovnom upravlenii, vybornoe nachalo i "sobornost'"* v *Kievskoi mitropolii v XVI i XVII vekakh* (Warsaw, 1930).

Ruthenian national consciousness based on the view of the church as properly a national institution.[18] The church had always been the Ruthenian church, the embodiment of the conversion of the Rus' rulers and their people in the tenth century. By the sixteenth century new conditions deepened the nation-bearing character of the church. The extinction of Rus' dynasties and polities made the church the only direct institutional link to Kyivan Rus'. The assimilation of many members of the secular elite to Polish culture, accompanied by religious conversions, augmented the role of the church as a spokesman for the Ruthenian tradition. Polish penetration of Ukraine, the development of a Polish vernacular literature and concept of nation, and the deprecation and later persecution of Orthodoxy by Polish clerical leaders and authorities combined to intensify national-religious feeling, in which the Ruthenian people and the Ruthenian church were viewed as one. The church not only embodied the national identity; it also frequently used the Ruthenian language in administration and publications, albeit without advocating the abandonment of the Church Slavonic language. All of these factors heightened Ruthenian national feeling and the identification of the church as the suprastructure of "Ruthenian nationhood." The mix of religious and national sentiment was especially apparent in the organization of church brotherhoods among the Ruthenian burghers, because these burghers, who were subject to discrimination, developed an intense ethno-religious sentiment in an environment in which they competed with other ethno-religious communities—Polish Catholics, Armenians, and Jews.

Even the Union of Brest, which divided the Ruthenians, worked to intensify the identification, as both sides strove that all Ruthenians should be one in faith. At the same time, however, it favoured more sophisticated thinking on Ruthenian national identity, since suddenly church and "nation" were not coterminous, and polemicists had to discuss the religious divide within the Ruthenian people. The essence of the debate was the historical question of which faith Grand Prince Volodymyr the Great had accepted. In Ukraine, therefore, it inspired knowledge of the Kyivan Rus' past as the cradle of Ruthenian national and religious culture. Even the Protestants occasionally invoked Volodymyr and the conversion as a means of securing legitimacy. While each church could deny the

---

18. On national consciousness in this period, see Teresa Chyńczewska-Hennel, *Świadomość narodowa szlachty ukraińskiej i kozaczyzny od schyłku XVI do połowy XVII wieku* (Warsaw, 1985).

other's legitimacy, it could not deny that there were Ruthenians of another religious persuasion. Orthodox might still see themselves as part of a greater Orthodox world, but they clearly viewed themselves as part of a Ruthenian (or, after the mid-seventeenth century, Ukrainian or Little Rus') division of that world, both as an ecclesiastical and a historico-linguistic community. After 1596 they also had to integrate into their worldview the adherence of fellow Ruthenians to Rome. At least the intellectuals, men such as Meletii Smotryts'kyi and Adam Kysil', articulated these issues, and Smotryts'kyi argued that conversion did not mean a change of nationality, since blood—not religion—defined nationality.[19] The concepts were amorphous, and the unstable political and religious situation prevented their crystallization. But Ukrainians had begun the discussions of religious, national, and cultural issues that have continued to the present. In modern times Ukrainians frequently invested the church with the national significance that it assumed in the sixteenth and seventeenth centuries, especially when other potential national institutions were abolished or usurped.

A fourth tradition, or rather experience, of the churches in Ukraine was that of accommodation or conflict of churches with state powers. The relations of a number of political entities (the Polish-Lithuanian Commonwealth, the Cossack Hetmanate, the Ottoman Empire, the Crimean Khanate, Muscovy/the Russian Empire) with the two Ruthenian churches were diverse and frequently contradictory. In general, however, the leaders of both churches of the Kyiv Metropolitanate found that their church structure and religious traditions had to be restructured in order to adjust to political rulers. Political power has determined much in Ukrainian religious history. Desire to obtain political influence and find favour with the ruler explains the Union of Brest to a considerable degree. Weak central government in the Commonwealth and successful utilization of internal centres of power (Prince Ostroz'kyi, the Zaporozhian Cossacks) and external ones (the Ottomans, Muscovy, the Eastern patriarchates) explain the reason for the survival of the Orthodox Church. Ultimately, however, that church could only ensure long-term existence by coming to terms

---

19. For Smotryts'kyi's works, as well as an introduction and bibliography by David Frick, see *The Works of Meletij Smotryc'kyi*, Harvard Library of Early Ukrainian Literature: Texts, vol. 1 (Cambridge, Mass., 1987). On Kysil', see my study *Between Poland and the Ukraine: The Dilemma of Adam Kysil, 1600–1653* (Cambridge, Mass., 1985).

with king and state—whether through the compromise of 1632 or the ostensible willingness to discuss a new union. In like manner, the Uniate Church survived assaults by Cossacks, nobles, and burghers because it had advocates in the government of the Commonwealth, kings, and senators, as well as Vatican nuncios, who influenced government policy.

Changes in political structures posed great problems and opportunities for the Churches of the Kyiv Metropolitanate. Had Polish control of Moscow continued or Władysław's candidacy to the Muscovite throne succeeded during the Time of Troubles, the church union would certainly have expanded beyond the metropolitanate to the Moscow Patriarchate. In contrast, the Cossack revolts and the Khmelnyts'kyi uprising endangered the very existence of the Uniate Church. Paradoxically, the uprising posed problems for the Orthodox Church, which it actively supported. Most of the Orthodox hierarchs viewed the rebellion with discomfort, particularly after the church obtained legal recognition in 1632, and were suspicious of the Cossack leaders as new political masters. They also feared that the political division of territories of the Kyiv Metropolitanate would undermine its ecclesiastical unity and that the revolt would weaken the position of the church in the lands that remained in the Commonwealth. Metropolitan Kosiv foresaw that Khmelnyts'kyi's turn to Muscovy and his oath of allegiance to the tsar would bring undesirable consequences for the church—above all the transfer of the Kyiv Metropolitanate from the jurisdiction of the Patriarchate of Constantinople to that of Moscow.

In the second half of the seventeenth century, metropolitans and bishops strove for stability amidst an unstable political situation. Uniate hierarchs sought to avoid the consequences of political compromises, such as the Union of Hadiach, which were deleterious to the interests of their church. Ultimately the division of Ukraine between the Polish-Lithuanian Commonwealth and Muscovy (1667, 1686) and the rise of Catholic intolerance in the Commonwealth worked to the Uniates' advantage. By the turn of the eighteenth century the sees of Peremyshl, Lviv, and Lutsk accepted the church union, and the real foundations of the Uniate Church were laid in the Ukrainian territories controlled by Poland.

The Orthodox clergymen and metropolitanate had greater options and more diverse constituencies. Metropolitan Kosiv sought to come to an accommodation with the Polish-Lithuanian authorities and to minimize the effect of the Pereiaslav Agreement, while Metropolitan Balaban supported Hetman Vyhovs'kyi's policy of reintegrating

Ukraine into the Polish-Lithuanian Commonwealth as the Duchy of Rus'. Bishops Metodii Fylymonovych and Lazar Baranovych adjusted to the influence of the Muscovite church and state in Ukraine, even at the price of undermining the unity of the Kyiv Metropolitanate. In general, all the Orthodox churchmen found that the church must eventually accommodate to political power, although the period contained many examples of attempts at avoiding this hard reality. Still, the subordination of the Kyiv Metropolitanate to Moscow in 1686, the loss of the western Ukrainian eparchies to the Uniates, and the church's anathema of its great patron, Hetman Ivan Mazepa, in 1708 revealed how political power would draw ecclesiastical boundaries and determine the role of the church.

Ultimately the failure to establish a political entity uniting the Ukrainian territories undermined the position of the local Orthodox church. In the late sixteenth century suggestions were made that the patriarch of Constantinople should migrate to the Ukrainian territories, and in the early seventeenth century various plans envisaged Kyiv as the centre of a patriarchate. Metropolitan Mohyla made Kyiv one of the major seats of the Orthodox world, and in the seventeenth century it appeared that the Kyivan metropolitans might see the prestige of their church raised by the formation of a new Orthodox state on their territory. That possibility receded rapidly after 1660.

Both the Orthodox and Uniate Churches were reorganized along the lines of dominance of Moscow-St Petersburg and Warsaw in Ukraine in the eighteenth century. By the early eighteenth century the Orthodox metropolitan residing in Kyiv had lost most of his metropolitanate's faithful, controlled by Poland, to the Uniates, while the Chernihiv Eparchy, though part of the Hetmanate, was subordinated directly to the Moscow Patriarchate. Kyiv might still be the home of great monasteries and churches, but the Kyiv Metropolitanate had been dismantled, and by the end of the eighteenth century even the particular practices of the Ukrainian church were largely abolished. In the Polish-controlled territories, the Kyiv metropolitan's Uniate competitor could only use Kyiv in his title, but not reside in the city. His large church in the Belarusian-Ukrainian territories was to a considerable degree Latinized and Polonized. The Uniate Church lost not only the upper classes to the Latin rite, but also much of its active self-identification as a Ruthenian national church that had inspired the formulators of the church union. In the eighteenth century it became the instrument for binding Ukrainians and Belarusians to the Commonwealth that some had hoped it would be in the late sixteenth century.[20]

A fifth tradition in Ukrainian church affairs of the period was the emergence of a religious, literary, and artistic culture that was specifically Ukrainian, rather than Ruthenian or Belarusian-Ukrainian. The centrality of the church, clergymen, and religious themes in intellectual and cultural pursuits permeated early modern Ukrainian culture. Indeed, religious culture influenced even secular cultural expression, such as administrative buildings, portraiture, or political tracts, because the clergymen and church schools controlled education. Political, economic, and social changes advanced the formation of new Ukrainian cultural models in the seventeenth century. The process, associated with the nationalization of the church as Ruthenian, had begun in the fifteenth century. By the late sixteenth century the common Belarusian-Ukrainian religious and secular culture had come to centre more and more in the Ukrainian territories as assimilation and conversion progressed more rapidly in the Belarusian territories. The political divide of the "Ruthenian" lands at the Union of Lublin (1569) advanced the differentiation of the Belarusian and Ukrainian cultures. In the early seventeenth century the political border to some degree mirrored religious divisions as the Ukrainian territories became the stronghold of Orthodoxy. More importantly, the religious institutions of Kyiv and Lviv, the nobles, burghers, and Cossacks of the Ukrainian lands, and the Cossack Hetmanate afforded new patrons and consumers of religious and secular culture.

By the second half of the seventeenth century a religious, Orthodox culture that may be called Ukrainian rather than Ruthenian had emerged. The limitation of the Kyiv metropolitan's title to "Little Rus'" after the Pereiaslav Agreement and the Muscovite church's claims to control Belarus reflected the predominantly Ukrainian nature of the church. In the new political and social environment of Ukraine, new literary and artistic forms, which have been called Cossack or Ukrainian baroque, arose. Histories, such as Archimandrite Teodosii Sofonovych's *Kroinika*, traced the history of Ukraine at the same time as the new Cossack

---

20. The relations of the Orthodox and Uniate Churches with the political entities that controlled Ukraine have not been sufficiently studied. On the Hetmanate, see Mykola Chubatyi, "Pro pravne stanovyshche Tserkvy v kozats'kii derzhavi," *Bohosloviia* 3 (1925): 19–53, 181-203.

elite provided patronage for art and music.[21] By the end of the century a specifically Ukrainian cultural model had matured. Centred in Kyiv, the Cossack Hetmanate, and Sloboda Ukraine, this "national" cultural style drew on the general Ruthenian tradition and continued to influence, and be influenced by, developments in the western Ukrainian and Belarusian territories. Just as the Ukrainian church and political entities were absorbed in the Russian church and Russian Empire, so this culture was absorbed into imperial Russian culture by the end of the eighteenth century. However, the existence of a national Ukrainian culture, closely allied with the church and religious culture, provided an enduring example for relations between church and culture and for styles in Ukrainian religious art, architecture, and music for subsequent generations.

A sixth tradition of the period was the formation of two churches—Orthodox and Catholic—that share the same religious culture. Both groups not only developed out of the church of St. Volodymyr, but were formed from similar influences and conditions in the century before and after the Union of Brest. Locked in heated combat, they were always aware that they were essentially one church and one tradition, distinct not only from the Western churches, but also from other Eastern churches. The Uniate Ruthenians did not easily fit into the norms and practices of the Roman church. The Orthodox had too fully imbibed the influences of the West and the political-social conditions of Ukraine to feel comfortable among other Orthodox churches. Institutions, men, books, practices, and ideas passed from one group to the other in this formative period of modern Ukrainian religious life. Catholic coreligionists have distrusted the Uniates' Catholicism, just as other Orthodox have been suspicious of the full Orthodoxy of Ukrainian believers. They have had some cause to do so, since shared Ukrainian religious characteristics and consciousness have waxed and waned, though they have never died out. In this way they have produced a certain internal Ukrainian ecumenism, despite confessional differences.

The first century after the Union of Brest, when both churches had salient national characteristics and even consciousness, was a

---

21.   For a discussion of Safonovych's work and of cultural processes in early modern Ukraine, see my article "The Cultural, Social and Political Context of Ukrainian History-Writing in the Seventeenth Century," in *Dall'Opus Oratorium alla Ricerca Documentaria: La Storiografia polacca, ucraina e russa fra il XVI e il XVIII secolo,* 285–310, ed. Giovanna Brogi Bercoff (Rome, 1986).

time when that which united the two churches seemed very real. Such characteristics, so often troubling to religiously homogeneous neighbours, give an especially modern ring to many statements of the age. Consider the declaration of Adam Kysil' before an Orthodox synod that was composed of clergymen and laymen calling for conciliation between Orthodox and Uniates in 1629:

> Gentlemen, you are not the only ones to weep. We all weep at the sight of the rent coat and precious robe of our dear Mother the Holy Eastern Church. You, Gentlemen, bemoan, as do we all, that we are divided from our brethren, we who were in one font of the Holy Spirit six hundred years ago in the Dnipro waters of this metropolis of the Rus' Principality. It wounds you, Gentlemen, and it wounds us all. Behold! There flourish organisms of commonwealths composed of various nations, while we of one nation, of one people, of one religion, of one worship, of one rite, are not as one. We are torn asunder, and thus we decline.[22]

Throughout this period, the struggle to re-unify the Kyiv Metropolitanate continued. Acceptance that two religious groups would arise where only one had existed came only slowly. Although subsequent divergence in religious culture and traditions has made the existence of Orthodox and Uniate believers among Ukrainians less difficult to accept, the continued instability in relations between the two groups derives in part from awareness of their common origins and shared characteristics. Consequently each group finds the existence of the other more troubling than it finds the existence of Roman Catholics, Protestants, or Greek and Russian Orthodox. Frequently, however, the two groups have found that the bond of shared religious culture and national loyalties is so strong that denominational affiliations are set aside.

A seventh tradition that arose in the period was an elevation of the Ukrainian churches to more than local significance. The Union of Brest constituted the largest lasting union of Eastern Christians with Rome and brought the Ukrainian and Belarusian territories to the attention of a wider Christian community. It served as a model for unionizing efforts among the Ukrainians of Hungary and the Armenians of the Polish Commonwealth. Clergymen who were active in promoting the church union, such as Metodii Terlets'kyi, used their experience in the Balkans. In discussions of how to gain

---

22. Sysyn, *Between Poland and the Ukraine*, 61.

acceptance of the church union, programmes for the erection of a patriarchate in Kyiv only loosely affiliated with Rome were formulated. Although these plans were never realized, they constituted a discussion of the structure of the Catholic Church that challenged the model of post-Tridentine Catholicism. The Eastern patriarchs and the Muscovite church were vitally interested in the church in the Kyiv Metropolitanate. They sought to keep it Orthodox and to draw upon its intellectual and institutional resources. The Kyiv Collegium made Ukraine a major centre of religious and intellectual culture.

Although the Ukrainian churches have never again occupied as important a place in the Christian community as they did in the sixteenth and seventeenth centuries, the experiments and plans of this age have inspired important modern, twentieth-century spiritual leaders and church movements. Iosyf Ruts'kyi served as a model of a Uniate hierarch with a broad vision of the relation between the Eastern and Western churches for Metropolitan Andrei Sheptyts'kyi. Petro Mohyla provided an example for making Kyiv the centre of a reformed, reinvigorated, virtually independent local Orthodox church for Metropolitan Vasyl' Lypkivs'kyi. Indeed, the modern religious leaders could even draw inspiration from religious figures who did not share their confessional adherence, but who had led the Ukrainian church at a time when it played a role of international importance.

The seven traditions outlined comprise only one method of assessing the significance of the sixteenth and seventeenth centuries in modern Ukrainian religious culture. All are not of equal importance, and each is but a means to analyze the rich Ukrainian religious experience of the early modern period. Other "traditions" can surely be added. However the components of the religious culture of the age are described, the picture will remain the same. Ukrainian religious culture underwent major changes in the sixteenth and seventeenth centuries that have shaped the Ukrainian religious experience throughout the remainder of its first millennium, and will continue to do so well into its second.

Frank E. Sysyn

The Ukrainian Autocephalous Orthodox Church and the Traditions of the Kyiv Metropolitanate[*]

Modern Ukrainian Orthodox churchmen and intellectuals have frequently looked to the early modern period as the model for the Ukrainian Orthodox revival. They have seen their goals of autocephaly, conciliarism, and Ukrainianization as rooted in the earlier period but undermined during the long intervening period of subordination to the Moscow Patriarchate and the Synodal Russian Church. They have sought to bring into harmony Ukrainian ecclesiastical institutions, cultural and educational advances, and sociopolitical reforms in a manner similar to that which they perceive to have occurred in an earlier period of Ukrainian religious ferment, cultural revival, and political renaissance. They have striven to return the Orthodox Church to that which they see as its proper and positive role in Ukrainian cultural, social, and political life and have turned to the past for affirmations of specifically Ukrainian traditions.

The vision of the Orthodox Church as a repository and patron of Ukrainian spiritual, cultural, and political life has been an enduring one in the twentieth century. It is primarily associated with the Ukrainian church movement that coalesced after 1917 and with the Ukrainian Autocephalous Orthodox Church (UAOC) established in the years 1919–21, but it has also sustained Ukrainianizing groups within other Orthodox churches in Ukraine. Stalin's brutal liquidation of the UAOC in the 1930s terminated this period of renewal. His subsequent accommodation with the Russian Orthodox Church (ROC) gave the newly elected Moscow patriarch a monopoly on Orthodox ecclesiastical life in Ukraine after the Second World War. Whenever conditions have permitted, however, attempts at bringing Orthodoxy and Ukrainian interests into a harmonious

---

[*]   This article was originally published in *Kirchen im Kontext unterschiedlichen Kulturen: Auf dem Weg ins dritte Jahrtausend. Alexander Men in memoriam (1935–1990)*, ed. Karl Christian Felmy et al. (Göttingen, 1991), 625–40. The article has been revised.

relationship have re-emerged. Examples of such strivings are the Ukrainian church movement in interwar Poland, the restoration of the UAOC during the wartime German occupation of the 1940s, and the church life of the Ukrainian diaspora.

In 1989 the Soviet policy of perestroika and glasnost permitted the resurrection of the UAOC, and in 1990 a sobor proclaimed the creation of the Kyiv Patriarchate. Metropolitan Mstyslav (Skrypnyk), the leader of the church in the West, returned to Ukraine to be enthroned as patriarch in October 1990. With over one thousand parishes, the UAOC re-emerged as an important element in religious life in Ukraine. As in the 1920s, the activity of the UAOC caused the ROC to rethink its policies toward Ukraine. The designation of the Ukrainian Exarchate of the Moscow Patriarchate as the "Ukrainian Orthodox Church" with certain autonomous rights may be seen as a reaction to the autocephalist revival. The re-emergence of the UAOC, which asserts its continuity with the church of the 1920s (though not necessarily with its more radical canons), makes an examination of the autocephalists' vision of the past essential to any discussion of current religious affairs.

Although the leaders of the modern Ukrainian Orthodox movement also turned to the Kyivan Rus' period as a source of inspiration, the early modern period, about which much more was known and which was so important in defining modern Ukrainian political and cultural life, offered a more immediate vision. The early modern period represented the rebirth of church and religious life after a time of stagnation. It also constituted the most recent period in which a distinct Ukrainian Orthodox Church, ecclesiastical institutions, and religious tradition had existed. Perception of analogous situations combined with the need for historical precedent to give the seventeenth and eighteenth centuries dominant influence as a model in religious matters, similar to the importance given the period in twentieth-century Ukrainian political and cultural affairs. The more scholarly and erudite might admit the existence of the important political, social, and cultural differences between the early modern period and the twentieth century. The more careful and detached might recognize how frequently information on the earlier period was fragmentary or contradictory, or how complex the realities of the early modern age were. All of the leaders of the Ukrainian church revival, however, used examples from the early modern church in shaping their own church life.

Since the Ukrainian church movement was closely related to the Ukrainian national revival, its intellectual leaders shared its desire to restore and develop authentic Ukrainian traditions. Just as churchmen such as Metropolitan Vasyl' Lypkivs'kyi and Archbishop Kostiantyn Krotevych sought to expound a theology and ecclesiology, composers such as Mykola Leontovych, Kyrylo Stetsenko, and Oleksander Koshyts' provided the church with its own music, artists, architects, and art historians such as Vadym Shcherbakivs'kyi and Iukhym Sitsins'kyi sought to define its iconography and architecture, linguists such as Ivan Ohiienko (later Metropolitan Ilarion) strove to forge a new liturgical language, and statesmen such as Symon Petliura and Oleksander Lotots'kyi sought to establish a conducive political climate. They all did so by attempting to "restore," as much as to create, something entirely new. So too, historians offered the church a historical tradition of legitimacy.

The most striking case is that of Orest Levyts'kyi, whose scholarship chronicled the development of the early modern Ukrainian church and whose religious and national loyalties brought him into the Ukrainian church community of the newly forming UAOC.[1] The creators of Ukrainian national historiography, with diverse religious views, examined the role of the Orthodox Church in the national past and thereby afforded a historical basis for those churchmen who wished to change the relationship of that church to Ukraine and the Ukrainian national awakening. The impetus for the Ukrainian church revival, however, also came from the nineteenth- and early twentieth-century historians of the *"Zapadno-russkaia Tserkov'"* (West Russian church), many of whom were Ukrainophiles and proponents of the specific characteristics of the Kyiv Metropolitanate, others of whom were all-Russian (or even "Great Russian") patriots and occasionally severe critics of the circumstances of that metropolitanate. In general, the detailed studies of scholars holding diverse religious and national viewpoints—namely, Metropolitan Evgenii Bolkhovitinov, Stepan Golubev, Platon Zhukovich, Mykola Sumtsov, Vitalii Eingorn, Kostiantyn Kharlampovych, Ivan Malyshevs'kyi, Gennadii Karpov, Vasyl' Bidn'ov, Fedir Titov, and others—provided a vast body of material in which the particular church life and traditions of Ukraine were portrayed. Some consciously and others almost against their will created the knowledge that informed the Ukrainian church movement.[2]

---

1. Levyts'kyi's reaction to the forming of the Ukrainian church is described movingly in an obituary by Mykola Vasylenko in *Zapysky Sotsiial'no-ekonomichnoho viddilu VUAN* 1 (1923): xcvii–xcviii.

2. The literature of Ukrainian church history is best approached through the bibliography of Isydor Patrylo, OSBM, *Dzherela i bibliohrafiia istorii*

The contribution of historical scholarship to the Ukrainian church revival has yet to be studied. It is certain, however, that the attention paid in nineteenth- and early twentieth-century scholarship to the period from the final division of the Kyivan metropolitan see into Russian and Ruthenian (Ukrainian-Belarusian) churches in 1458 to the subordination of the Kyivan see to Moscow in 1686, and the dismantling of the Kyiv Metropolitanate and the undermining of the traditions of Ukrainian-Belarusian Orthodoxy in the eighteenth century served to emphasize how different early modern Ukrainian Orthodoxy was from Russian Orthodoxy of that period, as well as from the ROC in Ukraine of the nineteenth and early twentieth centuries. These centuries of independent ecclesiastical development, especially the latter part, posed great problems for historians who sought to describe church history as one "Russian" ecclesiastical tradition. Discussion of subjects acceptable to an "all-Russian" identity, such as Catholic persecution of the Orthodox in the Polish-Lithuanian state, resistance to Uniate "schisms," the Pereiaslav Agreement, and the role of Ukrainians in the "All-Russian" church could not counterbalance awareness of the estrangement of the Muscovite and Ruthenian churches, of the unique religious traditions of Ukraine, and of the resistance of many Kyivan churchmen to alienation from Constantinople and absorption by Moscow.

Churchmen and historians of the Moscow Patriarchate have found the history of the Kyiv Metropolitanate in the fifteenth to eighteenth centuries so difficult to integrate into their vision of the "Russian" church's past that they have largely ignored the subject.[3] In contrast, modern Ukrainian Orthodox leaders such as Lypkivs'kyi, Chekhivs'kyi, Ohiienko (Metropolitan Ilarion), and Stepan Skrypnyk (later Metropolitan Mstyslav), and church historians such as Nataliia Polons'ka-Vasylenko, Ivan Vlasovs'kyi, and Dmytro Doroshenko, have lavished particular attention on this period.[4] While they concur

Ukraïns'koï Tserkvy (Rome, 1975), series 2, section 1, vol. 33 of *Analecta OSBM*; and his addendum in *Analecta OSBM* 10 (1979): 406–87.

3.   See, e.g., Archbishop Makarii, *The Eastern Orthodox Church in the Ukraine* (Kyiv, 1980) and my review of it in *Religion in Communist Lands* 14, no. 1 (1986): 73–6.

4.   See Dmytro Doroshenko, *Pravoslavna Tserkva v mynulomu i suchasnomu zhytti ukraïns'koho narodu* (Berlin, 1940); Nataliia Polons'ka-Vasylenko, *Istorychni pidvalyny UAPTs* (Munich, 1964); Ivan Vlasovs'kyi, *Narys istoriï Ukraïns'koï Pravoslavnoï Tserkvy*, 4 vols. in 5 bks. (New York and South

with the negative evaluations of Catholic and Polish dominance posed by Russian historians and churchmen, they view the period as one in which the faith of Kyivan Rus' endured and developed its own traditions in the heartland of the old Rus' state. They assert time and again that these traditions were more closely related to those of Kyivan Rus' than were the traditions of the Muscovite state, and they argue that by the sixteenth century Muscovite Orthodoxy was a particularly alien phenomenon for Ukrainians and Belarusians.

In the process of differentiating the Ukrainian church from the ROC and restoring Ukrainian Orthodoxy, the autocephalists evolved principles fundamental to their church. The separation of church and state, autocephaly, conciliarism, Ukrainianization, and the Christianization of life became tenets of what was even called the "ideology" of the UAOC.[5] The major historian of the church, Bohdan Bociurkiw, has described these principles as the basis of a renewal or "modernization" that transformed the Orthodox Church into an active and effective institution in Ukrainian society and consequently made it particularly dangerous to the Soviet regime.[6] However modernizing the principles were in practice, they drew their legitimacy by being cast as a return to earlier traditions. The autocephalists' insistence that the church base itself on the apostolic church gave their reforms a universal Christian basis. Their dedication to restoring the Ukrainian church's traditions stimulated them to search the history of the Kyiv Metropolitanate for evidence supporting their church reforms. Rather than investigating the nature and accuracy of the precedents utilized by the autocephalists,

---

Bound Brook, N.J., 1955–66), of which vols. 1–2 have been translated into English as Ivan Wlasowsky, *Outline History of the Ukrainian Orthodox Church* (New York and South Bound Brook, N.J., 1974, 1979); Ivan Ohiienko, *Ukraïns'ka Tserkva*, 2 vols. (Prague, 1942); and Vasyl' Lypkivs'kyi, *Istoriia Ukraïns'koï Pravoslavnoï Tserkvy, rozdil 7: Vidrodzhennia Ukraïns'koï Tserkvy* (Winnipeg, 1961), available in German translation as *Die Ukrainische Autokephale Orthodoxe Kirche* (Würzburg, 1982).

5.   See Archbishop Kostiantyn Krotevych, "Do ideolohiï U.A.P.Ts.," *Tserkva i zhyttia*, 1928, no. 1: 14–24.

6.   Bohdan R. Bociurkiw, "The Ukrainian Autocephalous Orthodox Church, 1920–1930: A Case Study in Religious Modernization," in *Religion and Modernization in the Soviet Union*, ed. Dennis J. Dunn (Boulder, Colo., 1977), 310–47. See also Friedrich Heyer, *Die Orthodoxe Kirche in der Ukraine von 1917 bis 1945* (Cologne-Braunsfeld, 1953); and my essay *The Ukrainian Orthodox Question in the USSR* (Cambridge, Mass., 1987), a revised version of which appears in this volume.

this article will discuss the degree to which the early modern period could serve as a model for the Ukrainian autocephalists' goals.[7]

Church and State

The Ukrainian Orthodox Church movement saw the bondage of the Orthodox Church to the Russian imperial state as a major failing of the old order. Forged in the struggle against the Russian state's assault on Ukrainian Orthodox traditions and against a Russian hierarchy that depended on the state to buttress its position, the Ukrainian Orthodox believed in benevolent state neutrality and religious toleration. The socialist cast of Ukrainian parties in the Ukrainian People's Republic (UNR) and the atheistic nature of the Ukrainian SSR meant that this principle represented the optimal situation for which the church could hope. Although we might assume that the autocephalist position would have moved toward seeking more active support for the church had there been an independent state with more powerful pro-religious political factions, we can be sure that the long negative experience of the Russian state's role in church affairs left an enduring mark on autocephalist thought.

The Ukrainian Orthodox turned to visions of Kyivan Rus' and Cossack Ukraine for a more positive model of church-state relations than that provided by the nineteenth-century Russian Empire. While Kyivan Rus' offered the example of a Ukrainian state that could be clearly contrasted with Muscovy, and in some cases with Byzantium, the early modern period presented a more contradictory image of church-state relations.[8] Modern church leaders condemned both the

---

7.   The basic works on Ukrainian church history are Vlasovs'kyi, *Narys;* Atanasii Velykyi, OSBM, *Z litopysu Khrystyians'koï Ukraïny,* vols. 4–6 (Rome, 1971–3); Michaele Harasiewicz [Mykhailo Harasevych], *Annales Ecclesiae Ruthenae* (Lviv, 1862); Hryhor Luzhnyts'kyi, *Ukraïns'ka Tserkva mizh Skhodom i Zakhodom:Narys istoriï Ukraïns'koï Tserkvy* (Philadelphia, 1954); Ludomir Bieńkowski, "Organizacja Kościoła Wschodniego w Polsce," in *Kościół w Polsce,* vol. 2, ed. Jerzy Kłóczowski ([Cracow], 1969), 733–1050; and Eduard Winter, *Byzanz und Rom im Kampf um die Ukraine, 955–1939* (Leipzig, 1942). Important works in East Slavic church history are Albert Maria Ammann, *Abriss der Ostslavischen Kirchengeschichte* (Vienna, 1950); Anton V. Kartashev, *Ocherki po istorii Russkoi Tserkvi,* 2 vols. (Paris, 1959); and Metropolitan Makarii (Bulgakov), *Istoriia Russkoi Tserkvi,* 12 vols. (St. Petersburg, 1864–86).
8.   On church-state relations, see Kazimierz Chodynicki, *Kościół Prawosławny a Rzeczpospolita Polska, 1370–1632* (Warsaw, 1934); Mykola Chubatyi, "Pro pravne stanovyshche Tserkvy v kozats'kii derzhavi," *Bohosloviia* 3 (1925): 19–53, 181–203; and Oleksander Ohloblyn, "Problema

Lithuanian and Polish states' discriminatory practices against the Orthodox, and the practice of kings' patronage rights, which undermined the election of hierarchs by the church. They especially censured King Sigismund III and the Polish-Lithuanian Commonwealth's Diet for their role in the Union of Brest and the persecution of the Orthodox Church. Yet, despite this negative appraisal, they approved of the privileges of self-administration granted the church and the traditions of legality that were lacking in Muscovy. The clear preference of Metropolitan Petro Mohyla and his successor Syl'vestr Kosiv for the Commonwealth over Muscovy slightly muted the modern churchmen's criticism of the policies of the Commonwealth, but greatly strengthened their argument that the Ukrainian Orthodox had disavowed subordination to the Russian church and state. Metropolitan Kosiv's insistence that he would not surrender church lands to tsarist officials, the decision of Metropolitan Dionysii Balaban to support Hetman Ivan Vyhovs'kyi's break with Moscow, and the action of Metropolitan Iosyf Tukals'kyi in siding with Hetman Petro Doroshenko indicated how deeply Ukrainian churchmen mistrusted the Muscovite pattern of church-state relations.

The modern Ukrainian churchmen sought to find positive aspects in the relations of the Cossack Hetmanate and the church, but the picture was a mixed one at best. The concept of "state" was even more tenuous as a description of the Hetmanate than it was of early modern Muscovy or the Commonwealth. The evolution of the Cossack Host into the political organizing structure of many Ukrainian territories was gradual. Even though Bohdan Khmelnyts'kyi governed the Hetmanate as a de facto independent state and was treated by some churchmen (Patriarch Paisios of Jerusalem and Paul of Aleppo) as a sovereign Orthodox prince, no assertion of full independent status with the hetman as a sovereign occurred before Ivan Mazepa's time. In many ways, the ideal hetman for the modern Ukrainian church movement was Petro Sahaidachnyi, who used his political power to secure the restoration of the church hierarchy and patronized educational and monastic institutions. Although Sahaidachnyi was the image of the righteous ruler, as a loyalist to the Commonwealth who led the Cossack Host before the establishment of the Hetmanate he was never a sovereign over Ukrainian territory. In looking for positive aspects of

---

derzhavnoï vlady na Ukraïnï za Khmel'nychchyny i Pereiaslavs'ka uhoda 1654 roku," *Ukraïns'kyi istoryk* 2 (1965), nos. 1–2: 5–13 and nos. 3–4: 11–16.

church-state relations, twentieth-century Ukrainian churchmen could point to the part the Khmelnyts'kyi uprising played in ending discrimination against the church, the solicitude of Khmelnyts'kyi and his successors for Orthodox ecclesiastical institutions, the support of the hetmans and the Cossack administration for church privileges, and the maintenance of electoral procedures in church life.

There were other incidents between hetmans and the church that were troubling to twentieth-century churchmen. Khmelnyts'kyi had threatened and bullied the metropolitan, and early indications that the hetman and the metropolitan would develop into complementary ruling authorities in Ukraine progressed no further. Khmelnyts'kyi had also entered into the Pereiaslav Agreement against the metropolitan's wishes; Hetman Ivan Briukhovets'kyi had requested that a metropolitan be sent from Moscow; and Hetman Ivan Samoilovych had taken an active part in subordinating the Kyiv Metropolitanate to Moscow in 1685–86. Criticism could also be levelled against the churchmen. Although the Orthodox bishops of Lviv and Lutsk were reported to have provided funds and munitions to the rebels in 1648, and the clergy and students of Kyiv greeted Khmelnyts'kyi as a liberator, Metropolitan Kosiv had been no real friend of the revolt and had feared bondage to the Cossacks. In 1651 he had tried to come to an accommodation with the victorious armies of the Commonwealth. Finally, numerous Orthodox clerics, including Bishop Metodii Fylymonovych, showed a willingness to serve the tsar and Muscovy rather than the hetman and the Hetmanate.

Had an enduring independent Ukrainian state emerged in the seventeenth century, twentieth-century churchmen would have had a more solid precedent to invoke. Instead they had to discuss an autonomous entity that existed in the ever-changing relations with Muscovite, Polish-Lithuanian, Tatar, and Turkish states and sovereigns. Just as importantly, they could only turn to a political entity that from the first had not encompassed all the Ukrainian lands, to say nothing of the even greater lands of the Kyiv Metropolitanate. Political divisions had presented the seven-teenth-century metropolitans with grave problems as they tried to keep the metropolitanate united despite the political fragmentation of their lands. As victorious Muscovite armies alienated episcopal sees in Belarus from Kyiv, metropolitans had to choose in which part of the metropolitanate they would reside at the cost of losing control of other areas (e.g., the appointment of administrators for the lands in the Left-Bank Hetmanate); thus they faced the losing battle of maintaining the integrity of a church without an independent

Ukrainian state and within the context of political divisions. It was an ominous precedent for twentieth-century Ukrainian church leaders, who could only hope that the modern separation of church and state would allow them to succeed in a venture (i.e., maintenance of a Ukrainian church without an independent Ukrainian state or without the unification of all Ukrainian lands) in which their seventeenth-century predecessors had failed.

Autocephaly

The modern Ukrainian church movement saw autocephaly, or self-rule, as the only form of administration that would permit the development of a national church free of manipulation by a Russian hierarchy, either synodal or patriarchal. It viewed—correctly, as time would show—the Moscow Patriarchate's concessions of autonomy to the church in Ukraine after 1917 as tactical manoeuvres to be withdrawn as soon as the opportunity arose. Ukrainian church leaders, above all Oleksander Lotots'kyi, studied the institution of autocephaly in the Orthodox world.[9] Modern autocephalous churches have appeared largely as a consequence of the emergence of new states; the collapse of the independent Ukrainian state occurred before an autocephalous Ukrainian church could gain recognition from the Constantinople Patriarchate. The Ukrainian church movement did not consider the Russian church, which had controlled Ukrainian Orthodoxy and had no desire to relinquish control, as the authority empowered to recognize autocephaly. Rather, it turned to the ecumenical Constantinople Patriarchate—the mother church of the Kyiv Metropolitanate—which had lost control of the metropolitanate to Moscow in 1686. Even though Constantinople never recognized the Ukrainian church as autocephalous, it strengthened the Ukrainian church movement greatly when, in 1924, it condemned the alienation of the Kyivan metropolitan see as simoniacal and uncanonical.

In all discussions of the autocephalous issue, the Ukrainian churchmen evoked historical precedents. They emphasized elements of autonomy in the relationship between Kyiv and Constantinople in the Middle Ages, and the virtual self-government of the various metropolitanates created for the Ukrainian and Belarusian lands in the fourteenth and fifteenth centuries. Essential to the autocephalist argument, however, was the extremely limited role of

---

9.   See Oleksander Lotots'kyi, *Avtokefaliia*, 2 vols. (Warsaw, 1935–8).

Constantinople in the sixteenth century. In reality, this situation had come about because of the weakness of the patriarchate and the increasing interference of Lithuanian and Polish rulers in church affairs. The late sixteenth-century Ukrainian church revival had, in fact, been marked by an increasing influence of the Constantinople and other Eastern patriarchs in Ukrainian church affairs, evident in the deposing of the Kyiv metropolitan in 1589, the granting of stauropegial rights to church brotherhoods and monasteries, and the appointment of exarchs. The modern autocephalist could, however, point to the virtual independence of the church, which was supported, but not controlled, by the patriarchate. Although the Mohylan hierarchy had been constituted in 1632 by direct intervention of the state, the Mohylan church did represent a virtually autocephalous church. After 1654 the Kyiv Metropolitanate had to defend its integrity against the Muscovite state and patriarchate (although Patriarch Nikon did uphold some of its rights). For the twentieth-century leaders there were clear-cut heroes and traitors; modern churchmen did little to understand the motivations of a Metodii Fylymonovych or a Lazar Baranovych, ignoring the fact that the seventeenth-century churchmen had real fears of Catholic or Islamic power and could not fully predict the outcome of their relations with Muscovy. For the modern autocephalists the dismantling of the Kyiv Metropolitanate and the subordination to Moscow (1685–86) destroyed a de facto autocephalous church.[10]

The early modern period offered an unfulfilled program to a Ukrainian autocephalous church—the project for a Kyiv patriarchate. Discussions in the 1580s proposing that the patriarch of Constantinople take up residence in Ostroh were followed in the 1620s by projects to elevate the metropolitan of Kyiv to patriarchal rank. They illustrated the growing importance of the Kyivan Orthodox see in the early seventeenth century. During the 1920s the possibility of such an innovation was discussed, and seventeenth-century precedents could be invoked.

The seventeenth century also served as a model for a pronounced Ukrainian, rather than Ruthenian (Belarusian-Ukrainian), character of the Kyiv Metropolitanate. Most historians of the Ukrainian Orthodox Church appropriate the entire metropolitanate to their

---

10. On the subjugation of the Kyiv Metropolitanate by the Moscow Patriarchate, see Natala Carynnyk-Sinclair, *Die Unterstellung der Kiever Metropolie unter das Moskauer Patriarchat* (Munich, 1970).

church. Yet the church of the fifteenth to seventeenth centuries should properly be referred to as Ruthenian, because it encompassed both Belarusians and Ukrainians. Indeed, the Belarusian territories of the Grand Duchy of Lithuania provided the centre of gravity for church life in the fifteenth and early sixteenth centuries, because the metropolitans resided in Vilnius and Navahrudak. However, by the end of the sixteenth century the Ukrainian territories rose to greater prominence in Orthodox church life: the metropolitans returned to Kyiv; Lviv and Kyiv emerged as major centres of ecclesiastical and intellectual activity; and the strongholds of Orthodoxy—the Lviv Dormition Brotherhood, the Zaporozhian Cossacks, and the nobility of the lands incorporated into the Kingdom of Poland at the Union of Lublin—were all in Ukrainian territories. With the establishment of the Kyiv Collegium, Ukraine became the intellectual centre of Orthodoxy for believers in the metropolitanate.

In the first stage of the Cossack revolt, the Ukrainian aspect of the church was reinforced as the Muscovite armies sought to subordinate Orthodoxy in Belarus directly to the Moscow Patriarchate. Thus the metropolitanate became more Ukrainian. Even the acceptance of "Little Rus'" in the title of the metropolitan of Kyiv defined the church as Ukrainian. Therefore, just as political (the existence of a Ukrainian polity) and social (the importance of the Cossacks in Ukraine) differentiation furthered the distinctiveness of the Ukrainian and Belarusian people, so too the rise of the Kyivan ecclesiastical centre and the evolution of the church in the political and social conditions of the Hetmanate led to a distinct Ukrainian, rather than Ruthenian, Orthodox tradition. Although the elements of virtual autocephaly, the delimitation of the Kyiv metropolitan see to the Ukrainian territories, and the evolution of a specific Ukrainian, rather than Ruthenian, tradition did not occur at the same time and were but certain phases of early modern developments, they did provide examples for the modern, twentieth-century autocephalists.

Conciliarism, or "Sobornopravnist'

The members of the modern Ukrainian church movement considered the interference of the state and the authoritarian policies of bishops responsible for the decay of Orthodoxy in the Russian Empire. As the secular clergy and laymen who backed the movement found the bishops and monks to be their antagonists, their belief in conciliar governance of the church increased. Conciliarism also influenced Russian church circles, but the Ukrainian church leaders saw their program not only as a movement of reform but as a movement of restoration of authentic Ukrainian traditions. They saw active participation by the laity, the election of hierarchs and clergymen, and governance by parish, eparchial, and national councils as ancient Ukrainian traditions. In practice, however, their precedents were drawn chiefly from the late sixteenth and seventeenth centuries. The Lviv Dormition Brotherhood, Hetman Sahaidachnyi, the enrolment of the Cossack Host into the Kyiv Epiphany Brotherhood, the participation of the nobility and Cossacks in church councils, and lay participation in electing clergy in the Hetmanate were held up as exemplary models for the present. The councils of the 1590s, the 1620s, and 1640 were seen as examples of the proper means of governance.

Influenced by Western cultural influences and organized along the lines of corporate orders, Orthodox nobles in the early modern period took a more active role in church affairs. Endowed with the rights of citizens of the Commonwealth, the nobles alone could guarantee security for the church. They could provide a safe haven for Orthodoxy on their estates, even when the church was illegal (1596–1632), and they could argue for church rights in the Diet. As the nobles assumed more important positions in the governance of the church, the clergymen were able to respond to government pressure by asserting that they could come to no decisions without nobiliary consent (e.g., the synod of 1629). The nobles, however, proved to be an uncertain bulwark for the church. Increasing numbers of conversions undermined the level of noble support for Orthodoxy, while, after the revolt of 1648, many Orthodox nobles chose the nobiliary Commonwealth over the Orthodox rebels. By the late seventeenth century, as resistance to the Union of Brest sputtered out, the loss of the Orthodox nobility sealed the fate of the church in the lands held by Poland.

The autocephalists, operating in a society where the upper classes were predominantly Russified, propagated "democratic" views that made them more favourably disposed to non-elite orders. In looking at early modern church affairs, they saw their counterparts in the burghers and the Cossacks. The burghers were indeed the organizers of the church brotherhoods, that unique contribution of the Ukrainians and Belarusians to ecclesiastical affairs.[11] They had also inaugurated schools and publishing enterprises that reformed religious life. Their delegates had taken part in church councils and

---

11. On the brotherhoods, see Iaroslav D. Isaievych, *Bratstva ta ïkh rol' v rozvytku ukraïns'koï kul'tury XVI–XVIII st.* (Kyiv, 1966).

contributed to organizing the political defence of Orthodoxy. The Cossacks appeared in the Ukrainian tradition as knights defending the nation and the church. Their stubborn adherence to Orthodoxy, their enrolment in the Kyiv Epiphany Brotherhood, and their support for the Orthodox Church before and after 1648 made them model lay activists. However, in their conservatism in ritual and their resistance to innovation the burghers and the Cossacks were far removed from the autocephalists' vision of renewal.

Most important to the autocephalists was the election of church officials as a tradition of the local churches. From the councils that met to elect metropolitans to the selection of priests by the parishes, the early modern church had strong traditions of democracy and community participation that could be invoked by the autocephalists. While it may be questioned how ancient these traditions were and how fully they diverged from the practices of the Russian church in all times and places, the election of clergy and hierarchs had indeed characterized the early modern Ukrainian church.

There were aspects of the early modern Ukrainian church that did not provide supporting examples for the autocephalists' program. Viacheslav Zaikin argued persuasively that many of these practices were not known in the early Christian church or in Kyivan Rus' and that they were often practical responses to difficult situations reluctantly embarked upon in early modern Ukraine.[12] It was indeed true that the laity became prominent because the early modern church was weak and poorly led by the clergy and because the rulers could not be trusted to act in the church's best interest. Throughout the early modern period some clergymen had resisted the influence of the laity in the governance of the church and resented their own dependence on laymen and church brotherhoods. Under Mohyla the church and the Cossack Host were at odds, and after 1648 hierarchs, such as Syl'vestr Kosiv, resented the influence of the Cossacks in church affairs.

The monastic tradition of early modern Ukraine presented particular difficulties to the autocephalist movement, which was deeply distrustful of the monks of the imperial Russian church as a group alienated from the faithful and antagonistic to Ukrainian aspirations. The late sixteenth and seventeenth centuries had been a time of monastic renewal in Ukraine. Founded frequently by the

---

12. Viacheslav Zaikin, *Uchastie svetskogo elementa v tserkovnom upravlenii, vybornoe nachalo i "sobornost'" v Kievskoi mitropolii v XVI i XVII vekakh* (Warsaw, 1930).

old Orthodox nobility and the Cossack elite, the monasteries had provided an important service not only as bastions of the faith, but also as centres of printing and learning. The archimandrite of the Kyivan Cave Monastery had been elected by clerical and lay dignitaries and functioned as a wider community leader. The great monasteries of Kyiv had initially opposed the extension of the Russian church's jurisdiction into Ukraine as undermining their autonomy. With its tradition of flight from the world, however, the monastic tradition contained an element antithetical to the Ukrainian autocephalists' vision. They found the pro-Russian sentiments of the trans-Dnipro monasteries of the 1630s and the eagerness of the great Kyivan monasteries to be directly subordinated to alien patriarchates—first Constantinople and then Moscow—troubling. These monasteries did eventually provide the cadres for the imperial Russian church, and in so doing they undermined Ukrainian church traditions.

The early modern Ukrainian church was one in which councils were used in governance and married clergymen and laymen had an important voice. Institutions such as the church brotherhoods were derived from reform movements in the laity. In the Hetmanate "national" and local assemblies met to fill civil and ecclesiastical posts. The autocephalists could find a great deal in the early modern period to affirm their vision of the church. They could not, however, draw upon a precedent entirely harmonious with their vision: bishops had resisted lay influence, church councils had not met after 1648, and monasteries and monasticism had had a much greater role in the church than the modern autocephalists wished them to play.

Ukrainianization

For the Ukrainian intelligentsia and certain segments of the peasantry, the Ukrainian church movement offered the benefit of Ukrainianization—a church in a comprehensible and national tongue. The Ukrainian Orthodox Church was the first Slavic church to abandon Church Slavonic in the liturgy and to accept the modern vernacular. Ukrainianization also involved incorporation of traditional and folk religious practices, approbation of national holidays and values in liturgical settings, and revocation of such anti-Ukrainian practices of the imperial church as the anathema against Hetman Ivan Mazepa.

From the perspective of the Ukrainian national movement, up-grading the status of the Ukrainian language so that it had a place in the UAOC was essential. The introduction of Ukrainian in the liturgy, therefore, did not stem only from the consideration of comprehensibility that churchmen in Russia offered in proposing the introduction of the Russian language. By replacing Russian with Ukrainian in sermons and church administration, the major characteristic of Ukrainian identity—the Ukrainian language—would be established as a central aspect of church life, and its status would be elevated. The autocephalists could not find a precedent for the use of early modern Ruthenian or Ukrainian in the liturgy; indeed, the seventeenth-century Ukrainian church reform concentrated on purifying Church Slavonic and improving its teaching. They could, however, point to the use of Ruthenian-Ukrainian in translations of the Scriptures, in composing sermons, and in church administration. It was among the Ruthenians that the question of the use of a vernacular literary language alongside Church Slavonic was first raised among the Orthodox Slavs. Ukrainian and Belarusian intellectuals discussed the relationship of two different languages—Church Slavonic and Ruthenian—and their spheres of use. Some sought to increase the sphere of Ruthenian (Meletii Smotryts'kyi), while others wished to hold firm to the use of Church Slavonic (Ivan Vyshens'kyi). In practice, however, all employed the vernacular.[13]

The modern Ukrainian church movement could also find precedents in the nativization of the church. In contrast to earlier periods in which Greek or South Slavic prelates had occupied major posts, in the seventeenth and eighteenth centuries almost all bishops and hegumens were Ukrainians or Belarusians. Metropolitan Mohyla was the notable exception, though the close relationship between the Moldavian and Ruthenian cultures and between the Mohyla family and the Commonwealth made him very close to a native. After 1654 the local clergy actively resisted any attempts at appointing Muscovites. The Ukrainianization in personnel paralleled an indigenization in rituals. Metropolitan Mohyla pursued an active policy of emphasizing the history and sanctity of the local church. He canonized the Fathers of the Kyivan Cave Monastery and refound the relics of St. Volodymyr. In practice, the church also incorporated local customs. Frequently this was not the result of a conscious policy, and at times seventeenth-century clergy even sought to purify practices by excluding local customs.

In general, the church of the seventeenth century was a specifically Ruthenian branch of Orthodoxy and, for reasons outlined

---

13. On the role of the church in cultural life, see Mykhailo Hrushevs'kyi, *Kul'turno-natsional'nyi rukh na Ukraïni XVI–XVII st.*, 2d ed. (n.p., 1919).

earlier, may be viewed as specifically Ukrainian even in customs and traditions. The art, music, and literature of the church integrated Byzantine traditions, Orthodox Slavonic culture, the legacy of Kyivan Rus', local customs, and Western influences into a distinctive Ukrainian synthesis. Autocephalists could appeal to the partial use of the vernacular language and to the patterns of Ukrainian church culture in their efforts to Ukrainianize the church.

Christianization of Life

The autocephalists' final principle was the Christianization of life. By offering instruction in the vernacular and reforming the church to address the needs of contemporary society, they sought to create Christian communities of dedication and conviction. They could find numerous precedents for their program in the early modern church. The church brotherhoods were communities dedicated to spiritual and intellectual renewal that emerged as a response of the society at large. The educational revival represented a movement to enlighten and had resulted in the Ukrainian church assuming leadership in the Orthodox world. The generous donations of the nobility and the Cossack officers had been accompanied by a general rise in religious interest and personal piety. The one model offered by the early modern period that the Ukrainian church movement rejected was that of the dominant role played by monasteries and monks in the seventeenth century. Generally, however, autocephalists could see the early modern period as one in which reform and revival had raised the level of religious thought and piety.

Conclusions

Despite contradictory tendencies in early modern church affairs, the Ukrainian church movement could find many authentic precedents for its program. The culture and faith of early modern Ukraine differed so markedly from imperial Russian Orthodoxy of the nineteenth century that they could serve as the basis for a modern Ukrainian Orthodox revival. In particular, the need to reform and adapt in the early modern period corresponded to the spirit of the Ukrainian church movement. There were, however, a few major differences. In the early modern period the church constituted the major intellectual and cultural institution of Ukrainian society, and it established values and norms. In the twentieth century the church was a peripheral institution for much of the population and had to compete with secular ideas and institutions. The establishment of the Ukrainian church movement was a means of returning the church to a more central position in society by realigning it away from Russian imperial traditions and toward the Ukrainian national awakening. The fundamental difference was that early modern Ukrainian Orthodoxy evolved under new political, cultural, and social circumstances without a program for change and innovation. Although the modern Ukrainian church movement looked to the past for precedents and legitimacy, the founders of the UAOC espoused an ideology that approved of innovation and change as positive aspects of renewal.

Serhii Plokhy

The Crisis of "Holy Rus'": The Russian Orthodox Mission and the Establishment of the Ukrainian Greek Orthodox Church of Canada[*]

The establishment of the Ukrainian Greek Orthodox Church (UGOC) in 1918–19 was an event whose significance went far beyond the confines of the ecclesiastical life of Canada's Ukrainian community. The conversion to Orthodoxy of a considerable number of the Ukrainian Greek Catholic intelligentsia and its founding of a new and independent church had a major influence not only on the development of Ukrainian Orthodoxy, but also of Russian Orthodoxy. Ever since the subordination of the Kyiv Metropolitanate to Moscow and the creation of the Russian Empire, the Russian Orthodox Church (ROC) had regarded Ukrainians as an inalienable component of "one Holy Rus'."[1]

The uniqueness of the situation in which the founding of the new Ukrainian church took place consisted above all in the fact that the

---

[*] Previously unpublished. Translated from the Ukrainian by Myroslav Yurkevich.

1. On the subordination of the Kyiv Metropolitanate to Moscow, see S[ergei] A. Ternovskii, "Issledovanie o podchinenii Kievskoi mitropolii Moskovskomu patriarkhatu," in *Arkhiv Iugo-Zapadnoi Rossii*, vol. 5 (Kyiv, 1873); K[onstantin] V. Kharlampovich, *Malorossiiskoe vliianie na Velikorusskuiu tserkovnuiu zhizn'* (Kazan, 1914), 149–249; and Ivan Vlasovs'kyi, *Narys istorii Ukraïns'koï Pravoslavnoï Tserkvy*, vol. 2 (New York and South Bound Brook, N.J., 1956), 292–343.

The idea of "one holy Rus'" as it existed in the Russian clerical milieu during the last years of the Russian Empire is conveyed to some extent in the works of Metropolitan Antonii (Khrapovitskii), one of the leading figures of the ROC in Ukraine during the Revolution of 1917. In one of the circular letters he composed as an émigré, he wrote: "Rus' united gradually from the time of Tsar Aleksei Mikhailovich, then Peter I, Catherine II, and before the last war. Only the thrice-damned revolution again dismembered Holy Rus', once again placing significant areas of Russian population under foreign and un-Orthodox rule and leaving our people divided among various states of un-Orthodox faith to the present day" (Bishop Nikon [Rklitskii], *Zhizneopisanie blazhenneishago Antoniia, mitropolita Kievskago i Galitskago*, vol. 9 [New York, 1962], 112).

North American continent became the meeting place of political and confessional currents that had never been able to interact freely in Ukraine while it was divided by imperial boundaries. In North America, on the common ground of Orthodoxy, traditionalists and renovationists coexisted, ideas of Ukrainian ecclesiastical autonomy were beginning to develop, and former Greek Catholics were active— Galician Russophiles and members of the populist intelligentsia who sought in Orthodoxy greater scope for the expression and profession of their Ukrainian ideology. The conflict of various Orthodox currents and the diversity of national approaches to the Orthodox idea on the North American continent virtually modeled a situation that might have arisen in a united Ukraine and is, therefore, of particular interest to the student of Ukrainian history.

It was the Ukrainian Greek Orthodox Brotherhood, which openly declared its existence after the "confidential" meeting of July 1918, that initiated the formation of the Ukrainian Greek Orthodox Church of Canada. Its leaders, prominent among whom were the young Galician populists Myroslaw Stechishin [Stechyshyn] and Wasyl Swystun [Vasyl' Svystun], reflected the interests of the secular intelligentsia, the students, and to some extent the Galician immigrant community in Canada generally. The Galician immigrants wanted to rid themselves of the authority of the Greek Catholic clergy, which seemed to them too indifferent to Ukrainian problems and too Rome-oriented, in order to transform the Greek Catholic Church into a Ukrainian national church. They turned in the direction of Orthodoxy as the faith adopted by St. Volodymyr the Great, prince of Kyivan Rus', a faith subsequently professed and defended by the Ukrainian Cossacks. Striving to establish an independent Ukrainian Orthodox Church based on the principles of popular rule, i.e., the broad participation of the secular element in matters of church administration, the initiators of the "confidential" meeting of 1918 also understood the importance of the institutions of the episcopacy and the clergy, without which the church could not exist.[2] The need for episcopal organization within the future church prompted the initiators of the UGOC to turn to Bishop Aleksandr (Nemolovskii) of the ROC.

---

2.   On the initiators of the UGOC and its early activity, see Iurii Mulyk-Lutsyk, *Istoriia Ukraïns'koï Hreko-Pravoslavnoï Tserkvy v Kanadi*, vol. 3, *Ukraïns'ka Hreko-Pravoslavna Tserkva v Kanadi v iurysdyktsiï Mytr. Germanosa* (Winnipeg, 1987), 159–203, 263–96; and Paul Yuzyk, *The Ukrainian Greek Orthodox Church of Canada, 1918–1951* (Ottawa, 1981), 90–6.

The propagation of Orthodoxy in North America began in 1794 with the establishment of the Russian Orthodox mission to Alaska. Soon after the sale of Alaska to the United States in 1867, the Russian Holy Synod created the Eparchy of the Aleutians and Alaska, with its seat initially in Sitka and later in San Francisco. With the beginnings of Ukrainian immigration to North America, the Russian Orthodox mission, which gave rise to the ROC's Eparchy of the Aleutians and North America, began its work among the immigrant Ukrainians. This involved not only dealing with Orthodox Bukovynians, but also a mission to the Greek Catholic Galician and Transcarpathian immigrants. The ROC's interests were advanced by conflicts between the Greek Catholic and Roman Catholic clergy in North America and by the fact that the services of Orthodox clergymen, who received salaries from the tsarist government, could be purchased much more cheaply by the faithful.

Successful missionary activity among Ukrainians was one of the reasons for the conversion of the ROC's Eparchy of North America into an archeparchy in 1905, during the tenure of the future patriarch of the ROC, Tikhon (Belavin). It was also under Tikhon's administration that the seat of the archeparchy was transferred from San Francisco to New York, which was further evidence of the re-orientation of the Russian mission from the former Russian settlements in Alaska to the Ukrainian immigrants on the eastern seaboard of the United States and Canada. In 1908 the new ruling hierarch, Archbishop Platon (Rozhdestvenskii), established a separate administration of the Russian mission for Canada.[3]

The events of the Revolution of 1917 and subsequent civil war in the Russian Empire confronted the Russian mission in North America with an unexpected challenge. The Orthodox Church in Russia split into three independent sections: the Renovationist

---

3.   In the United States the year 1891 marked the beginning of Greek Catholic conversion to Russian Orthodoxy. There the process involved mainly settlers from the Lemko region. In Canada the first conversion of Greek Catholics to Russian Orthodoxy took place in 1897. On the origins and history of the Russian Orthodox mission in North America, see *Ocherk iz istorii Amerikanskoi Pravoslavnoi Dukhovnoi missii, 1794–1837: K stoletnemu iubileiu pravoslaviia v Amerike, 1794–1894* (St. Petersburg, 1894); Archimandrite Serafim, *The Quest for Orthodox Church Unity in America: A History of the Orthodox Church in North America in the Twentieth Century* (New York, 1973); Constance J. Tarasar et al, eds., *Orthodox America 1794–1976: Development of the Orthodox Church in America* (Syosset, N.Y., 1975); and Mulyk-Lutsyk, *Istoriia*, 3: 204–45.

Church, which was supported by the Bolsheviks; the Church Abroad, which was overtly anti-Bolshevik and active within the Russian émigré community; and the Patriarchal Church headed by Patriarch Tikhon, who initially responded to Bolshevik pressure by declaring the church's neutrality on political questions and later was forced to recognize Soviet power.[4] The revolution opened the way for an unprecedented growth of the Ukrainian national movement and Ukrainian consciousness, which did not fail to take account of the church and served to promote the development of Orthodoxy both in Ukraine and in the immigration.[5] The rise of Ukrainian consciousness among the clergymen and faithful of the Russian Orthodox mission in Canada who had come from Ukraine occurred at a time when important changes were taking place in the mission's leadership. In June 1917 the ruling hierarch of the North American Archeparchy, Archbishop Evdokim (Meshcherskii), left for Russia to take part in a sobor in Moscow. His temporary replacement as head of the archeparchy became the administrator of the Russian mission in Canada, Bishop Aleksandr (Nemolovskii). Aleksandr, who was born in Volhynia, had long served in North America; as subsequent events showed, he took a sympathetic attitude to the Ukrainian movement.[6]

Evdokim's departure for the sobor and Aleksandr's accession to the seat of the archeparchy in New York made possible the emergence of Archimandrite Adam (Phillipowsky [Fylypovs'kyi]) as a leading figure in the administration of the Russian mission in Canada. A former Greek Catholic, Adam converted to Orthodoxy because of his Russophile convictions. He was an ardent supporter of the idea of "one Holy Rus'."[7] With his appointment as administrator of the Russian mission in Canada, two centres of authority—New York and

---

4.   On the split in the Russian Orthodox Church during the revolution, see Dimitry Pospielovsky, *The Russian Church under the Soviet Regime, 1917–1982*, vol. 1 (New York, 1984), 25–162, 255–300.

5.   The history of the Ukrainian Orthodox movement during the revolution is best presented in Bohdan R. Bociurkiw, *The Politics of Religion in the Ukraine: The Orthodox Church and the Ukrainian Revolution, 1917–1919*, Kennan Institute for Advanced Russian Studies, Occasional Paper no. 202 (Washington, D.C., 1985); and in Vasyl' Ul'ianovs'kyi, *Tserkva v ukraïns'kii derzhavi 1917–1920 rr. (Doba Het'manatu Pavla Skoropads'koho)* (Kyiv, 1997).

6.   Biographical information about Aleksandr can be found in Mulyk-Lutsyk, *Istoriia*, 3: 421, 239–41.

7.   For an account of Phillipowsky's career, see Mulyk-Lutsyk, *Istoriia*, 3: 238–42.

Winnipeg—emerged within the North American Archeparchy. The conflict between those centres, and between Aleksandr and Adam personally, was deepened by Adam's ambitions, the insecurity of Aleksandr's tenure at the archeparchial seat in New York (he was not elected the ruling hierarch there until March 1919), and the division of the archeparchy between two countries, the United States and Canada. The ideological roots of the conflict, however, lay in the opposing views of the bishop and the archimandrite on the Ukrainian question and its role in the Orthodox Church.

Open conflict between Aleksandr and Adam began in June 1917 at the Orthodox congress in Winnipeg, when Aleksandr provoked a wave of discontent among the Russian and Russophile clergy with his support of the Ukrainian faction at the congress. When he was asked whether he considered himself a Ukrainian, the bishop replied, "I was born in Volhynia. We call it 'Little Russia,' while you call it 'Ukraine.' Thus you may call me a Ukrainian bishop."[8] Apparently Aleksandr considered the congress a fitting occasion for the first open manifestation of his pro-Ukrainian sympathies, but the reaction of the Russian and Russophile circles proved so sharp that the bishop found himself obliged to take a much more cautious stand. Approached in the summer of 1918 with the first proposal of the initiators of the UGOC to take the church under his pastoral care, the bishop responded with an indefinite "Why the divisions?"[9]

After considerable hesitation, Aleksandr posed the question of the establishment of a Ukrainian Orthodox Church (UOC) in Canada for consideration at the second sobor of the Russian Orthodox mission,

8. See Archimandrite Adam, "Zlobnyia intrigi na menia za zashchitu russkago dela pered mazepinstvom," *Svet*, 1919, 9–11; reproduced in Mulyk-Lutsyk, *Istoriia*, 3: 527–8. Adam writes that when the Ukrainians at the meeting sang their national anthem "Shche ne vmerla Ukraïna" (Ukraine Has Not Yet Died) and the Russophiles responded with the song "Pora, pora za Rus' sviatuiu" (It Is Time, Time on Behalf of Holy Rus'), "The Bishop approached our singers and said aloud, 'Be quiet and do not hinder them (i.e., the Mazepists), [but] let them sing, for they sing the same thing in Petrograd.'" According to the principal Russophile newspaper in Canada, Aleksandr "ordered that the speech at the Winnipeg Congress be written in phonetic script and that Ukrainian newspapers be distributed. Also, on the first day of the congress, when the Russian boys sang 'Pora, pora za Rus' sviatuiu' and the Ukrainians belted out 'Ne pora' [It Is Not Time], the bishop told the Russians to remain silent and asserted that 'Ne pora' should be sung, for he ... himself had sung 'Ne pora' when he was a student in Petrograd" (*Russkii narod*, 17 April 1919).

9. Aleksandr's letter to Myroslaw Stechishin, 4 (17) July 1918, in Mulyk-Lutsyk, *Istoriia*, 3: 422.

held in Cleveland in March 1919. The sobor elected Aleksandr archbishop for North America and approved the establishment of a Ukrainian church under his authority. In organizational terms, the question was to be resolved according to the previous practice of subordinating certain non-Russian Orthodox Churches, such as the Serbian, Albanian, and Syrian, to the Russian mission. The Ukrainian church was to be regarded not as a national body but as a political, and hence temporary, one. The conditions under which Archbishop Aleksandr agreed to take the UOC under his authority were that church's acceptance of Orthodox dogmas and rituals, the supremacy of Patriarch Tikhon and the Russian archbishop in North America, and the assignment of all church property to the archbishop.[10]

The sobor's decision on the Ukrainian church and the de facto victory of Aleksandr's supporters brought forth a storm of protest from the Russophile camp. Archimandrite Adam's attacks on Aleksandr forced the latter to seek another solution to the Ukrainian question. In time the Ukrainian clerical milieu in the Russian mission came up with the idea of creating a UOC in Canada as a component of the autonomous Orthodox Church in Ukraine that had been proclaimed at the Kyiv sobor of 1918. This was entirely plausible in terms of church canons and was intended to neutralize Russophile attacks on the decision of the Cleveland sobor. A stimulus to the emergence of this plan was the arrival in the United States in June 1919 of the former archbishop of North America, Platon (Rozhdestvenskii), who had since become the metropolitan of Odesa and Kherson. On 30 June Archbishop Aleksandr sent a telegram to the secretary of the Ukrainian Greek Orthodox Brotherhood, Myroslaw Stechishin, informing him that he had spoken with Platon, who had listened with approval and considered that there was a way to resolve the Ukrainian problem. Aleksandr asked the brotherhood to send a delegate to New York immediately.[11]

Wasyl Swystun was dispatched as the Canadian delegate. He arrived in New York on 16 July and conducted negotiations with Archbishop Aleksandr (Metropolitan Platon was out of town at the time), signing an agreement with him on the establishment of a Ukrainian church in Canada.[12] Metropolitan Platon later acquainted

---

10.   On the Cleveland sobor's decision, see Mulyk-Lutsyk, *Istoriia*, 3: 485–87; and Yuzyk, *The Ukrainian Greek Orthodox Church*, 178.

11.   For the text of the telegram, see Mulyk-Lutsyk, *Istoriia*, 3: 496.

12.   Ibid., 506–7. Cf. the text of the agreement in Swystun's own account, *Kryza v Ukraïns'kii Pravoslavnii (Avtokefal'nii) Tserkvi* (Winnipeg, 1947), 82–4.

himself with the agreement and gave it his general approval, with the reservation that certain details would have to be discussed at the sobor. In time the details were concretized. Platon wanted the brotherhood to send him a petition on the formation of a UOC in Canada and to recognize the canons of the Russian church.[13] The actual point at issue was the liquidation of all the particular rights of the UGOC guaranteed by the agreement between Swystun and Aleksandr and the establishment of an ordinary eparchy of an autonomous UOC in Canada. The brotherhood never replied to the conditions Platon laid down.

The stimulus for a complete breach of relations between the brotherhood and the Russian mission was Archbishop Aleksandr's pastoral letter of 10 (23 N.S.) September 1919, in which he asserted that the Ukrainians were not a distinct people but merely one of the political parties of Russia. This letter, which Aleksandr wrote under pressure from his Russian and Russophile opponents, gained widespread notoriety in Canada and was exploited by the Greek Catholic clergy in their campaign against the formation of the UGOC. The brotherhood's rift with Aleksandr and the Russian mission became inevitable. In November 1919 the newly established UGOC came under the pastoral authority of Metropolitan Germanos (Shegedi), who was under the jurisdiction of the patriarch of Antioch. Thus, the conflict within the Russian mission came to an end: the UOC of Canada was established outside the bounds of the Moscow patriarch's authority.[14]

What were the views of the Russian mission's leading circles on the challenge that the growing Ukrainian movement presented?

One of the articles in the newspaper *Ukraïns'kyi holos*, the principal mouthpiece of the initiators of the UGOC, defined the composition of the clergy serving in the Russian mission in Canada as Muscovite, Little Russian and Russophile (*"moskal', maloros i moskvofil"*).[15] That designation referred not only to the ethnic origin

---

13.   For the text of Rev. Panteleimon Bozhyk's letter to Swystun presenting Metropolitan Platon's conditions, see Mulyk-Lutsyk, *Istoriia*, 3: 519.

14.   For information about Metropolitan Germanos and documents on his recognition of the UGOC, see Mulyk-Lutsyk, *Istoriia*, 3: 610–81; Yuzyk, *The Ukrainian Greek Orthodox Church*, 103–5; and Roman Yereniuk, "Church Jurisdiction and Jurisdictional Changes among Ukrainians in Canada, 1891–1925," in *The Ukrainian Religious Experience: Tradition and the Canadian Cultural Context*, ed. David J. Goa (Edmonton, 1989), 121–2.

15.   *Ukraïns'kyi holos*, 29 October 1919.

of the mission's clergymen but also to their political, national, and ecclesiastical orientation. However, even if one accepts the division of the Orthodox clergy in Canada proposed by *Ukraïns'kyi holos*, it should be noted that there were considerable differences in the attitudes of the "Muscovites" (ethnic Russians), "Russophiles" (Galicians who had converted to Orthodoxy), and "Little Russians" (clergymen from Russian-ruled Ukraine) to the Ukrainian question.

The idea of a single Russian people divided into three branches, one of which was the "Little Russians" or Ukrainians, but united by a single Orthodox Church was the fundamental idea of Russian Orthodoxy during its synodal period. Hostility to the Ukrainian movement, a typical attitude among the higher Russian clergy, was based on the view that the Ukrainian movement was an attempt at splitting one people, "one Holy Rus'." In Ukraine that view was shared by Metropolitan Vladimir (Bogoiavlenskii) of Kyiv, an ethnic Russian. According to a participant in the Ukrainian Orthodox movement, the metropolitan simply could not understand what the supporters of Ukrainian autocephaly were accusing him of. At a meeting with a Ukrainian delegation in 1917, he asked in bewilderment, "What is Ukraine? What is the Ukrainian people? Are not the Little Russians the same as the Russian people?" In a pastoral letter written in the summer of 1917, he wrote in particular, "Love of one's native land cannot overshadow or overcome love for all of Russia and the one Orthodox Russian Church."[16]

During the revolution, under pressure by the growing Ukrainian movement, the idea of "Holy Rus'" underwent some modification at the Moscow and Kyiv sobors of 1917–18. The change in attitude toward the Ukrainian idea on the part of Metropolitan Platon, who participated in both sobors and then became directly involved in the negotiations with the founders of the UGOC, perhaps best demonstrates the changes that were taking place in the attitude of the Russian hierarchy toward the Ukrainian Orthodox movement.

In December 1917 Metropolitan Platon left Moscow for Ukraine as the plenipotentiary representative of the newly elected Patriarch Tikhon and head of the delegation of the Moscow Orthodox sobor. He was to ensure that the Kyiv sobor, whose convocation was demanded by the supporters of Ukrainian ecclesiastical autonomy, was conducted "according to the canons." Platon's general policy in Ukraine was determined by Tikhon's instructions: yes to the

---

16.   See Bociurkiw, *The Politics of Religion,* 10 and 51.

broadest autonomy, no to autocephaly. The Kyiv sobor proclaimed the establishment of an autonomous Orthodox Church in Ukraine, and it elected Platon to the Supreme Church Council, the governing body of the UOC, which was headed by Metropolitan Antonii (Khrapovitskii). Besides Antonii and Platon, Archbishop Evlogii (Georgievskii) of Volhynia and one other bishop were members of the council.[17]

In December 1918, with the overthrow of Hetman Pavlo Skoropads'kyi's regime by the forces of the Directory of the Ukrainian People's Republic (UNR), Metropolitan Antonii and Archbishop Evlogii were arrested and Metropolitan Platon became the de facto head of the Supreme Church Council. But soon Platon left Kyiv, heading first to Odesa, then to Istanbul, and finally to the United States, where he arrived in June 1919.[18] During his stay in

17. Metropolitan Platon, who hailed from the Kursk region, spoke Ukrainian well. In 1895 he graduated from the Kyiv Theological Academy, where he remained as an inspector, and in 1902 he was appointed its rector. When he first came to the United States in 1908, he was vicar of the Kyiv Eparchy and a deputy to the Second Russian State Duma. Recalled to the Russian Empire in 1914, he was first appointed to Kishinev (Chişinau) and then became exarch of the Georgian Orthodox Church. When the February Revolution erupted, he was in Georgia. After the Georgian church proclaimed its autocephaly, Platon was arrested, but later he was released and allowed to travel to Petrograd. See Vlasovs'kyi, *Narys*, 4, pt. 2 (1966): 45; and Bociurkiw, *The Politics of Religion*, 53.

18. According to a contemporary, Platon was present at Antonii's arrest: "After Archbishop Evlogii's arrest, Metropolitan Platon spent the night in Metropolitan Antonii's office, but neither of them slept. On the evening of 5 [18] December a truck arrived with five Petliurites, who said that they had come to arrest 'Citizen Metropolitan Antonii as a dangerous enemy of our country and of the Ukrainian people.'... After the vehicle departed, there were various rumours. Some said that the metropolitan had already been killed, while others said that he was being tortured in some prison—in short, each rumour was more terrible than the last" (Nikon, *Zhizneopisanie blazhenneishago Antoniia*, 4: 240).

During the rule of Hetman Skoropads'kyi, Platon demonstrated considerable flexibility on the issue of Ukrainian independence. It was he who welcomed the hetman as a guest at the Kyiv sobor on 23 July 1918, and he endorsed the idea of an independent Orthodox Ukraine in his address to Skoropads'kyi. For the text of this address, see Vasyl' Ul'ianovs'kyi and Bohdan Andrusyshyn, "Tserkva v Ukraïns'kii het'mans'kii derzhavi: Poperedni notatky ta dokumenty," in *Ostannii het'man: Iuvileinyi zbirnyk pam'iati Pavla Skoropads'koho* (Kyiv, 1993), 353.

Oleksander Lotots'kyi, who was acting minister for religious affairs under the Directory of the UNR and subsequently the UNR's ambassador

America, Platon remained generally true to the views on the Ukrainian church he had developed in 1917 and 1918. Evidence of this is to be found in the long excerpts from his Kyiv speeches and declarations cited in Archbishop Aleksandr's pastoral letter of 10 September 1919.[19] The first document written by Platon that is cited in the pastoral letter was an appeal to the Ukrainian Church Council dated 22 December 1917. There Platon, following the guidelines of the Moscow sobor, came out in favour of autonomy for the Ukrainian church but rejected the idea of its autocephalous status. His refusal to countenance autocephaly was based on three grounds: canonical—the Ukrainian church was not recognized as possessing the authority of apostolic founding; historical—the Ukrainian church had not previously enjoyed autocephalous status; and juridical—Platon insisted on a referendum on the question of autocephaly involving the entire Orthodox population.

The other document cited extensively in Aleksandr's pastoral letter is Platon's speech at the opening of the Kyiv sobor on 7 January 1918. The speech provides evidence of a certain change in the higher Russian clergy's treatment of the Ukrainian ecclesiastical movement—a change that had led to modification of the idea of "one and indivisible Orthodox Rus'." The term "Little Russia" had been changed to "Ukraine," with the latter bearing the same significance and meaning as the former. In particular, observed Platon in his speech, "There will be rejoicing among those creators

---

to Turkey, left the following reminiscence of his contacts with Platon: "Back in Kyiv, when he visited me at the ministry, I gave him to understand that I was in possession of the original appeal against the Directory written in his hand. On the same day he disappeared from Kyiv, having pleaded his way into the compartment of a foreign diplomat who was leaving Kyiv for Odesa.... From Odesa, which was then in the hands of the [Russian] Volunteers, who had taken charge under the protection of Entente troops, Metropolitan Platon related and wrote fantastic tales of Ukrainian 'bestialities.' The Ukrainian ambassador in Athens, F[edir] P. Matushevs'kyi, later told me about ... Platon's letter to the Greek metropolitan, in which he related that on the orders of the Ukrainian authorities the hair and beard of Metropolitan Antonii had been plucked out one hair at a time in order to violate his Orthodox hierarchical dignity by giving him the appearance of a Catholic priest. It is thus easy to imagine what this unworthy hierarch related in person once he found himself in the favourable atmosphere of the [Russian] Volunteer [Army] in Constantinople" (Oleksander Lotots'kyi, *Storinky mynuloho*, vol. 4, *V Tsarhorodi* [Warsaw, 1939], 92).

19.   For the text of Aleksandr's pastoral letter, see Mulyk-Lutsyk, *Istoriia*, 3: 533–6.

of Ukraine's history, fighters for its civil and ecclesiastical life, our fathers and grandfathers, who always considered themselves Orthodox, always Russian, and always children of their homeland—their native Ukraine, their native Holy Rus'."[20] Such were the changes and concessions that the Russian episcopate was prepared to make on the Ukrainian question.

In defining the ideology of those who favoured the establishment of a UOC in North America, two of Archbishop Aleksandr's pastoral letters about the UGOC are especially significant. One was written on 21 February 1919 after the Cleveland sobor ended; the other was the 10 September 1919 letter mentioned above and was written after Metropolitan Platon arrived in the United States and the Russophile party's attacks on Aleksandr intensified. Both letters are interesting because they document the Russian and Russophile view of the Ukrainian problem, to which Aleksandr was obliged to adhere and to which he had to appeal. They are also important because they describe his efforts at justifying and substantiating the right of a Ukrainian Orthodox Church to exist within the bounds of that official ideology.

In his February letter, Aleksandr stressed that the motto of the Orthodox remained unchanged: "One indivisible Orthodox Rus'." Appealing to views and conceptions widespread in the Russian and Russophile milieu, he emphasized that the Ukrainians were sons of Holy Rus' who came from the same Russian roots and constituted a political party, not a distinct people. "It is our opinion," wrote Aleksandr, "that the Russian people living in Russia (Little Russia) created Ukraine for the sole purpose of saving themselves from Lenin and Trotsky."[21]

Having accepted and proclaimed the thesis of the indivisibility of Holy Rus' and the political, rather than national, character of Ukrainian identity, Aleksandr was obliged to base his justification for the formation of a UOC on that thesis. According to him, because the goal was to convert Greek Catholics to Orthodoxy, certain concessions could be made for that purpose and the Greek Catholics could be allowed to call their church Ukrainian if they were so used to that name. The letter expressed the hope that the "Ukrainians," once converted to Orthodoxy, would in time become "one with our American Orthodox Rus'." Given that there were already two political parties, Republican and Democratic, in the United States, there would be no point in maintaining the old political division

---

20. Ibid., 3: 535.

21. The text of the first pastoral letter is also reproduced in ibid., 3: 487–8.

transplanted into the immigrant milieu from the homeland.[22] Thus, the central idea of the pastoral letter was that of making a tactical concession to the Ukrainian movement in order to ensure the success of the Orthodox mission among Greek Catholics and obtain their adherence to "one Orthodox Rus'."

While the decision of the Cleveland sobor on the establishment of a separate Ukrainian eparchy was widely disseminated and discussed in the press, Archbishop Aleksandr's pastoral letter remained little known to the general public. It is even unlikely that members of the Ukrainian Greek Orthodox Brotherhood read it, for there was no reaction on their part to the offensive formulation about the Ukrainians being a political party rather than a people. Only when Aleksandr repeated the same assertion in his subsequent pastoral letter and again when he was in Canada did a harshly negative reaction from the initiators of the UGOC ensue.

Archbishop Aleksandr's pastoral letter of 10 September 1919 also repeated the formula of "one indivisible Orthodox Rus'" as its leading idea and again stressed that "Ukrainians are not a distinct people, a nation, but only one of the Russian political parties ... [and] the children of one mother, Holy Rus'."[23] Moreover, in this letter Aleksandr spoke more boldly about Ukraine and the Ukrainian church than in his previous one. The grounds for this were the Kyiv sobor's decision and Patriarch Tikhon's recognition of the UOC's autonomy. Aleksandr's references to the sobor's decision were undoubtedly associated with Metropolitan Platon's arrival in New York. By citing Platon's Kyiv speeches in his letter, Aleksandr was clearly trying to kill two birds with one stone—to please the more senior hierarch and to defend the decision of the Cleveland sobor on the Ukrainian question.

The acceptance of the term "Ukraine" for everyday use and the removal of its negative, abusive connotation confronted imperial Orthodoxy with the task of developing new concepts and a new terminology in order to do battle with the Ukrainian movement per se, i.e., the movement for Ukrainian state sovereignty and ecclesiastical independence. The supporters of the all-Russian ideology began dividing Ukraine and Ukrainianism into positive (pro-Russian or "Little Russian") and negative (anti-Russian) camps. Aleksandr solved the problem for himself—more precisely, for his opponents—as follows: "there is a profound distinction between Orthodox Russian Ukraine, which we clearly understand as an

---

22. Ibid., 3: 533–4.
23. Ibid., 3: 535.

inalienable part of Holy Rus', and Uniate Swabian Ukraine, 'cut off,' independent, [and] hating all that is Russian."[24]

Archbishop Aleksandr was actually articulating the notion, subsequently adopted by many Russian Orthodox thinkers, of eastern and central Ukraine as an inalienable component of Rus' and Russia, and of Galicia as an element foreign to "Holy Rus'" in both religious and political terms. In associating the movement for Ukrainian independence with the "Swabians," i.e., the Germans, Aleksandr was alluding to the accusation, common during the First World War, that the Ukrainian movement was acting in German interests and was indeed a product of German intrigue. But in referring to anti-Russian sentiments only in Uniate "Swabian" Ukraine, he was certainly being disingenuous, the better to deflect such accusations from the Ukrainian movement in Orthodox Russian Ukraine.

As concerns terminology and, to some extent, ideology, Aleksandr's second pastoral letter was a step in the direction of the Ukrainian movement: under the influence of events in Ukraine, the letter propagated the idea of an autonomous UOC. In practical terms, however, the letter marked the archbishop's breach with the initiators of the UGOC. In it Aleksandr stated that he had consecrated no Ukrainian priests and would not give Ukrainians the right of free action within the Orthodox mission. The letter justifies this abrupt change of position on his part by citing Ukrainian efforts to organize parishes not among Uniates but among Orthodox who belonged to the Russian mission. This accusation that Ukrainians were proselytizing among the faithful of the Russian mission served to prepare the formal grounds for Aleksandr's abandonment of the principal argument that he had given in his first pastoral letter in favour of the establishment of a Ukrainian church—that of converting Greek Catholics. Now the archbishop took a diametrically opposite position. He wrote, in particular, "Better that thousands should die for Orthodoxy, but I shall not permit that a wedge be driven into the body of Christ—the church."[25]

It is not known to what extent these arguments of Aleksandr were sincere. The development of Ukrainian Orthodoxy within the framework of the Russian mission and at its expense (most of its faithful were from Ukraine) was indeed a mortal danger to the mission. Both of Aleksandr's pastoral letters were written with an eye to the circumstances and attitudes that were then developing

24. Ibid., 3: 536.
25. Ibid.

within the Russian Orthodox mission. Even though the recognition of Orthodox ecclesiastical autonomy in Ukraine theoretically broadened opportunities for the establishment of Ukrainian church institutions within the framework of the Russian Orthodox Archeparchy in America, in practice the opposite tendency prevailed—the confrontation between the Ukrainian and pan-Russian currents ended with the complete victory of the latter.

Generally speaking, the clergy of the Russian mission proved much more conservative on the Ukrainian question than the Russian clergy in Ukraine. The reasons for this should be sought above all in the fact that in Ukraine, as opposed to Canada and the United States, the Ukrainian movement developed into a political force represented by state power, unstable though it was. The Hetman government and the Directory of the UNR constituted a force with which the Russian hierarchs had to reckon. Secondly, the autocephalist movement in Ukraine grew and developed within the imperial Orthodox Church, and it was impossible simply to close the door in its face, as was done to the initiators of the UGOC. Another important reason for the failure of the Ukrainian movement within the Russian mission was the presence of an element that was absent in Ukraine, or in any event was not decisive for the fate of Ukrainian Orthodoxy. This element consisted of the Orthodox Galician Russophiles, who were extraordinarily active in Canada and far more anti-Ukrainian in their attitude than was imperial Russian Orthodoxy. It was the Galician Russophiles, represented by Archimandrite Adam (Phillipowsky), who were the principal force that did not permit the development of the Ukrainian movement within the Russian mission.

One of the reasons for the spread of Russophile sentiments and the conversion of Galicians to Russian Orthodoxy in Canada was the general political situation that developed there during the First World War. As part of the British Empire, Canada fought with the Entente against Germany and Austria-Hungary, from which the Galician immigrants in Canada had come. Thus, Galicians were considered a hostile element in Canada, and Russophile propaganda, which treated Galician Ukrainians as part of the Russian people and favoured the annexation of the Carpathian region by Britain's ally, Russia, could hardly remain without influence on the Galicians, threatened as they were by the Canadian authorities.[26]

26. On the fate of Ukrainian immigrants in Canada during the First World War, see Frances Swyripa, "The Ukrainian Image: Loyal Citizen and

The principal mouthpiece for the Russophile movement in Canada was the newspaper *Russkii narod* (The Russian People), edited by Viktor Hladyk and Roman Samilo. It was they who determined the newspaper's line and created a mass base for Archimandrite Adam's activity. For *Russkii narod*, the most authoritative figure was the Galician Russophile Dimitrii Markov, a deputy to the Austrian Parliament and the Galician Diet and one of the leaders of the "new course," a radical current in the Russophile movement that wholly identified Galicians with Russians and favoured the introduction of Russian as the literary language in Galicia. In Galicia, as in Canada, the complete identification of Galician Ruthenians with Russians was accompanied by the conversion of the leading representatives of the "new course" to Orthodoxy. This movement was much more successful in Canada than in Galicia.[27]

The Russophile movement, known in Canada as the "Russo-Carpathian movement," manifested its loyalty to Russia and Russian Orthodoxy in every way and was negatively disposed toward the Bolsheviks. In 1919 the Russophiles declared their solidarity with General Denikin and his army, which was supported by the Entente. The "Russo-Carpathians" considered the Ukrainian movement their principal opponent and sought to discredit it ideologically and politically by every means possible. The Russophiles' anti-Ukrainian credo was rather comprehensively formulated in a resolution adopted at a "Russo-Carpathian" convention held in Chipman, Alberta, in April 1919. The text of the resolution, prepared by Roman Samilo, proclaimed, "The convention decisively protests against Ukrainian separatism, as Ukraine has been conceived by the Germans in order

---

Disloyal Alien," in *Loyalties in Conflict: Ukrainians in Canada during the First World War*, ed. Frances A. Swyripa and John Herd Thompson (Edmonton, 1983), 47–68; and Peter Melnycky, "The Internment of Ukrainians in Canada," in ibid., 1–24.

27.   On the Russophile movement, see Mykola Andrusiak, *Narysy z istoriï halyts'koho moskvofil'stva* (Lviv, 1935); Stepan Ripets'kyi and Ostap Sereda, "Russophiles," in *Encyclopedia of Ukraine*, vol. 4, ed. Danylo Husar Struk (Toronto, 1993), 473–5; John-Paul Himka, *Religion and Nationality in Western Ukraine: The Greek Catholic Church and the Ruthenian National Movement in Galicia, 1867–1900* (Montreal and Kingston, Ont., 1999); and Anna Veronika Wendland, *Die Russophilen in Galizien: Ukrainische Konservative zwischen Österreich und Russland, 1848–1915* (Vienna, 2001). The ideas of those who supported the "new course" are presented best in Dimitrii Markov, *Russkaia i ukrainskaia ideia v Avstrii* (Lviv, 1915).

to divide the one Russian people into several parts. The Ukrainians are traitors to the entire Russian people and to all of Slavdom. Ukraine has never constituted an independent state."[28]

The view of the Ukrainian movement as a German intrigue was actively promoted in many items in *Russkii narod*. In an article published on 23 May 1918, the newspaper stated that "it was not in vain that Hrushevs'kyi fed at the Austrian trough; not for nothing did Austria give comfort to that Ukrainian 'activist.' A blind instrument in the hands of German politicians, he was preparing the triumph of the German imperialists the whole time."[29] Political accusations of this kind were accompanied in the newspaper by accusations that the Ukrainian movement was betraying the Russian (*russkii*) people. An article titled "Let Us Be Russians and Canadians" stated that "fat Germans, Austrians, and Jews, together with the traitors to the Russian people—all kinds of Skoropads'kyis, Vasyl'kos, and other Mazepist traitors ... sold the Little Russian people of Ukraine to the Swabians with the peace of Brest-Litovsk."[30] Since the supporters of the "new course" propagated the idea of the complete identity of the "Carpatho-Russians" with the "Great Russians," there was virtually no mention of the "Little Russians" in this context: given the presence of the Ukrainian movement in Russian-ruled Ukraine, this was a rather delicate question. Emphasis was placed directly on union with Russia.

In the eyes of the leaders of the Russophile movement, the very recognition of Ukraine's existence was a crime with a perfectly specific designation—treason to the Russian people. This approach to the problem of Ukrainian identity became the point of departure for Russophile attacks on the Ukrainian Orthodox movement and its supporters or even very cautious sympathizers. Archbishop Aleksandr became the principal target for attack by the Russophile clergy, both because the pro-Ukrainian position of the ruling hierarch was a real threat to the Russophile movement and because Archimandrite Adam himself was planning to head the Orthodox eparchy in Canada. The banner under which this struggle for the episcopacy proceeded was the defence of the idea of "one Orthodox Rus'."[31]

---

28. *Russkii narod*, 1 May 1919.

29. *Russkii narod*, 23 May 1919.

30. *Russkii narod*, 17 April 1919.

31. Later, in 1923, when Aleksandr was finally replaced in New York by Platon, who had again returned to the United States, Adam entered into a

The campaign to discredit Aleksandr, which was initiated by Archimandrite Adam's supporters as early as 1917, went into full swing in the spring of 1919, after the Cleveland sobor. The organizers of the campaign accused Aleksandr of recognizing the UOC, which implied recognition of Ukraine and consequently betrayal of the "Russian people." In the "Easter greetings" published in *Russkii narod* on 17 April 1919, it was noted that Aleksandr "is not recognized and will continue not to be recognized by the Russian people, he who gave recognition to some 'separate Ukrainian church' and thus to Ukrainian separatism, even as the glorious army of Gen. Denikin is fighting against intended Ukrainian separatism, and who, according to English and Russian newspapers, has separated himself from the mother church in Rus'."[32] An appeal to Aleksandr from the Galician Orthodox community of Wostok, Alberta, stated: "we ask Your Grace to break all ties with the traitors to the Russian people, the Mazepist Ukrainians…"[33]

Thus, the recognition of the UOC's right to exist implied the recognition of Ukraine, which amounted to "Mazepism," separatism, and treason. It is quite clear that the Russophiles were not prepared to make even the slightest ideological or organizational concession to the Ukrainian movement. The tactical compromise proposed by Russian circles, which involved the formal recognition of the terms "Ukraine" and "Ukrainian" used in the same sense as "Little Russia" and "Little Russians," and the recognition of Ukrainian ecclesiastical autonomy while retaining the dependence of the Ukrainian church on Moscow, was completely rejected by the Orthodox Russophile movement. One of the reasons for this was the Russophiles' recognition of the threat posed to them by the Ukrainian movement. They had already lost the battle in Galicia and were now trying to take their revenge in Canada, resolutely maintaining the Orthodox Church as their principal strong point.

The conflict between the Ukrainian and Russophile movements in Canada became, in practice, a continuation of the old Galician conflict over the self-identification of the Galician Ruthenians. The national revival that began in Galicia in the early nineteenth century produced several programs of Galician nation building. The idea of

---

struggle against the latter. By this point the issue could no longer have been that of defending Russian unity.

32. *Russkii narod*, 17 April 1919.

33. *Ukraïns'kyi holos*, 29 October 1919.

a distinct Ruthenian people, which had some success in Transcarpathia, was virtually absent from the sphere of political struggle in Galicia, where two alternative identities—the Ukrainian and the Russian—were in conflict. The activists of both camps, which took shape at first in the Greek Catholic Church's sphere of influence, later turned their gaze in the direction of Orthodoxy. But their views of Orthodoxy and what they sought in it were diametrically opposed. For the Russophiles, their breach with the Greek Catholic Church was the next logical step in their identification with the Russians, while the "Ukrainians," i.e., the Galician populists, wanted to establish their own national church and sought a return to the "popular" religion, which they considered to be the Orthodoxy of the times of Volodymyr the Great.

* * *

The appeal of the initiators of the UGOC to Archbishop Aleksandr became a challenge on the part of the Ukrainian movement, which was gathering strength and knocking ever more insistently on the door of the imperial Orthodox Church. The appeal provoked a deep division within the ranks of the Russian Orthodox camp, which had maintained formal unity until then. Three possible reactions to the Ukrainian challenge were formulated. The first was represented by Aleksandr and supported by the "Ukrainophile" clergy within the mission; the second belonged to Metropolitan Platon and was associated with the compromise attained by the Ukrainian sobor in Kyiv in 1918; and the third was formulated by the Russophile grouping headed by Archimandrite Adam. The very fact of the formulation of these programs, which testified to the divergences of opinion that had arisen in the Russian mission over the nationality question, gave evidence of the seriousness and profundity of the crisis in which the proponents of the idea of "indivisible Holy Rus'" found themselves. The victory of Adam's faction actually deepened the crisis, accelerating the process that led to the establishment of an independent UOC in Canada. The founding of that church preceded the organizational consolidation of the Ukrainian Autocephalous Orthodox Church in Ukraine, and the circumstances of its emergence modeled to some extent not only the development of Russo-Ukrainian ecclesiastical relations, but also the prospects of Orthodox-Greek Catholic relations in a future Ukraine.

Serhii Plokhy

In the Shadow of Yalta: International Politics and the Soviet Liquidation of the Ukrainian Greek Catholic Church[*]

In 1996 the Ukrainian Greek Catholic Church (UGCC) marked two important dates in its history: the four hundredth anniversary of the Council of Brest, which united that church with Rome, and the fiftieth anniversary of the Lviv Sobor of 1946, which terminated that church's legal activity on the territory of Ukraine for almost half a century. The Lviv Sobor was masterminded by the Soviet secret police, and it crowned the Stalinist policy of the liquidation of the church by its "reunification" with the Russian Orthodox Church (ROC).[1]

For more than forty years the history of the liquidation of the UGCC was more an object of ecclesiastical and political struggle than of scholarly study. Only in the course of the last decade since the rebirth of this church in Ukraine in 1989 has the political atmosphere in Ukraine permitted scholars to go beyond a one-sided approach to the history of the UGCC. In his presentation at the Second International Congress of Ukrainian Studies, held in August 1993 in Lviv, the late Bohdan R. Bociurkiw, the pre-eminent authority in the field, denounced both the mythological approach created by the Soviet counter-propagandistic literature and the

---

[*] An earlier version of this article was published in *Logos: A Journal of Eastern Christian Studies* (Ottawa) 35 (1994), nos. 1–4: 59–76. It has been revised.
1. On the history of the UGCC under the Soviet regime, see the writings of Bohdan R. Bociurkiw, the principal authority on the subject: "The Uniate Church in Soviet Ukraine: A Case Study in Soviet Church Policy," *Canadian Slavonic Papers* 7 (1995): 89–113; "The Suppression of the Ukrainian Greco-Catholic Church in Postwar Soviet Union and Poland," in *Religion and Nationalism in Eastern Europe and the Soviet Union*, ed. Dennis J. Dunn (Boulder, Colo., 1987), 97–119; "The Ukrainian Catholic Church in the USSR under Gorbachev," *Problems of Communism*, November–December 1990, 1–19; and above all *The Ukrainian Greek Catholic Church and the Soviet State (1939–1950)* (Edmonton and Toronto, 1996).

martyrological approach that has dominated Ukrainian diaspora writings on the topic.[2]

Despite obvious differences between these two approaches to the history of the liquidation of the UGCC, both share the view that the main reason for the liquidation was the UGCC's close association with the Ukrainian national movement. This article proposes to challenge that position and to examine one of the long neglected aspects of the liquidation of the UGCC, namely, the influence of international politics on the Soviet decision to put an end to the activity of that church.

The Decision to Liquidate the Church

On 2 March 1945 Joseph Stalin and Viacheslav Molotov, deputy head of the Soviet government and people's commissar for foreign affairs, ordered Georgii Karpov, the head of the Council for the Affairs of the ROC (CAROC) and a colonel in the NKGB (the People's Commissariat for State Security), to prepare a memorandum that would include historical data and current information on the ROC's relations with the Vatican and proposals as to how that church could be used to fight Catholicism. Karpov submitted the memorandum to Stalin, Molotov, and Lavrentii Beria (head of the NKGB) on 14 March 1945. It was approved by Stalin on 16 March. From that time on the memorandum functioned as an instruction that co-ordinated the activity of the different government bodies and the ROC in their assault on the Catholic Church.

Karpov's memorandum was divided into four parts: (1) on the unification of the UGCC with the ROC; (2) on Soviet government support for Old Catholics and other measures to fight the Roman Catholic Church; (3) on support for ROC activity abroad; and (4) on the organization of the World Council of Christian Churches. The first part not only formulated the main goal of government policy

---

2. Bociurkiw's paper, "Mitolohiia chy martyrolohiia? Dosvid i problemy naukovykh doslidzhen' stalins'koï likvidatsiï Hreko-Katolyts'koï Tserkvy v Halychyni, 1944–1946," was distributed among the participants of the congress. He mentions Serhii Danylenko's books *Dorohoiu han'by ta zrady: Istorychna khronika* (Kyiv, 1970) and *Uniaty* (Moscow, 1972) as examples of the Soviet "mythological" approach to the topic. The "martyrological" tendency is represented by *First Victims of Communism: White Book on the Religious Persecution in Ukraine* (Rome, 1953) and *Martyrolohiia ukraïns'kykh Tserkov u chotyr'okh tomakh*, vol. 2, *Ukraïns'ka Katolyts'ka Tserkva: Dokumenty, materiialy, khrystyians'kyi samvydav Ukraïny*, comp. and ed. Osyp Zinkevych and the Rev. Taras Lonchyna (Toronto and Baltimore, 1985).

toward the UGCC—that is, its liquidation via "reunification" with the Moscow Patriarchate—but also proposed a number of measures to achieve it. These included the creation of an Orthodox eparchy in Lviv; the issuing of a patriarchal appeal to Ukrainian Greek Catholics to "reunite" with the Moscow Patriarchate, and the formation of an "Initiative Group" within the UGCC that would declare the termination of the church's links with the Vatican.[3]

Once approved by Stalin, Karpov's proposals acquired the force of official government policy and had to be implemented by all possible means. In his letters dealing with the memorandum, Karpov stressed that his proposals had been approved by Stalin.[4] It appears that on the lower level those instructions had been accepted as Stalin's personal orders.[5]

According to the Soviet legislation that was in place in 1945, the state body directly responsible for the government's policy toward the UGCC was the Council for the Affairs of Religious Cults (CARC). It had been established by Stalin in the fall of 1944 to control the activity of non-Orthodox denominations. In reality, the CARC was only a minor and insignificant player in Stalin's game. The head of the council, NKGB Col. Ivan Polianskii, had sent his subordinates the first instructions regarding the anti-Catholic offensive only in May 1945, when the entire Greek Catholic hierarchy had been in prison for more than three weeks and the anti-Uniate campaign had been underway in Galicia for more than a month. In order to respond to Polianskii's letter, his Ukrainian subordinate, Petro Vil'khovyi, had to go on a fact-finding mission to Lviv, and only subsequently did he report to his chief about the assault on the UGCC.[6] According to the memoirs of Metropolitan Iosyf Slipyi, the head of the Ukrainian "Committee for Religious

---

3.   The text of the memorandum has been published with some minor omissions in Ivan Bilas's article "Trahediia Tserkvy," *Patriiarkhat*, 1993, nos. 5: 16–19, 6: 18–21, and 7: 8–11. A modified version of this article appeared as "Moskovs'kyi patriiarkhat, karal'ni orhany SRSR ta znyshchennia UHKTs u 1940-ykh rokakh," *Logos* 34, nos. 3–4 (1993): 532–76.

4.   Bilas, "Trahediia Tserkvy," 1993, no. 6: 18.

5.   In the Ternopil region, one of the lower-ranking Soviet officials in charge of religious affairs told Greek Catholic priests that she personally did not care about any differences between Orthodoxy and Greek Catholicism as long as the priests fulfilled Stalin's wishes. See Vasyl' Hrynyk, "Tserkva u ridnomu kraiu i Polshchi," in *Martyrolohiia ukraïns'kykh Tserkov*, 2: 246.

6.   Bilas, "Trahediia Tserkvy," no. 6: 20–1.

Affairs" (probably Vil'khovyi) was very surprised when he learned of Slipyi's arrest.[7]

It appears that because the whole action was aimed at converting the Ukrainian Greek Catholics to Russian Orthodoxy, the CAROC was assigned to play a major role in the operation. When the Initiative Group was formed within the UGCC, its appeal for recognition was granted not by the CARC, but by the CAROC. The CAROC official, Pavlo Khodchenko, and not Vil'khovyi, signed a letter in which the Initiative Group was recognized as the highest administrative body of the UGCC and was instructed to co-ordinate its activity with CAROC representatives.[8] In the final account, however, the institutions that supposedly had to play the most important role in the whole action were in reality almost removed from the stage. Khodchenko and Vil'khovyi, the two writers who were promoted to their high government posts together with a number of other representatives of the Ukrainian cultural elite to demonstrate the national character of the Soviet Ukrainian state and to secure for Stalin an extra seat at the United Nations, served as a cover for other, much more powerful, government bodies that actually "ran the show."[9]

Karpov's memorandum was presented not only to Stalin and Molotov but also to Beria, the head of the Soviet secret police. This is not surprising, since both Karpov and Polianskii remained high-ranking NKGB officers after their appointment to government posts. Polianskii was Karpov's subordinate in the NKGB's religion department, and thus Karpov was directly responsible for the outcome of the whole action. Karpov probably did not differentiate much between the functions of the CARC and the CAROC. The task he initially gave Polianskii—the formation of the Initiative Group—belonged more to the realm of secret-police activity than of a normal government body. These facts help to explain Polianskii's reluctance to give instructions to his subordinates in the CARC. The

7. "Spohady Patriiarkha Iosyfa," *Patriiarkhat*, 1993, no. 6: 18.

8. See the text of Khodchenko's letter to the members of the Initiative Group, in *Diiannia Soboru Hreko-Katolyts'koï tserkvy u L'vovi 8–10 bereznia 1946* (Lviv, 1946), 19–20.

9. On Vil'khovyi's and Khodchenko's careers, see Bociurkiw, *The Ukrainian Greek Catholic Church*, 67, n. 18. During the war another Ukrainian writer, Oleksandr Korniichuk, was promoted to the post of minister of foreign affairs of Soviet Ukraine. See Orest Subtelny, *Ukraine: A History* (Toronto, 1988), 478.

main assault on the church was conducted by the NKGB, the institution responsible for the covert operations not only within the boundaries of the USSR, but also abroad.

Foreign-Policy Considerations

The text of Karpov's memorandum indicates that his main concern was the Vatican's "attempts at influencing the postwar world order." Stalin and Molotov's request for the memorandum came less than a month after the end of the Yalta Conference. Although the Vatican's policy was not officially on the agenda at the conference and there is no mention of the Vatican or the pope in any official documents of that meeting, apparently the Vatican's position on the issue of Europe's future was discussed there. Stalin allegedly posed his famous question about the pope—"How many divisions does he have?"—and President Franklin D. Roosevelt asked Molotov to discuss the future of the Catholic Church in the Soviet-occupied areas with his special envoy to the USSR.

1. President Roosevelt and Changes in Soviet Religious Policy

In 1941 the Soviet religious record had proved crucial to the success of President Roosevelt's attempts at securing the Lend-Lease Agreement for the USSR: there was a danger that American aid to the atheistic Soviet Union might meet with strong opposition in the United States. Roosevelt was especially concerned with a potentially negative reaction on the part of the Roman Catholic Church, whose faithful constituted an important part of the Democratic electorate.

In his 29 June 1941 address to the world, Pope Pius XII neither supported the German attack on the USSR nor declared a new crusade against Communism, as had been expected by some of Roosevelt's opponents. This gave Roosevelt some breathing space. On 8 July 1941 he sent a note to the Vatican confirming the United States' commitment to help the victims of German aggression, and the American diplomat at the Vatican was instructed to reveal at the time of the presentation of this note that "the principles and doctrines of communistic dictatorship are as unacceptable and as alien to the American people as are the principles of Nazi dictatorship."[10] In his letter of 3 September 1941 to the pope,

---

10. Raymond H. Dawson, *The Decision to Aid Russia, 1941: Foreign Policy and Domestic Politics* (Chapel Hill, 1959), 148.

however, Roosevelt compared two "forms of dictatorship," the German and the Russian, and came to the conclusion that the Russian one presented a lesser evil. He wrote: "I believe that the survival of Russia is less dangerous to religion, to the church as such, and to humanity in general than would be the survival of the German form of dictatorship. Furthermore, it is my belief that the leaders of all churches in the United States should recognize these facts clearly and should not close their eyes to these basic questions and by their present attitude on this question directly assist Germany in her present objectives."[11] Clearly Roosevelt tried to achieve one of the goals of his domestic policy with this statement.

In response to the president, Pope Pius XII expressed his support for American assistance "in the mission of mercy,"[12] but the presidential envoy was informed that, in the Vatican's opinion, the Bolsheviks were continuing to pursue their anti-religious policy and that only two Catholic churches were open in the entire USSR.[13] To secure the Vatican's support or at least to ensure its neutrality on the issue of American aid to the USSR, Roosevelt decided to send Myron C. Taylor, his personal representative to the pope, on a new mission to the Vatican. Taylor, who was a Protestant and a member of the board of directors of several major American corporations, was beyond suspicion of selling out American interests to Pius XII or to Stalin; therefore he was an ideal candidate for the planned mission.[14]

While sending his representative to the pope, Roosevelt also tried to influence Stalin to improve church-state relations in the USSR. Before his departure to Rome at the end of August 1941, Taylor wrote a letter to Roosevelt in which he drew the president's attention to Article 134 of the Soviet Constitution, which declared freedom of religion, a right that was not generally known in the United States. He also proposed to persuade Stalin to issue a declaration on the matter. That task was assigned to W. Averell Harriman. But even before Harriman's departure the Soviet

---

11.   Myron C. Taylor, ed., *Wartime Correspondence between President Roosevelt and Pope Pius XII* (New York, 1947), 62.

12.   Ibid., 64.

13.   Hansjakob Stehle, *Eastern Politics of the Vatican, 1917–1979*, trans. Sandra Smith (Athens, Ohio, and London, 1981), 221.

14.   Robert E. Sherwood, *Roosevelt and Hopkins: An Intimate History* (New York, 1950), 384.

ambassador to the United States, Konstantin Oumansky, was summoned to the White House. Roosevelt told him "that if Moscow could get some publicity back to this country regarding freedom of religion," it would help Congress to approve the next lend-lease bill. The president wanted the "publicity" to come as soon as possible, even before Harriman's arrival in Moscow.[15]

The Soviet response to Roosevelt's suggestion came only after the president on his own, without any "publicity" from the Soviet Union, declared at a press conference in Washington that freedom of religion was guaranteed by the Soviet Constitution. On 4 October the Soviets called a press conference for foreign journalists and the head of the USSR information agency, Solomon Lozovskii, announced that religion was considered to be a private matter in the USSR. Lozovskii's announcement followed Harriman's meeting with Stalin on 28 September, where the issue of freedom of religion had been raised. After the meeting Harriman discussed the same question in his talks with Molotov and Oumansky.[16] Harriman was obviously right when, after his return from Moscow in 1941, he wrote in an internal memorandum that in the USSR "religious worship will be tolerated only under the closest G.P.U. scrutiny."[17]

Though the immediate Soviet response to President Roosevelt's diplomatic pressure was by no means impressive, in the long run the pressure produced remarkable results and contributed immensely to the revision of Soviet policy toward the ROC. In December 1941 Pavel Sudoplatov, a high-ranking official of the Soviet secret police, met Oumansky, who revealed that Roosevelt had insisted on the dissolution of the Comintern and the improvement of church-state relations in the USSR.[18] Those requests had been duly fulfilled by the time Roosevelt and Stalin first met in Tehran in December 1943. The Comintern ceased to exist in May 1943, and the Soviet rapprochement with the ROC took place

15. Dawson, *The Decision to Aid Russia*, 236.

16. W. Averell Harriman and Elie Abel, *Special Envoy to Churchill and Stalin 1941–1946* (New York, 1975), 103.

17. Ibid, 103. In the 1920s the Soviet secret police was known as the Glavnoe politicheskoe upravlenie or GPU (Main Political Directorate).

18. Pavel Sudoplatov and Anatolii Sudoplatov, with Jerrold L. and Leona P. Schecter, *Special Tasks: The Memoirs of an Unwanted Witness—A Soviet Spymaster* (Boston, 1994), 222. Sudoplatov met Oumansky in Beria's office. Roosevelt's representative in the matter of the Comintern's dissolution was Harry Hopkins.

in September of that year.[19] The dissolution of the Comintern, which was announced in Moscow on 22 May 1943, allegedly raised some hopes in the United States that a concordat could be reached between the USSR and the Vatican. Around the same time rumours began spreading in New York, according to which Archbishop Francis Spellman, who was then on a visitation of American troops in Turkey, was a possible intermediary arranging the Vatican-Soviet agreement.[20]

2. The Yalta Conference and Edward Flynn's Mission to Moscow

On the eve of the Yalta Conference Sudoplatov had lunch with Harriman in the Aragvi restaurant in Moscow. One of Sudoplatov's tasks during that meeting was to reassure Harriman that the Soviet government was committed to the "tolerance of Catholics, Protestants, and Orthodox priests, even those who had collaborated with the Germans in the occupied territories during the war." Harriman apparently did not want to discuss that topic, being more interested in business opportunities in the Soviet Union after the war ended. He only mentioned that "the recent meeting to elect a patriarch for the [Russian Orthodox] Church had produced a favourable impression on American public opinion."[21]

The issue of Soviet church policy, Harriman's lack of interest notwithstanding, was of special concern to President Roosevelt on the eve of the Yalta summit, where the future of postwar Europe was to be decided. Significant concessions to Stalin, whose armies had marched victoriously to the West, were almost inevitable, and Roosevelt wanted to secure the Vatican's support for, or at least neutrality on, the decisions reached at the conference.

On 30 January 1945, on his way to Yalta, Roosevelt's adviser and special representative, Harry Hopkins, visited Pius XII at the Vatican. The twenty-minute audience was organized by Roosevelt's representative at the Holy See, Myron Taylor, who was present at

---

19.   On the role of the international factor in Stalin's decision to allow the elections of the patriarch of Moscow in September 1943, see Dimitry Pospielovsky, "The 'Best Years' of Stalin's Church Policy (1942–48) in the Light of Archival Documents," *Religion, State and Society* 25, no. 2 (June 1997): 139–62, here 140–3.

20.   Robert A. Graham, S.J., *Vatican Diplomacy: A Study of Church and State on the International Plane* (Princeton, 1959), 377.

21.   Sudoplatov and Sudoplatov, *Special Tasks*, 224.

the meeting.[22] Hopkins allegedly tried to persuade the pope to support the Allied plan for the division of Europe.[23] The pope's opposition to the plan was probably known in Washington long before Hopkins's visit to Rome. Early in January 1945 Roosevelt had invited his Catholic advisor and one of the leaders of the Democratic party, Edward J. Flynn, to go to Yalta to negotiate with Stalin and Molotov on the future of the Catholic Church in Eastern Europe and the Balkans. According to Flynn, the president believed that there could not be a lasting peace in Europe unless Catholics in those regions were granted freedom of religion.[24]

Flynn's mission had been prepared by Roosevelt in an atmosphere of strict secrecy. The president decided to inform Pius XII about the mission, but Flynn's name was not included on the list of the members of the American delegation to Yalta. Flynn entered the Soviet Union only with a letter signed by Roosevelt, and later he was issued an American passport in the American Embassy in Moscow.[25] Despite the secrecy surrounding Flynn's mission, information about its purpose was eventually leaked to the press. According to the Religious News Service, Flynn raised the following questions in Moscow: (1) permission for the Vatican to send clergy into Soviet-occupied Eastern Europe; (2) permission to reopen Roman Catholic institutions there; and (3) the issue of Italian prisoners detained in the USSR.[26] Considering that the idea of Flynn's mission to the USSR was expressed by Roosevelt in connection with the future of the church in Soviet-controlled Eastern

---

22.   Sherwood, *Roosevelt and Hopkins*, 848. Writing his book during the Cold War, when Roosevelt's concessions to Stalin were coming under attack in the West, Sherwood did not mention the future of Europe as a topic of discussion between Hopkins and the pope.

23.   Later the pope was praised for his objections to the plan. See Stehle, *Eastern Politics*, 250.

24.   See Edward Flynn's memoirs, *You're the Boss* (New York, 1947), 185.

25.   Ibid., 186–7. Secretary of State Edward Stettinius described the situation in relation to Flynn's mission in the following words: "The President said that he had a critical, urgent, and top-secret matter for the State Department. He had decided at the last minute to take Flynn on the trip to Crimea, and Flynn had no passport. The President added that he did not want Flynn to spend the rest of his days in Siberia. Steps were taken immediately to secure the passport" (*Roosevelt and the Russians: The Yalta Conference* [Garden City, 1949], 69).

26.   Graham, *Vatican Diplomacy*, 380.

Europe and the Balkans, the Religious News Service's account seems to be quite accurate.

It was only on his way to Yalta that Roosevelt decided that Flynn would go on a fact-finding mission to Moscow and other parts of the USSR after the conference. We know very little about Flynn's negotiations in Moscow. Neither in his letters to members of his family nor in his memoirs did he present any direct information on the purpose of his mission; he stated that "at this writing, my mission has not been completed and I shall have to omit a full account of progress."[27] However, he mentions some details that can help to explain the genesis of Karpov's memorandum to Stalin that initiated a major attack on the Catholic Church in the USSR.

Stalin ordered the memorandum during Flynn's mission to the Soviet Union. Flynn arrived in Moscow on 12 February, immediately after the Yalta Conference, and left the Soviet capital on 9 March 1945.[28] In Moscow he met Molotov, Karpov, and Polianskii.[29] All of them were involved in the preparation of the memorandum. According to Flynn's letters, he met with Molotov before 2 March, the date when the task to prepare the memorandum was assigned by Stalin and Molotov to Karpov, and was far from satisfied with his talks in the Kremlin. In a letter to his wife, Flynn noted: "I visited Mr. Molotoff [Molotov] at the Kremlin[,] and while conversations were not entirely successful I believe something was

---

27. Flynn, *You're the Boss*, 190. The twelve letters Flynn wrote during his mission to Europe between January and March 1945 to his wife Helen and other members of the family are preserved in the Franklin D. Roosevelt Library, Edward J. Flynn Papers, container 25. The papers also contain the diplomatic passport issued to Flynn in Moscow; the numerous visa stamps therein and the letters help to establish the exact dates of Flynn's mission in Moscow and Rome. I would like to thank Mr. Raymond Teichman and other members of the staff of the Roosevelt Library for helping me to obtain copies of the documents pertaining to Flynn's mission to Yalta.

28. The dates were established on the basis of the visa stamps in Flynn's passport and his letters to his family. For the date of Flynn's arrival to Moscow, see his letter to his wife dated 12 February 1945. His diplomatic passport was issued on 13 February, and a Soviet entry visa was issued to him on 17 February. On Flynn's departure date, see his letter to his wife of 8 March 1945, and the visa stamps in his passport. He was issued a Soviet exit visa on 8 March and an Egyptian entry visa by the Egyptian Embassy in Moscow on 9 March 1945.

29. Flynn's memoirs contradict Stehle's statement, based on Graham's information, that Flynn was allowed to talk only with Moscow city officials. See Stehle, *Eastern Politics*, 421.

accomplished."[30] It was also before 2 March that Karpov arranged Flynn's meeting with the new Moscow patriarch, Aleksii. Karpov was quite helpful in providing information on the activities of the ROC, but he denied any knowledge of other denominations. This was quite strange to Flynn; he writes in his memoirs that "Karpov, the government representative of the Orthodox Church, who had previously disclaimed all knowledge of other churches, was located in the same building on the floor above Pol[i]ansk[ii]."[31] Flynn's interview with Polianskii appeared to be even more peculiar. "For a chairman of a commission," wrote Flynn, "he seemed to know little or nothing about what was going on...[...] Throughout the conversation Pol[i]ansk[ii] was very nervous, vague, and either did not have the desired information or had determined not to give it. The interview was most unsatisfactory."[32]

Flynn left the USSR for Tehran and then Cairo, arriving in Rome on 21 March 1945. At the Vatican he met the pope twice and conducted talks with two Vatican representatives, Msgrs. Domenico Tardini and Giovanni Battista Montini (the future Pope Paul VI).[33] But the Soviet authorities apparently did not consider the Vatican's reaction to the results of Flynn's negotiations in Moscow to be of any importance to them: their decision to launch a major attack on the Catholic Church was made before Flynn reached Rome.

The Vatican's attempts at preventing Roosevelt from reaching an agreement with Stalin in Yalta and Flynn's attempts at negotiating the new concessions on the part of the Soviets should be listed among the immediate reasons that led to the preparation of Karpov's

---

30.   The letter is dated 2 March 1945 in Moscow.

31.   Flynn, *You're the Boss*, 194. In the account of his talks with Karpov, Flynn speaks about the difference between Karpov's role and that of the tsarist procurator of the Holy Synod (ibid., 192). That comparison can apparently be traced to the instructions Stalin gave Karpov on 4 September 1943. According to the minutes of the meeting, Stalin reminded Karpov that he was not supposed to act as procurator of the Holy Synod.

32.   Flynn, *You're the Boss*, 195.

33.   Ibid., 205–6. Flynn's letters and the visa stamps in his passport indicate that he left Baku for Tehran on 13 March. He arrived in Cairo on 15 March 1945. Flynn mentioned his one-hour meeting with the pope and his negotiations with Msgrs. Tardini and Montini in an undated letter to his wife from Rome. The letter was postmarked in Washington on 6 April 1945. On the results of Flynn's mission, see Peter C. Kent, *The Lonely Cold War of Pope Pius XII: The Roman Catholic Church and the Division of Europe, 1943–1950* (Montreal and Kingston, Ont., 2002), 82 and 272.

memorandum. Flynn's mission to Moscow dealt with the future of the Catholic Church in Eastern Europe and the Balkans and apparently did not target the issue of the church's future in the USSR. Karpov's memorandum did not discuss the future of the Catholic Church in Eastern Europe and concentrated instead on the anti-Catholic assault on the territory of the USSR. The latter was viewed within borders that were more reminiscent of the provisions of the Ribbentrop-Molotov Pact than those of the Yalta Conference. Though the conference recognized eastern Galicia as part of the Soviet Union and thus gave Stalin a free hand in conducting his anti-Catholic policy in that region, it did not recognize the abolition of the independence of the Baltic states, whose territories were also included in Karpov's plan. There could be only one explanation for the territorial dimensions of Karpov's memorandum: it covered those territories that constituted the USSR in June 1941.

The adoption of Karpov's memorandum as the basis for Soviet policy on the Catholic Church marked a clear departure from previous policy. Before the Yalta Conference, Stalin was apparently looking for opportunities, if not to win the pope's favour, then to neutralize the Vatican so that the Soviet Union could obtain approval from its Western allies for its territorial acquisitions in Eastern and Central Europe. At that time the Catholic Church (including the UGCC) was tolerated, and in April 1944 Stalin even agreed to meet the Catholic priest Stanisław Orlemański. To Orlemański's question, "Do you think that collaboration with the Holy Father, Pope Pius XII, is possible in the struggle against the oppression and persecution of the Catholic Church?" the Soviet dictator answered, "I believe that is possible." A photo of Stalin and Orlemański appeared in the 28 April 1944 issue of *Pravda*.[34]

The new Soviet policy toward Catholics in the territories recaptured from the Germans came as a surprise to local church authorities. In his memoirs Metropolitan Slipyi recalls a conversation with the head of the Soviet body in charge of religious matters (probably Vil'khovyi), who tried to persuade Slipyi that the previous persecution would not be repeated, that the church would regain its buildings, and that the Greek Catholics in Poland would be subordinated to the Lviv see in order to secure Soviet influence in that country. Slipyi also mentions a conversation that took place near St. George's Cathedral in Lviv with a Soviet officer in the summer of 1944. The officer promised that the policy conducted in Western

---

34.   Stehle, *Eastern Politics*, 230–1.

Ukraine during the years 1939–41 would be abandoned.[35] In
November 1944 the Soviet government allowed a public funeral for
Metropolitan Sheptyts'kyi, and in December 1944 it reassured a
visiting Uniate delegation that the UGCC would not be persecuted
by the Soviet regime.[36] The same attitude was demonstrated by the
Soviet military authorities toward the Greek Catholic Church in
Transcarpathia.[37] The Roman Catholics in Poland were treated with
special caution. Cardinal Adam Stefan Sapieha of Cracow, the
mentor of the future Pope John Paul II, was even praised by the new
Polish authorities as a member of the anti-Nazi resistance.[38]

These changes in Soviet religious policy had little impact on the
Vatican. The pope was deeply convinced that the same Soviet anti-
religious policy that was conducted in the 1930s would be re-
introduced after the war. During the years 1942–44 the Vatican
repeatedly denounced rumours of a possible Vatican-Soviet
rapprochement. Even after the Allies occupied Rome in the summer
of 1944 the Vatican spokesman reacted rather ambiguously to
information about Soviet toleration of the Catholic Church: "Certain
developments have been noted with interest; we assume that one
can observe certain signs of change. But up to now there are, to be
precise, no new facts for the Vatican."[39] The same attitude remained
dominant in the Vatican on the eve of the Yalta Conference, and the
American president could do little about it.

Nevertheless, Flynn's mission to Moscow was not entirely
unsuccessful, since the Catholic Church (including the UGCC) was
generally tolerated in Eastern Europe for the next couple of years.
Although that policy cannot be attributed solely to Flynn's mission,
it may be suggested that in March 1945 Stalin decided to satisfy the
Americans and not antagonize the Catholics of Eastern Europe. It
should be mentioned, however, that overall American efforts to
improve Soviet-Vatican relations and thereby introduce at least some
elements of freedom of conscience in the USSR produced

35. "Spohady Patriiarkha Iosyfa," 18.

36. On the delegation's visit to Moscow, see the collection of documents
from the Soviet archives published in M. I. Odintsov, "Uniaty i sovetskaia
vlast' (vstrecha v Moskve, dekabr 1944)," *Otechestvennye arkhivy,* 1994, no. 3:
56 ff.

37. "Holhofa Ukraïnskoï Tserkvy v Karpats'kii Ukraïni," in *Martyrolohiia
ukraïns'kykh Tserkov,* 2: 293–4 and 298–9.

38. Stehle, *Eastern Politics,* 244–50.

39. Ibid., 249.

contradictory results. President Roosevelt, who tried to please American Catholics, in fact helped to improve Stalin's relations with the ROC and thus to create the anti-Catholic alliance between that church and the Soviet state. His attempts at securing the future of the Roman Catholic Church in Eastern Europe provoked Stalin to launch a major attack against both the Roman and the Greek Catholics in the USSR.

Conclusions

If anything else, the circumstances of Flynn's mission to Moscow and Rome in the spring of 1945 prove that the international factor played a much more important role in the Soviet liquidation of the UGCC than was previously believed.

The Soviet takeover of Western Ukraine in 1944 evoked two opposite reactions from the Catholic authorities. The first came from Metropolitans Sheptyts'kyi and Slipyi. The leadership of the UGCC was doing its best to secure the position of their church under the new circumstances. At the request of the Soviet military command, Metropolitan Slipyi helped to organize a meeting of Soviet representatives with the leadership of the Ukrainian Insurgent Army (UPA). He also issued pastoral letters encouraging UPA fighters to cease their military resistance. The UGCC donated 100,000 rubles to the Soviet Red Cross Committee and asked for permission to open a hospital for soldiers and officers of the Red Army, but was denied that "privilege."[40]

The second response came from the Vatican. The pope, apparently, was more concerned with looking for ways to fight Communism than with saving his church under Soviet rule. There remains little doubt that it was the diplomatic actions of the Vatican, and not the policy of Metropolitans Sheptyts'kyi and Slipyi, that contributed to the liquidation of the UGCC in 1945–46.[41] Although accusations that the church hierarchy and activists had collaborated with the Nazis and the nationalist underground played an important role in the propagandistic campaign against the UGCC, in reality they were

---

40.   The collection of church money was initiated by Slipyi's predecessor, Metropolitan Sheptyts'kyi, who, in seeking a modus vivendi for the UGCC, sent a letter to Stalin thanking him for the "reunification" of Ukraine. On Sheptyts'kyi's and Slipyi's attempts at saving the UGCC under Soviet occupation, see Stehle, *Eastern Politics*, 214–15; Bilas, "Trahediia Tserkvy," no. 6: 21; and Bociurkiw, *The Ukrainian Greek Catholic Church*, 84–101.

41.   Stehle considers the Vatican's policy toward the USSR to have been a major mistake. See his chapter "Papal Error and First Consequences in Poland" in *Eastern Politics*, 250–6.

not the crucial factor behind the March 1945 Soviet decision to liquidate it.

If the Vatican had gone along with the United States and Great Britain on the decisions reached at Yalta and Potsdam, it could probably have avoided the liquidation of the UGCC. But there is no clear answer to the question whether the policies of Metropolitans Sheptyts'kyi and Slipyi and a more realistic policy on the part of the Vatican could have saved that church in the long run. Indeed, there is some evidence that the Soviet authorities were planning to liquidate the UGCC as early as the years 1939–41 and that they resumed their efforts to that end immediately after the recapture of Lviv in the summer of 1944.[42]

The international factor in the liquidation of the UGCC remained extremely important in the development of Soviet policy toward the remnants of that church in later years. As Sudoplatov's memoirs appear to indicate, the decision to assassinate Bishop Teodor Romzha of Uzhhorod and Mukachiv and thereby to destroy the Greek Catholic Church in Transcarpathia came as a reaction to information that had been gathered by Soviet intelligence abroad.[43] The history of the imprisonment and release of Metropolitan Slipyi

---

42.   Bociurkiw, "The Uniate Church in Soviet Ukraine," 90–7; idem, "Sheptyts'kyi and the Ukrainian Greek Catholic Church under the Soviet Occupation of 1939–1941," in *Morality and Reality: The Life and Times of Andrei Sheptyts'kyi*, ed. Paul Robert Magocsi with the assistance of Andrii Krawchuk (Edmonton, 1989), 101–23; and idem, *The Ukrainian Greek Catholic Church*, 57–61.

43.   "Our reassurances to Roosevelt before Yalta that Soviet citizens now enjoyed religious freedom did not end our problems with the Ukrainian Greek Catholic Church, or Uniates. Our agent in Rome, Joseph Grigulevich, who had acquired Costa Rican citizenship and became ambassador from Costa Rica to both the Vatican and Yugoslavia right after the war, reported that the Vatican would take a strong stand against us because of Moscow's treatment of the Ukrainian Catholic Church.... Grigulevich's information, received in 1947, that the Vatican was lobbying American and British officials to render assistance to the Ukrainian Catholic Church and the guerrilla movement supporting it, was directed not only to Stalin and Molotov but also to Khrushchev in the Ukraine. Khrushchev's response was to ask Stalin to sanction the secret liquidation of the Uniate Church leadership in the formerly Hungarian city of Uzh[h]orod" (Sudoplatov and Sudoplatov, *Special Tasks*, 250 and 252).

On the plans to liquidate the Greek Catholic Church in Transcarpathia in 1947, see the collection of documents from Soviet archives, "Dokumenty vidnosno likvidatsiï Hreko-Katolyts'koï Tserkvy na Zakarpatti," *Logos* 34, no. 3–4 (1993): 639–50.

may also serve as an example of the continued importance of the international factor in the formulation of Soviet policy toward the church. In April 1945 he was arrested together with other UGCC bishops, and after a secret trial he was sent to a labour camp. Slipyi was summoned to Moscow for the first time in the spring of 1953, when Beria wanted to use him as an intermediary to improve Soviet-Vatican relations. The metropolitan was released by Khrushchev in January 1963 only to please the pope and improve Soviet relations with the West.[44] It is well known that Gorbachev legalized the UGCC in 1989 largely under pressure from the West and against the will of the conservative Communist Party apparat in Ukraine.[45] In all these cases, foreign-policy considerations played an important, if not a decisive, role. The UGCC, viewed by the Soviet authorities as an agent and product of the West, inevitably became a hostage that was held to ransom by the USSR in its relations with the West and probably suffered more than any other denomination during the iciest years of the Cold War.

---

44.   On Slipyi, see Jaroslav Pelikan, *Confessor between East and West: A Portrait of Ukrainian Cardinal Josyf Slipyj* (Grand Rapids, Mich., 1990).

45.   On the legalization of the UGCC in the USSR, see Myroslaw Tataryn, "The Re-emergence of the Ukrainian (Greek) Catholic Church in the USSR," in *Religious Policy in the Soviet Union*, ed. Sabrina Petra Ramet (Cambridge, 1993), 292–318.

Frank E. Sysyn

The Ukrainian Orthodox Question in the USSR[*]

In 1977 Father Vasyl' Romaniuk, a prisoner in the Soviet Gulag because of his struggle for religious rights, addressed a letter to Metropolitan Mstyslav (Skrypnyk), leader of the Ukrainian Autocephalous Orthodox Church (UAOC) in the West:

> Your Grace! First of all, I assure you of my devotion and humility. I declare that I consider and have always considered myself a member of the UAOC in spite of the fact that I formally belonged to a different hierarchy, for it is well known that the Ukrainian Church, Orthodox as well as Catholic, is outlawed in Ukraine. Such are the barbaric ethics of the Bolsheviks.[1]

Father Romaniuk's appeal was remarkable testimony to the fact that almost fifty years after the destruction of the original UAOC established in the 1920s, and more than thirty years after the eradication of the second UAOC that had been restored and functioned for a few years during the Second World War, loyalty to Ukrainian Orthodoxy remains alive among Ukrainian believers. It also demonstrates how shared persecution has brought new ecumenical understanding between Ukrainian Orthodox and Ukrainian Catholics.

To discuss the position of Ukrainian Orthodoxy in the Soviet Union is a difficult task, because since the destruction of the UAOC in the early 1930s, dozens of its bishops, hundreds of its priests, and

---

* This article originally appeared in *Religion in Communist Lands* 11, no. 3 (Winter 1983): 251–63, and was reprinted in my brochure *The Ukrainian Orthodox Question in the USSR* (Cambridge, Mass., 1987), 9–22. The current version has been abridged (it does not include the original extended historical introduction) and revised. The speculations and observations I made in 1983 have been retained.

1. Vasyl Romaniuk, *A Voice in the Wilderness: Letters, Appeals, Essays*, trans. and ed. Jurij Dobczansky (Wheaton, Ill., 1980), 45.

thousands of its lay activists (and the liquidation of its successor restored during the Second World War), it exists more as a preference and a tradition than as an active movement. But it is clear that substantial numbers of Orthodox believers in Ukraine see themselves as Ukrainian Orthodox and that numerous believers would be attracted to a movement to establish a Ukrainian Orthodox Church if it were feasible to do so.

In any examination of the Ukrainian Orthodox issue among contemporary Soviet believers, political, cultural, and ecclesiastical factors predating Soviet rule must be taken into account, above all the relation of Russian Orthodoxy and Russian nationalism to Ukrainian Orthodoxy, and the interrelations between Ukrainian Greek Catholics and Ukrainian Orthodox.

The twentieth-century experience of Orthodox believers Ukraine was one of struggle over whether the church should represent the interests of Russian nationalism or the Ukrainian national movement. Political goals, ecclesiastical laws, and religious dogmas have intertwined in determining believers' choices, but the Russian trend has usually had the advantage of representing the status quo. By the early twentieth century, both in Russia and in Ukraine, a church reform movement sought to revitalize religious life and remove the dead bureaucracy that governed the imperial church. But whereas in Russia this movement remained a controversy between reformers and conservatives, in Ukraine it took on a national coloration. In the nineteenth and twentieth centuries, movements in Ukraine to improve the spiritual, cultural, and material life of the masses usually assumed a Ukrainian patriotic stance and opposed the Russificatory policies of the tsars. In the early twentieth century most of the hierarchs and monks of the official church in Ukraine defended the old regime and its policies. The reformers who sought liturgical, constitutional, and attitudinal changes in the church came largely from the married clergy and the laity. In Ukraine a segment of the reformers sought use of the Ukrainian language in sermons, religious texts, and the liturgy, and a reorganization of the church's government. They were opposed by those bishops and clergymen who had sought to strengthen the position of the Russian Orthodox Church (ROC) by allying it with the Russian nationalist and Black Hundreds movements. These activists, who had begun transforming the imperial Russian church into an instrument of Russian mass national politics, were profoundly Ukrainophobic, and they used their influence in the church to persecute Ukrainian culture and Ukrainian patriots.

The collapse of the tsarist regime offered great opportunities for the Ukrainian national movement. The rapid spread of Ukrainian national consciousness and patriotism was soon manifested in Orthodox Church affairs. After 1917 the Ukrainian church movement demanded Ukrainianization of the church, a greater role for the married clergy and laity in its governance, and autocephaly.[2] Persecuted by the conservative and Russian chauvinist bishops who even opposed the use of the Ukrainian language in the liturgy, the Ukrainian church movement became more and more radical. The Russian leadership sought to use the church for Russian political purposes, particularly support of the monarchists, and the fall of the Ukrainian People's Republic, which had adopted a decree declaring the autocephaly of the Ukrainian church in January 1919, undermined the Ukrainian church movement's position. At the same time, the Bolshevik triumph over the Russian Whites had also weakened the ROC. A deadlock ensued in which the Ukrainian Orthodox activists, unlike the Georgian Orthodox who re-established their church after the collapse of tsarist rule, found it impossible to win existing bishops over to the idea of establishing a Ukrainian Orthodox Church. Determined not to capitulate to the Russian hierarchs, a church council held in the St. Sophia Cathedral in 1921 resorted to the "Alexandrine" precedent, i.e., the consecration of a bishop through the laying-on of hands by the clerical and lay members of the sobor.[3] It declared the 1686 submission of the Kyivan metropolitan see to Moscow as forcible and illegal, and saw Ukrainian Orthodoxy as always having existed but having lacked its own hierarchy.

In the 1920s the Bolshevik regime favoured competition between Orthodox religious groups. It also embarked on a Ukrainianization program to win the support of the Ukrainian populace. The UAOC was thus allowed to develop: it gathered Ukrainian patriots around

---

2.   The standard history of the church is Iwan Vlasovs'kyi, *Narys istoriï Ukraïns'koï Pravoslavnoï Tserkvy*, 4 vols. in 5 bks. (New York and South Bound Brook, N.J., 1955–66). Volumes 1–2 have been published in English translation as Ivan Wlasowsky, *Outline History of the Ukrainian Orthodox Church* (1974, 1979). On the history and traditions of the Ukrainian church movement, see Dmytro Doroshenko, *Pravoslavna Tserkva v mynulomu i suchasnomu zhytti ukraïns'koho narodu* (Berlin, 1940); and Nataliia Polons'ka-Vasylenko, *Istorychni pidvalyny UAPTs* (Munich, 1964).

3.   For the church's justification of this practice, see Ivan Teodorovych, *Blahodatnist' iierarkhiï UAPTs* (Regensburg, 1947). On the issue of autocephaly, see Oleksander Lotots'kyi, *Avtokefaliia*, 2 vols. (Warsaw, 1935–8).

itself and by its activities even induced the Russian jurisdictions in Ukraine to make concessions to Ukrainian sentiment. By 1927 Soviet policies began to change, and the revered Metropolitan Vasyl' Lypkivs'kyi was forced to resign. In 1929 the church was accused of involvement in the purported underground activities of an "Association for the Liberation of Ukraine" and condemned as a "Petliurite" institution. It was forced to declare its self-liquidation in 1930, and its clergymen and activists were annihilated in the arrests and purges of the early 1930s. While all Orthodox groups were persecuted, only the Ukrainian Autocephalous Orthodox were selected for total destruction, thus indicating the increasing Russificatory tendencies of Stalinism.[4]

The annexation of Volhynia and Polissia by Poland after the First World War had placed about 2.5 million Orthodox Ukrainians in the Polish state. In 1924 the Constantinople Patriarchate established a Polish Autocephalous Orthodox Church, explaining its right to determine the fate of former territories of the ROC as deriving from the powers of the ecumenical Constantinople Patriarchate, the canons of the church, and the uncanonical means by which the Kyivan metropolitan see was transferred in 1686 from the jurisdiction of Constantinople to that of Moscow. In the interwar period the increasing national consciousness of the Ukrainian population was manifested in a movement to Ukrainianize the church and challenge the Russian nationalists' control of the hierarchy and the institutions. By the outbreak of the Second World War the Ukrainian church movement had achieved considerable successes, including the appointment of a Ukrainian bishop in Volhynia.

It was from the Polish Orthodox Church, with its hierarchy consecrated in the traditional manner, that a new hierarchy was

---

4.   On the history of the church in this period, see Vasyl' Lypkivs'kyi, *Istoriia Ukraïns'koï Pravoslavnoï Tserkvy, rozdil 7: Vidrodzhennia Ukraïns'koï Tserkvy* (Winnipeg, 1961); Friedrich Heyer, *Die Orthodoxe Kirche in der Ukraine von 1917 bis 1945* (Cologne-Braunsfeld, 1953); and the following articles by Bohdan R. Bociurkiw: "The Issues of Ukrainization and Autocephaly of the Orthodox Church in Ukrainian-Russian Relations, 1917–1921" in *Ukraine and Russia in Their Historical Encounter*, ed. Peter J. Potichnyj et al (Edmonton, 1992), 245–76; "The Church and the Ukrainian Revolution: The Central Rada Period, " in *The Ukraine, 1917–1921: A Study in Revolution*, ed. Taras Hunczak (Cambridge, Mass., 1977), 220–46; and "The Ukrainian Autocephalous Orthodox Church, 1920–1930: A Case Study in Religious Modernization," in *Religion and Modernization in the Soviet Union*, ed. Dennis J. Dunn (Boulder, Colo., 1977), 310–47.

consecrated for a restored UAOC in 1942. With the question of the apostolic succession of the hierarchy now resolved, the UAOC began setting up a church structure in the former Soviet Ukraine, although harassment from the Nazi occupation authorities and competition from an "Autonomous" Orthodox Church that wished to remain loyal to the ROC hindered its activities. Meanwhile, Stalin had come to an accommodation with the ROC in 1943, largely in order to obtain support for his war effort. A new patriarch was elected that year, and as the Red Army swept westward, all Orthodox believers in Ukraine were incorporated into the patriarchal ROC. In 1946, after a period of persecution and intimidation, the Soviet authorities staged the spurious Lviv Sobor, which incorporated the Ukrainian Greek Catholics into the ROC. Similar measures were adopted in Transcarpathia in 1949. Since the Second World War only the ROC has been allowed to serve Ukrainian Orthodox and Ukrainian Greek Catholic believers.

In discussing the present fate of Ukrainian Orthodox believers, one must see them as sharing the difficulties of all members of the ROC—discrimination in education and employment, pressure on clergy, difficulty retaining houses of worship, and constant demands for demonstrations of Soviet patriotism. Within the structure of Russian Orthodoxy, Ukraine and Ukrainians occupy a position far greater than their proportion in the general population. This is due to the greater strength of religious activity in Ukraine than in Russia, particularly because of the reopening of churches during the Second World War and because of the desire to convert Ukrainian Greek Catholics to Orthodoxy. It has been estimated that over fifty percent of the functioning Orthodox churches in the USSR are in Ukraine (with over twenty-five percent of the all-Soviet total in the western and, by tradition, predominantly Ukrainian Greek Catholic regions, which have a mere seven to eight million inhabitants).[5] In addition, Ukrainians provide a very large percentage of vocations. In short, the postwar period has repeated the processes of the late seventeenth and eighteenth centuries, when Ukrainians played an important role in the Russian church. But unlike that period, when Ukrainian learning and ecclesiastical practices supplanted Muscovite ones, no such tendencies are apparent yet in the USSR. The church in eastern Ukraine remains a bastion of Russification, using the

---

5.   For statistics on the churches, see Bohdan R. Bociurkiw, "The Orthodox Church and the Soviet Regime in the Ukraine, 1953–1971," *Canadian Slavonic Papers* 14, no. 2 (Summer 1972): 193–4 and 196.

Russian pronunciation of Church Slavonic and Russian as the languages of preaching and administration. Only in western Ukraine, prompted by fear of widespread Ukrainian Greek Catholic sympathies among Orthodox believers, does the church use the Ukrainian variant of Church Slavonic in church services and Ukrainian in sermons and allow the retention of local liturgical practices, including markedly Uniate ones.

How does the Ukrainian Orthodox problem affect the position of believers in Ukraine, and what significance does it hold for the future? First, the Ukrainian question remains one of the major unresolved issues for the Orthodox world. The 1924 decree of the Constantinople Patriarchate questioning the transfer in 1686 of the Kyiv Metropolitanate casts doubt on the canonicity of the Russian church's position in Ukraine.[6] On a more basic level, however, Ukrainians face the problem of being the second most numerous national body of Orthodox believers, yet have no church of their own in Ukraine. However fictitious their republic's autonomy may be, they cannot help contrasting the position of their fifty-million-strong homeland with the tiny Georgian republic of the USSR, which has its own patriarchate.

The problem is far more than a question of national pride. As long as Russian Orthodoxy, whether official or dissident, remains the instrument of Russian nationalism, it inevitably evokes resentment from Ukrainian believers. It is but one more sign that the formally atheistic, internationalist Soviet regime uses one measure for Russians and their culture, and another for non-Russians. In addition, Russian nationalist trends among Orthodox dissenters, including Aleksandr Solzhenitsyn, can only trouble Ukrainian believers.

At a time when the ROC is becoming more Ukrainian in its constituency, pressures are inevitable. So far the official church has made a few concessions: the active role permitted Metropolitan Filaret (Denysenko) of Kyiv, exarch of all Ukraine, in international forums, the publication of a Ukrainian-language journal of the patriarchate, *Pravoslavnyi visnyk* (The Orthodox Herald), a limited edition of a Ukrainian prayer book, and the retention of Ukrainian Church Slavonic in Uniate areas. Many of these gestures, like pamphlets issued by the Society for Contacts with Ukrainians Abroad entitled "Eastern Orthodoxy in Ukraine" (instead of

---

6.   A Ukrainian translation of the Tomos of 13 November 1924 may be found in Polons'ka-Vasylenko, *Istorychni pidvalyny UAPTs*, 113–16.

"Russian Orthodoxy"), may be seen as intended for the Ukrainian diaspora, but they inevitably strengthen the position of Ukrainians in the church.[7]

What is harder to judge is the effect of the increasing number of Ukrainian clergymen, above all from patriotic western Ukraine, including traditionally Orthodox (Volhynia, Bukovyna) and Catholic (Galicia, Transcarpathia) regions. As these clergymen, as well as believers from western Ukraine, have fanned out throughout Ukraine, they have undoubtedly disseminated their patriotism and non-Russian liturgical practices. (Anyone who has attended church in Kyiv and Lviv knows how substantial the differences still remain.)

We have information from testimony provided by Orthodox believers from central and eastern Ukraine that the KGB is concerned about the increase of western Ukrainian clergy and is trying to stop the practice of candidates from the vocation-rich western eparchies going east to be ordained. In 1977 the bishop of Poltava, Feodosii (Dykun), a native of the former western Ukrainian stronghold of Ukrainian Orthodoxy in Volhynia, wrote a lengthy letter of protest to Leonid Brezhnev on the position of the church in his eparchy. In it he recounts the following confrontation with the authorities:

I. Ia. Nechytailo says that I am "enticing clergy to Poltava from the western oblasts of Ukraine." At present two priests from western Ukraine serve in Poltava oblast—neither of whom I knew [previously] and therefore could not "entice" them. It seems to me that one should not be surprised that two priests from the western regions of Ukraine are serving in Poltava oblast, but rather [one should be surprised] why they should not serve here. Why does the [oblast] plenipotentiary [Nechytailo] divide Ukraine into two when it is one [whole]? And why should one part be set against the other? What crime did the plenipotentiary see in that people of some oblasts, let us say the western ones, go to live in other, eastern, oblasts or the reverse?[8]

7. On the policies and situation of the church, see Vasyl Markus, "Violation of Religious Rights in Ukraine," in *Ukraine and the Helsinki Accords: Soviet Violations of Human Rights*, ed. Marco Carynnyk (Toronto and New York, 1980), 94–127; and the bibliography *Soviet Persecution of Religion in Ukraine* (Toronto, 1976). See also the booklet by Archbishop Makariy, *The Eastern Orthodox Church in the Ukraine* (Kyiv, 1980); and my review of it in *Religion in Communist Lands* 14, no. 1 (1986): 73–6.
8. "Zvernennia iepyskopa Feodosiia do Brezhnieva,' *Suchasnist'*, 1981, nos. 7–8: 159–85, here 172; reprinted in *Martyrolohiia ukraïns'kykh Tserkov u*

If Bishop Feodosii seems concerned about treating all believers equally as his faithful, other bishops remain closer to the official church's and the regime's traditions of Russian chauvinism. In the spring of 1974 the editors of the underground journal *Ukraïns'kyi visnyk* (The Ukrainian Herald) challenged Metropolitan Filaret:

> And maybe the Exarch will tell us what he did with Father Sava of St. Volodymyr's Cathedral in Kiev, after the Reverend [Sava] began delivering his sermons in Ukrainian? Maybe he can also tell us why in 1972 only four students from the Lviv Region were accepted into the Odessa Theological Seminary? Why an atmosphere of [Russian] chauvinism pervades the seminary? Why services in the Churches of Ukraine are conducted in Russian, with the exception of the western regions, and even there not in all areas? In Volyn, for example, only Russian is used in almost all the Churches. Why is there no religious literature published in the Ukrainian language? No, the Exarch will not answer these questions. We will do this for him. It is because there is no official Ukrainian Church in Ukraine. Moscow usurped the Ukrainian Orthodox Autocephalous Church in Eastern [i.e, Soviet] Ukraine in the thirties and the Greek-Catholic Church in Western Ukraine in the forties. Moscow's Orthodox Church is an instrument of Russification. Key administrative positions in the Church are held by obedient lackeys who care only about their earthly comforts and who receive a dole from the satanical regime for their black hypocritical deeds.[9]

Essential to the question of Ukrainian Orthodoxy is the Ukrainian Greek Catholic issue. It is clear that the regime has allowed the Orthodox Church a Ukrainian face in western Ukraine, in order to win over the suppressed Ukrainian Greek Catholics. For every active member of the clandestine Ukrainian Greek Catholic Church (UGCC), there are many priests and believers in the official Orthodox Church who would return to the UGCC immediately if the church became legal. For the present this element, as well as the real converts to Orthodoxy, form a strong lobby, which views the

---

chotyr'okh tomakh, vol. 1, *Ukraïns'ka Pravoslavna Tserkva: Dokumenty, materiialy, khrystyians'kyi samvydav Ukraïny*, comp. and ed. Osyp Zinkevych and Oleksander Voronyn (Toronto and Baltimore, 1987), 779–808, here 794.

9.   *The Ukrainian Herald, Issue 7–8: Ethnocide of Ukrainians in the U.S.S.R. Spring 1974. An Underground Journal from Soviet Ukraine,* comp. Maksym Sahaydak (Baltimore, Paris, and Toronto, 1976), 157.

proper role of the Orthodox Church as similar to that of the traditionally patriotic and activist UGCC. They press for the pursuit of this role at least at the parish level. The tremendous increase in activity of the clandestine UGCC in the last few years will obviously strengthen this party's hand.

Although in recent years there have been a number of noble protests by Orthodox Russian believers in defence of Ukrainian Greek Catholics, it is still safe to say that most Russian Orthodox (like Russian atheists) find the Uniates alien and incomprehensible.[10] In contrast, throughout the twentieth century common patriotism and common suffering have drawn Ukrainian Orthodox and Ukrainian Greek Catholics together. In the 1930s the Ukrainian Greek Catholic metropolitan, Andrei Sheptyts'kyi, defended Orthodox believers against Polish religious persecution. To this day the Ukrainian Orthodox hierarchy in the West condemns the forcible conversion of the Ukrainian Greek Catholics in 1946. Father Romaniuk's statement is, I believe, indicative of a widespread sentiment, particularly among intellectuals. Even the most ardent Orthodox believer cannot but have respect for the tenacious struggle of his fellow Christians, the Ukrainian Greek Catholics. Whether Russian Orthodox believers can fully understand this ecumenical drift among the Ukrainian Orthodox is a major question.

In recent years it has become clear that young Russians have turned more and more to the church for spiritual and national values. Here, as always, Ukrainian youth are in a difficult position, particularly in central and eastern Ukraine, where the church is so Russian. It is indicative that when Valentyn Moroz, a son of Orthodox Volhynia, defended the spiritual legacy of Ukrainians as represented by the church of the Hutsul mountaineers in Kosmach, he asserted: "In 1773 it was reconsecrated as a Uniate Church but by this time this had lost its former significance. Galicia had become a province of Austria. Polish rule had come to an end. The Uniate movement had become integrated into Ukraine's spiritual life. The struggle against it and defence of Orthodoxy ceased to be a national problem. On the contrary, Russia soon began to use Orthodoxy as a means of Russification in the lands taken from Poland. The most important task was the preservation of the Church."[11]

---

10. See Elena Sannikova's letter to Pope John Paul II in *Religion in Communist Lands* 11, no. 3 (1983): 293–4.

11. *Report from the Beria Reserve: The Protest Writings of Valentyn Moroz, a Ukrainian Political Prisoner in the USSR,* ed. and trans. John Kolasky (Toronto, 1974), 58.

Moroz's statement reflects how differently a Ukrainian and a Russian patriot must view the role of the Orthodox Church in the past. The Russian can see it as a national church that defended his people's cultural legacy, but the Ukrainian has two national churches and cannot forget the official Orthodox Church's alien nature and negative role in the nineteenth and twentieth centuries. There has yet to be a study of the spiritual and cultural values of Ukrainian intellectuals and dissenters.[12] Some, such as Levko Lukianenko, have demanded the restoration of a Ukrainian Orthodox Church. In general, it seems clear that the Ukrainian intelligentsia's search for spiritual values leads more to the past (Mohylan Orthodoxy, the church brotherhoods, the Ukrainian baroque) and the rich Christian folklore of the people (Christmas Eve supper, carols, *pysanky* or Easter eggs, *vertep* or holiday puppet theatre, and so on), than to official Russian Orthodoxy. Anyone who has seen *Shadows of Forgotten Ancestors* and other Ukrainian ethnography-based films of the 1960s and early 1970s cannot but feel this strongly.

The Ukrainian intelligentsia has also turned to its spiritual roots in the broad cultural sense in an attempt at preserving its legacy. Here it is at a great disadvantage compared with the Russian intelligentsia, since historical, literary, and art history works that would be permitted and even encouraged in Russia are forbidden as "nationalist" in Ukraine. The pogrom of intellectuals in the early 1970s brought research in fields such as pre-1917 Ukrainian history to a halt and destroyed almost all historical journals: *Seredni viky na Ukraïni* (The Middle Ages in Ukraine), *Istorychni dzherela ta ïkh vykorystannia* (Historical Sources and their Utilization), *Kyïvs'ka starovyna* (Kyivan Antiquities), and others.[13] While scores of art books are published in Leningrad and Moscow, it was only the appearance of a book on Ukrainian icons in the United States that forced the Soviet authorities into allowing one to be published in Kyiv. The vast icon collections assembled by Metropolitan Sheptyts'kyi remain stored haphazardly in church basements in Lviv. While destruction of churches and other cultural monuments is an all-Soviet phenomenon, the KGB works with particular zeal in Ukraine, accusing opponents of "Ukrainian bourgeois nationalism."

---

12.   For a bibliography of Ukrainian religious dissent, see George Liber and Anna Mostovych, *Nonconformity and Dissent in the Ukrainian SSR, 1955–1975: An Annotated Bibliography* (Cambridge, Mass., 1978).

13.   I discuss these problems in my review of *Ukraïns'ka poeziia*, comp. V. P. Kolosova and V. I. Krekoten', in *Kritika* 16, no. 1 (Winter 1980): 24–40.

Those interested in Ukrainian spiritual and artistic culture inevitably turn to the "Second Jerusalem"—Kyiv. Here the situation is catastrophic, since Communist plans to build a new Soviet capital led to virtual cultural genocide in the City of the Golden Domes in 1934 and 1935. St. Michael's Monastery, St. Basil's Church, the Epiphany Brotherhood Monastery, St. Nicholas's Collegiate Church, SS. Borys and Hlib Church, and many other edifices were destroyed, and in the end nothing was built in their place.[14] Interestingly enough, while Ukrainian medieval and baroque churches were removed from the face of the earth, the nineteenth-century synodal-period Cathedral of St. Volodymyr was left standing and now serves as the metropolitan's seat.

In the last few years there has been a spate of publishing activity connected with the rather arbitrarily proclaimed 1,500th anniversary of Kyiv in 1982.[15] New books on Kyiv and its art have been published, and for the first time modern Ukrainian translations of the chronicles have appeared: the Primary, the Kyiv, and the Galician-Volhynian. While the authorities intend the anniversary to affirm "East Slavic" (read "all-Russian") unity throughout the ages, the Ukrainian intelligentsia has used it to provide at least a little access to Ukraine's spiritual and cultural legacy. The 1,500th anniversary of the city must also be seen in connection with the impending millennium of Kyivan Christianity in 1988. It is, of course, painful for the Ukrainian Orthodox to remember that in the city of Metropolitans Ilarion, Petro Mohyla, and Vasyl' Lypkivs'kyi now resides a mere exarch of the Moscow Patriarchate. Pope John Paul II's call to Ukrainians to prepare for the celebration of the millennium of their Christianity has resonance not only for Ukrainian Greek Catholics but also for Ukrainian Orthodox. The Ukrainian Orthodox and Ukrainian Catholic Churches in the West will be joining together for conferences and scholarly publications intending to reaffirm their spiritual legacy and bring their churches' plight to the world's attention.[16] It is clear that this will sustain their believers in Ukraine. It will be interesting to see how far the

14. See the catalogue of a photo exhibition at the Ukrainian Museum in New York: Titus D. Hewryk, *The Lost Architecture of Kiev* (New York, 1982).

15. Roman Solchanyk, "Literature, History and Nationalities Policy in the Ukraine," *Radio Liberty Report*, no. 318/82 (9 August 1982).

16. For the 27 June 1981 announcement of the Ukrainian Orthodox and Ukrainian Catholic Churches' joint plans to celebrate the millennium, see *The Ukrainian Quarterly* 38, no. 3 (Autumn 1981): 325.

Soviet authorities will go in allowing the Moscow patriarch to celebrate the millennium of "Russia's" Christianity in order to combat Ukrainian activities.

As with all Soviet policies on religion, foreign affairs play a major role in calculations. Patriarch Pimen and Metropolitan Filaret of Kyiv have important parts to play in "ecumenical contacts" and "peace offensives." Obviously, the existence of large and active Ukrainian Catholic and Ukrainian Orthodox Churches in the West is extremely troublesome to them. The Ukrainian Greek Catholics, with their support from Pope John Paul II and their access to Vatican Radio, are the greater problem. Still, the existence of 300,000 to 400,000 Ukrainian Orthodox believers in the West poses a major problem for the Soviet authorities.[17] The Ukrainian Orthodox Churches, based primarily in the United States and Canada (where the Ukrainian church is the largest Orthodox Church), challenge the Russian church's legitimacy in Ukraine.

At his election in 1971 Pimen, the new patriarch of Moscow, announced the "reunion" of Ukrainian Orthodox abroad with his church as a major goal. Indeed, Moscow's recognition of the Russian Orthodox Greek Catholic Metropolia as the Orthodox Church in America in 1970, with the program of gathering all Orthodox believers in the United States and Canada, cannot be seen as divorced from the Soviet government's and the Moscow Patriarchate's plans to undermine Ukrainian Orthodoxy abroad.[18] During a visit to the United States in the 1970s, Metropolitan Filaret of Kyiv, facing thousands of protesters demanding the rights of the Ukrainian Orthodox and Ukrainian Greek Catholic Churches, mendaciously asserted that all Ukrainians wish to belong to the ROC.[19] The resolution of the U.S. Congress calling for religious freedom for the Ukrainian Orthodox and Ukrainian Greek Catholic Churches

---

17.   On the problems of Ukrainian Orthodoxy in the West, see my article "The Ukrainian Orthodox Churches and the Ukrainian Diaspora," 16-25, and Petrusia Markowsky, "The Rise of Ukrainian National Consciousness and the Formation of the Ukrainian Greek Orthodox Church of Canada," both in *Vitrazh* (London), no. 11 (June 1980). See also Paul Yuzyk, *The Ukrainian Greek Orthodox Church of Canada, 1918–1951* (Ottawa, 1981); and Odarka S. Trosky, *The Ukrainian Greek Orthodox Church in Canada* (Winnipeg, 1968).

18.   I discuss this problem in "The Ukrainian Orthodox Churches," 22–4.

19.   On Filaret's statements and the demonstrations against him, see "Chronicle of Current Events," *The Ukrainian Quarterly* 31, no. 1 (Spring 1975): 103–7.

obviously causes discomfort to Filaret and his superior, Patriarch Pimen.[20] Regrettably, until now many of the Western broadcasting companies that transmit information on religion and religious services to the USSR have seen Orthodoxy as only Russian in culture and language, thus depriving Orthodox Ukrainian believers and Ukrainian Orthodoxy of support. Consequently the Ukrainian Orthodox Church of Canada has begun its own transmissions.

All too often Ukrainian Orthodoxy and Ukrainian believers are forgotten in discussions of religious problems in the USSR. The Ukrainian Orthodox issue takes on complexity because it is not merely an issue of Soviet denial of religious freedom. Russian Orthodox émigré leaders, who are otherwise critical of Soviet religious policies and the accommodations of the Moscow Patriarchate with the regime, approve of any measures against "Ukrainian nationalism." Few Russian Orthodox leaders have concurred with the late Alexander Schmemann in declaring the annexation of the Ukrainian church by the Russian church in the seventeenth century uncanonical and in condemning the Russian hierarchy's opposition to the restoration of an independent Ukrainian Orthodox Church in the twentieth century.[21] A more typical response has been the virulent attack by Ludmilla Sergeeva, editor of the journal *Posev*, on Michael Bourdeaux of Keston College, for having even discussed the Ukrainian Orthodox issue in an interview for Radio Liberty.[22]

While the discussions in émigré and Orthodox circles in the West will influence the Ukrainian Orthodox issue in the Soviet Union, they will not be decisive. At present the firm alliance between the Soviet state and the ROC on the Ukrainian Orthodox issue appears likely to continue, and indeed strengthen as the millennium

---

20. For the full text of Senate Congressional Record 18 (27 April 1981) and House Congressional Record 123 (1 May 1981), see *The Ukrainian Quarterly* 38, no. 4 (Winter 1982): 353–70.

21. Aleksandr Shmeman, "Ukraïns'ko-rosiis'kyi dialoh: Relihiinyi aspekt," *Vidnova*, no. 2 (Winter 1984–Spring 1985): 52.

22. See Bohdan Nahaylo, "An Interview with the Reverend Michael Bourdeaux," *Radio Liberty Research*, no. 297/84 (2 August 1984); and the primitive attack on Bourdeaux by Sergeeva, "Komu eto na pol'zu," *Posev*, 1984, no. 10. Even the Orthodox Church of America continues to publish tendentiously anti-Ukrainian materials, such as Dimitry Pospielovsky, *The Russian Church under the Soviet Regime, 1917–1982*, 2 vols. (Crestwood, N.Y., 1984). See my review of this work in the *Russian Review* 45, no. 1 (1986).

celebrations near. However, the existence of a disproportionately large Ukrainian constituency in the ROC, the continued discontent of Ukrainian patriots with the Soviet regime's policies of Russification, the contacts with Ukrainian Orthodox abroad, and the very identification of the millennium with Kyiv will likely engender opposition to the current situation. One can agree with the evaluation of Bohdan Bociurkiw, the distinguished scholar of twentieth-century Ukrainian Orthodoxy:

> When the Second World War brought about a dramatic reversal in Stalin's religious policy and gave a new lease of life to the Russian Orthodox Church, the latter was unabashedly put to use as an instrument for the Sovietization and Russification of the Ukrainian Orthodox and Ukrainian Greek Catholics. As in the secular sphere, so, too, in ecclesiastical life the very concept of "Ukrainization," let alone independence, has assumed a "nationalist" and "subversive" connotation. But behind the facade of the "monolithic unity" of the regime and the Russian Church, Ukrainization remains a very much alive, if suppressed, idea and an unfulfilled popular aspiration.[23]

---

23. Bohdan Bociurkiw, "Ukrainization Movements within the Russian Orthodox Church, and the Ukrainian Autocephalous Orthodox Church," in *Eucharisterion: Essays Presented to Omeljan Pritsak on His Sixtieth Birthday by His Colleagues and Students*, ed. Ihor Ševčenko and Frank Sysyn with the assistance of Uliana M. Pasicznyk, vols. 3–4 (1979–80), part 1 of *Harvard Ukrainian Studies*, 111.

Frank E. Sysyn

The Third Rebirth of the Ukrainian Autocephalous Orthodox Church and the Religious Situation in Ukraine, 1989–1991[*]

Since 1988 the religious situation for Eastern Christians has changed more radically in Ukraine than in any other area of the former Soviet Union. Until the celebrations of the millennium of East Slavic Christianity and the delayed beginning of perestroika and glasnost in Ukraine, the Russian Orthodox Church (ROC) was the only Eastern Christian institution with legally recognized congregations in Ukraine. By 24 August 1991, when Ukraine declared its independence, the Ukrainian Greek Catholic Church (UGCC), the Ukrainian branch of the Moscow Patriarchate, and the Ukrainian Autocephalous Orthodox Church (UAOC) maintained competing organizations with legally registered parishes.

Descending from the Union of Brest of 1596, the UGCC, also known in the West as the Ukrainian Catholic Church, had been the dominant church among Eastern Christian believers in Galicia and Transcarpathia until these areas were annexed by the Soviet Union during the Second World War. The Soviet authorities forcibly liquidated the UGCC and incorporated it into the ROC. Despite decades of persecution, an underground church had been maintained and a considerable portion of the ostensibly Russian Orthodox clergy and believers continued to be loyal to the Union of Brest. Galicia and Transcarpathia were especially important for the ROC in Ukraine, because they contained almost half of its parishes and generally the best organized ones.

Organized under the leadership of the metropolitan of Kyiv as the exarch of Ukraine, the ROC had controlled the Orthodox of Ukraine since the transfer of the Kyiv Metropolitanate from the jurisdiction of the Moscow Patriarchate in 1685–86. Despite

---

[*]   This article originally appeared in *Seeking God: The Recovery of Religious Identity in Orthodox Russia, Ukraine, and Georgia*, ed. Stephen K. Batalden (DeKalb, Ill., 1993), 191—219. It has been revised.

short-term concessions to aspirations for Ukrainian religious autonomy in 1918 and during the Second World War, the ROC succeeded in maintaining itself as a unified, centralized institution. Although the UAOC sees itself as the heir of the Kyiv Metropolitanate as it existed before its incorporation into the ROC, its more modern institutional antecedents is the original UAOC that was formed out of the Ukrainian church movement in 1921, suppressed in the 1930s, and re-established in 1942 during the German occupation of Ukraine. The original UAOC combined aspirations for an independent Ukrainian church with a movement for radical religious reform. The establishment of a hierarchy without consecration by bishops led to its appellation as "self-consecrators." The UAOC, liquidated under pressure from the Soviet authorities in the 1930s, survived within the Ukrainian émigré communities in the West. After it was revived in Ukraine in 1942, its hierarchy was consecrated in the traditional manner and was more conservative in its theology and adherence to traditional Orthodox canons than its predecessor of the 1920s. Though it was abolished and destroyed in Ukraine with the Soviet reoccupation in 1944, the UAOC came to play a dominant role in the postwar Ukrainian Orthodox communities in the West.

As was universally expected, the abatement of active persecution led to the re-emergence of the UGCC from the underground in the western Ukrainian regions of Galicia and Transcarpathia.[1] With the defeat of the Communist Party in the three Galician oblasts in March 1990, the UGCC no longer faced local government opposition to reclaiming the churches that it had possessed before 1946, so that by 1991 the archbishop major of Lviv, Myroslav Ivan Cardinal Liubachivs'kyi, who had returned from exile in Rome, headed about two thousand Greek Catholic congregations. Although the Ukrainian Exarchate of the Moscow Patriarchate lost hundreds of congregations and churches to the Ukrainian Greek Catholics, the ROC benefited from the new religious policies by obtaining permission to establish

---

1. For a recent discussion of the UGCC's situation, see Bohdan R. Bociurkiw, "The Ukrainian Catholic Church in the USSR under Gorbachev," *Problems of Communism*, November–December 1990, 1–19. On 1 January 1991, 1,912 Ukrainian Greek Catholic parishes were registered, and eighty-nine others had applied for registration. See "Über 10.000 staatlich registrierte religiöse Gemeinden derzeit in der Ukraine—ukrainische katholische Kirche verfügt über 1.912 Gemeinden," *Informationsdienst Osteuropäisches Christentum* (Munich), no. 9–10/91 (May 1991): 32.

new congregations and take over hundreds of church edifices. The renaming of the exarchate as the Ukrainian Orthodox Church (UOC) and the granting of broad autonomy by the patriarchate in 1990 were more unexpected.[2] Nevertheless, the most unexpected event on the Ukrainian religious scene was the rapid development of the UAOC following the declaration by the first parish in August 1989 that it was breaking with the Moscow Patriarchate.[3]

Unlike the UGCC, which had maintained a continuous underground organization after 1946, and the UOC, which merely assumed the institutions of the Moscow Patriarchate, the UAOC had to establish its structure in entirety. Other than certain references in dissident literature and the activities of Father Vasyl' Romaniuk, who affirmed his allegiance to the UAOC, no organized movement to reestablish the UAOC existed as late as 1988.[4] Yet students of Ukrainian church history realized that diminution of political repression and a Ukrainian cultural revival had twice before stimulated the establishment of the UAOC in the twentieth century.[5] Even they could hardly have predicted how rapidly it would regenerate.

---

2.   The documentation on the granting of a new status to the UOC in October 1990 and the report of a press conference with Metropolitan Filaret are in *Pravoslavnyi visnyk* (Kyiv), 1991, no. 1 (January): 2–13. "Ukrainian Orthodox Church" was approved as an alternative official name of the Ukrainian Exarchate at the ROC hierarchs' council of 30–1 January 1990. See *Pravoslavnyi visnyk*, 1990, no. 5 (May): 29–30, translated from *Moskovskii tserkovnyi vestnik*, 1990, no. 4.

3.   Gerd Stricker, a specialist on Soviet religious affairs and a keen observer of Ukraine, described the movement for the UAOC as something that only émigré Ukrainians had believed in. See his "Ist die Ukrainische Kirche zugelassen? Unklarheiten nach Gorbachevs Besuch im Vatikan," *Glaube in der 2 Welt* 18, no. 1 (1990): 23.

4.   See Vasyl Romaniuk, *A Voice in the Wilderness: Letters, Appeals, Essays*, trans. and ed. Jurij Dobczansky (Wheaton, Ill., 1980), 45. On the situation of Ukrainian Orthodoxy in the early 1980s, see my article "The Ukrainian Orthodox Question in the USSR" in this volume. The first initiative group for the restoration of the UAOC appeared in February 1989. See Bohdan Nahaylo, "Initiative Group Seeks Renewal of Ukrainian Orthodox Church," *The Ukrainian Weekly* (Jersey City), 5 March 1989.

5.   In 1980 Bohdan R. Bociurkiw wrote: "But behind the facade of the 'monolithic unity' of the regime and the Russian church, Ukrainization remains a very much alive, if suppressed, idea and an unfulfilled popular aspiration" ("Ukrainization Movements within the Russian Orthodox Church, and the Ukrainian Autocephalous Orthodox Church," *Harvard Ukrainian Studies* 3–4 [1979–80]: 111).

The failure of the Moscow Patriarchate to learn from the lessons of 1917–21 and 1942, the years of the two earlier establishments of the UAOC, and to make concessions to Ukrainian ecclesiastical aspirations was fundamental to the rebirth of the UAOC.[6] Even though in the 1970s and 1980s over fifty percent of the parishes of the patriarchate were in Ukraine, with twenty-five percent in nationally conscious western Ukraine, the ROC permitted very few Ukrainian elements.[7] Indeed, in the Brezhnev-Suslov years, when the Soviet government embarked on more intensive Russification, including the attempt at forming one "East Slavic nation," the church eliminated some of the concessions it had made to Ukrainians in ritual and the assignment of cadres. Its Russian-language seminaries, including the one in Ukraine, did not teach the Ukrainian language and culture, much less examine specifically Ukrainian spiritual and ecclesiastical traditions.

Despite the decree of autonomy proclaimed in 1918 and the titles of exarch and exarchate, the church in Ukraine was fully subsumed into the ROC. The ROC remained the only Russian imperial structure in the Soviet period; it did not adjust in either name or structure to the recasting of the Russian Empire as the Soviet Union, except for its loss of the Georgian Orthodox Church. The church in some way mitigated this affiliation by using the term "Rus'ka Pravoslavna Tserkva" (Rus' Orthodox Church) in Ukrainian instead of "Rosiis'ka Pravoslavna Tserkva" (Russian Orthodox Church). It did so to evoke Kyivan or Old Rus', though in nineteenth- and early twentieth-century western Ukrainian usage the term would mean "Ukrainian," excluding Russians. In fact, in contemporary usage even in western Ukraine, the term "Rus'ka" had come to signify "Russian," and the church was perceived as such. In practical terms, the church used the Russian pronunciation of Church Slavonic everywhere except in Galicia and Transcarpathia, and Russian as the language of preaching in urban areas and even at times in rural

6.   The authors of some recent writings issued by the Moscow Patriarchate and the UOC have admitted that the striving for "pure Orthodox" practices alienated the population of western Ukraine. See, for example, Oleksandr Makarov, "Bid na stupeniakh viry," *Pravoslavnyi visnyk*, 1990, no. 3: 24, translated from *Moskovskii tserkovnyi vestnik*, 1989, no. 17 (December).
7.   See Bohdan R. Bociurkiw, "The Orthodox Church and the Soviet Regime in the Ukraine, 1953–1971," *Canadian Slavonic Papers* 14, no. 2 (Summer 1972): 193–4 and 196.

areas outside western Ukraine. In liturgy, music, architecture, and iconography it adhered to norms that were portrayed as Orthodox, but were in fact imperial Russian. Its historical and cultural self-conception was as an all-Russian Orthodox Church, so much so that it emphasized the traditions of the church of Muscovy to the neglect of those of the Kyiv Metropolitanate. The major features distinguishing the exarchate from the general ROC, aside from its greater density of parishes and numbers of vocations, were that it devoted greater attention to anti-Uniate polemics and that in the former Uniate regions priests were permitted to incorporate some local religious and artistic traditions. Nevertheless, with the greater mixing of cadres and the striving for "pure Orthodox practices," even these were concessions made under pressure.

An interview with Patriarch Aleksii published in *Literaturnaia gazeta* on 28 November 1990 most clearly demonstrated the degree of alienation of the leadership of the ROC from Ukrainian religious aspirations. By then the new patriarch had travelled twice to Ukraine. In the summer he had to answer requests by clergymen gathered at the Pochaiv Monastery that autocephaly be granted to the church in Ukraine as a way of saving Orthodoxy's position.[8] In the autumn he had come to Kyiv to grant the church autonomy and had been confronted by large crowds of believers and Ukrainian activists objecting to Aleksii's use of the St. Sophia Cathedral in Kyiv, which, until its closure in the early 1930s, had belonged to the UAOC.[9] Still, in describing the situation in Ukraine, the patriarch said:

> In regard to the so-called Ukrainian autocephalists, these people wish to see in Christ not their Lord and Judge, but an ally. An ally in political struggle. Two thousand years ago people also treated Christ as a political figure: some placed hope in Him as a political leader, [while] others feared Him also as a dangerous political criminal. And as a result, together they crucified Him.... The subordination of Church interests to political

---

8.   See the report by Valerii Liubats'kyi, "Where Is the Split?" *News from Ukraine* (Kyiv), 1990, no. 37: 1 and 7.

9.   For the UOC's version of the conflict over Aleksii's service at the St. Sophia Cathedral, see "Zolotyi homin Sofiï," *Pravoslavnyi visnyk*, 1991, no. 1: 15–16; and V. Andriievs'kyi, "Shche raz pro podiï bilia Sofiï," *Radians'ka Ukraïna*, 29 January 1991. For another version by two parliamentarians, see Leonid Taniuk and Zinovii Duma, "Konfliktu mohlo b ne buty: Vysnovky Komisiï z pytan' kul'tury ta dukhovnoho vidrodzhennia z pryvodu podii v Kyievi 28 zhovtnia 1990 roku," *Kul'tura i zhyttia* (Kyiv), 9 December 1990.

interests, the transformation of the Church into an instrument of politics, always constitutes violence against the faith and the Church, [and] always leads the Church to Golgotha.[10]

Given the ROC's traditional link to the Russian Empire and the Soviet Union, Aleksii was arguing from a position of weakness. His church's active agitation for an all-Union Soviet treaty demonstrated that no such break had occurred even in 1990. Just as significant was Aleksii's interpretation of the religious situation:

If the Ukrainian autocephalists could clearly explain in what way unity with the Russian church hinders the act of their spiritual salvation and in what way they would be spiritually richer dividing themselves off from their Russian brothers, I would try to understand them. In the Ukrainian church there are its own specific complications [slozhnosti], its own traditions. Knowing of this, we granted it independence [nezavisimost'] and autonomy [samostoiatel'nost'] in matters of administration.[11]

As of November 1990, Aleksii had not tried to understand the autocephalists' position, and his mention of "specific complications" rang truer than that of "its own traditions" in explaining why autonomy had been granted to a newly named "Ukrainian Orthodox" Church in late 1990.

That the newly elected patriarch of the ROC had not yet considered the autocephalists' views and did not seem to have reflected deeply on the traditions of a UOC can hardly be surprising when one examines how late the concept of a UOC emerged among the leaders of the exarchate in Ukraine. In the early 1980s even in writing for the Ukrainian diaspora, which belonged in large part to Ukrainian Orthodox Churches, leaders of the exarchate would go no further than entitling their works "Orthodoxy in Ukraine," with the accompanying assertion that the exarchate was an inseparable part of the ROC.[12] Accounts of the history of Orthodoxy, far from

---

10.   *Literaturnaia gazeta* (Moscow), 1990, no. 48 (28 November).

11.   Ibid.

12.   See, for example, Archbishop Makariy, *The Eastern Orthodox Church in the Ukraine* (Kyiv, 1980); and my review of it in *Religion in Communist Lands* 14, no. 1 (1986): 73–6. Even in his address to the sobor that elected the patriarch of Kyiv on 7 June 1990, Metropolitan Filaret did not mention a "Ukrainian Orthodox" Church or any desire for its autonomy; see *Pravoslavnyi visnyk*, 1990, no. 9: 13–17. In a 1989 interview he described the merits of Germogen, the early seventeenth-century Russian Orthodox

discussing the evolution of a Ukrainian Orthodox tradition or of the Kyiv Metropolitanate, concentrated on Muscovy-Russia in the fifteenth to seventeenth centuries, viewing the period of clear and stable separation of the Metropolitanates of Kyiv and Muscovy (1458–1686) as negative and examining events in Ukraine only episodically. In his work "On the Question of the History of the Kyiv Metropolitanate," written after the proclamation of the UOC, Metropolitan Filaret (Denysenko) of Kyiv did not depict the history of a continuously developing ecclesiastical tradition, but confined himself to answering the autocephalists' views of specific incidents (such as "the separation of the Rus' Orthodox Church into two metropolitanates" in the fifteenth century, "the reunification of the Kyiv Metropolitanate with the Moscow Patriarchate" in 1685–86, and above all the events of the twentieth century and the rise of the UAOC) without diverging from usual interpretations or admitting that the policies of the ROC erred in any way on Ukrainian issues.[13]

In general, the Moscow Patriarchate belatedly reacted to Ukrainian religious and national aspirations. Deeply imbued, even in Ukraine, with its identity as the ROC and devoid of any conceptualization of a legitimate Ukrainian ecclesiastical culture, the church leadership was ill-prepared for responding to the renewed autocephalist movement or for establishing a UOC. Linguistically Russified in central and eastern Ukraine and immersed in Russian ecclesiastical and secular culture, many clergymen lacked both the knowledge and the desire to respond to the Ukrainian national revival. Because the autocephalists won over clergy and believers in western Ukraine and the intelligentsia throughout Ukraine in 1990, the Moscow

---

patriarch, in the liberation of the "Fatherland," despite the fact that Ukraine was not part of the Russian state in 1612 and Ukrainians were fighting for the state they inhabited, the Polish-Lithuanian Commonwealth, against Muscovy. See H. Chornomors'kyi, "'Ne ubyi' ne oznachaie 'ne zakhysty,'" *Pravoslavnyi visnyk* 1989, no. 7: 29, translated from *Sovetskii patriot*, 9 April 1989. As late as 9 May 1989 Filaret argued that a UOC was unnecessary. Questioned on the issue of the UAOC, he replied, "And our Church, as is known from history, does everything for the union of peoples. Therefore it is against autocephaly" ("Za iednist' i perebudovu," *Pravoslavnyi visnyk,* 1989, no. 8: 22, reprinted from *Radians'ka Ukraïna*).

13.   Metropolitan Filaret, "Do pytannia pro istoriiu Kyïvs'koï mytropolii," *Pravoslavnyi visnyk*, 1991, no. 2: 37–49; no. 3: 38–49; and no. 4: 44–52. For another history of the Kyiv Metropolitanate, which views the "union" of 1685–86 as positive, see Archpriest Mykola Novosad, "Moskovs'kyi patriarkhat i Kyïvs'ka mytropoliia," *Pravoslavnyi visnyk*, 1990, no. 8: 31–4.

Patriarchate lost a component that was most attuned to Ukrainian aspirations.[14] At the same time, its leaders became more suspicious of Ukrainian issues as promoting schism and more dependent on maintaining the old political order to buttress their position.[15]

If the Moscow Patriarchate provided an environment conducive to the rebirth of the UAOC, the national revival in Ukraine advanced knowledge and reverence toward the UAOC. With the renewal of Ukrainian culture and national awareness in the 1980s, attention focussed on the 1920s. Although the original intention may have been to rehabilitate the so-called Ukrainian national Communists of the 1920s in order to legitimize Soviet Ukrainian patriotism, the renewal soon expanded into a return to the Ukrainian cultural flowering of that decade. This period, frequently called the "executed rebirth," ended with the Stalinist destruction of the Ukrainian intelligentsia and the man-made famine of 1932–33. As the focus shifted to the study of the non-Communist element of that revival and the process of Ukrainian-ization of the masses, intellectuals paid more attention to the role of the UAOC. With the increased discussion of the crimes of Stalinism, the accusations against the UAOC at the show trials of the Association for the Liberation of Ukraine in 1930 and the ruthless persecution and destruction of the UAOC and its leaders in the 1930s gave that church authority as a national institution and an aura of martyrdom.[16]

The general Ukrainian historical and cultural renewal also made the Ukrainian intelligentsia more favourable to the UAOC and the traditions and views it had espoused. As the Soviet interpretation of Kyivan Rus' as the cradle of the "Old Rus' nationality" that spawned the three "fraternal" East Slavic nations was questioned, the ROC's principal theoretical underpinning was challenged. When historians and political leaders could once again discuss Russification in the

---

14. The importance of western Ukraine in advocating Ukrainianization can be seen in an article by Archpriest Sozont Chobych of the Lviv Eparchy, "I Tserkvy torknulasia perebudova," *Pravoslavnyi visnyk*, 1990, no. 2: 25–6.

15. For the UOC's conflict with Rukh, the Ukrainian popular movement for Perestroika, see Metropolitan Filaret, "Liudy, bud'te oberezhnymy!" *Pravoslavnyi visnyk*, 1990, no. 5: 26–7.

16. On the increase in information on the UAOC in the publications of the intelligentsia, see Fedir Turchenko and Oleksandr Ihnatusha, "Ukraïns'ka avtokefal'na tserkva," *Vitchyzna*, 1989, no. 12 (December): 166–75. For an example of the Ukrainian intelligentsia's reaction to the UAOC in its initial stages, see V. Stel'makh, "Druhe voskresinnia," *Kul'tura i zhyttia* (Kyiv), 24 June 1990. For the increasing interest in Metropolitan Vasyl' Lypkivs'kyi, see the reprint of his works in *Slovo* (Kyiv), no. 21 (November 1990): 8.

nineteenth-century Russian Empire, they inevitably condemned the ROC's role as a major proponent and instrument of these policies. The most important impetus for the Ukrainian national revival to take interest in religious affairs and in the UAOC was its focus on the "Cossack Age," the sixteenth to eighteenth centuries, as the source of Ukrainian identity. Not only was this period one in which religious affairs were central, but also one in which the Kyiv Metropolitanate was separate from the church in Muscovy (entirely until 1686) and in which Ukrainian religious culture—literary, artistic, and musical—was quite distinct from the Russian. The UAOC had revived these traditions in the 1920s, while the ROC had largely suppressed them. The Ukrainian cultural revival and growth of historical consciousness inevitably led even those distant from church affairs to view the UAOC positively and the ROC negatively.[17]

The UAOC revived so rapidly because it had survived outside the Soviet Union, and churches in the West could serve as models, financial supporters, and sources of literature and cadres. The history of the Ukrainian Orthodox Churches in the West has involved the complex evolution of a number of organizations, reflecting religious developments in Ukraine and conditions in the countries of settlement.[18] By the 1980s the great majority of Ukrainian Orthodox belonged to three metropolitanates—the UAOC (Europe, South America, Australia), the Ukrainian Orthodox Church of the United States, and the Ukrainian Orthodox Church of Canada—which, though administratively separate, considered themselves in spiritual unity as one church. With about 300,000 believers, 400 churches, 200 priests, and two seminaries, the three metropolitanates constituted both a significant component of the Orthodox diaspora and a major institution in Ukrainian community life. In Canada the UOC was the largest Orthodox jurisdiction, while in the United States the church's centre in South Bound Brook, New Jersey, with its memorial church, museum, archive, seminary, cultural centre, and Ukrainian national cemetery, served as a focal point for the Ukrainian diaspora.

---

17. For a criticism of the role of the ROC in Ukrainian history, see Anatolii Shcherbatiuk, "Rosiis'ke pravoslav'ia," *Za vil'nu Ukraïnu* (Lviv), October 1990.

18. For a discussion of the Ukrainian Orthodox Churches in the West, see my article "The Ukrainian Orthodox Churches and the Ukrainian Diaspora," *Vitrazh* (London), no. 11 (June 1980): 16–25; and Paul Yuzyk, *The Ukrainian Greek Orthodox Church of Canada, 1918–1951* (Ottawa, 1981).

Metropolitan Mstyslav (Skrypnyk) closely linked the metropolitanates of the UAOC and the UOC in the United States because he served as metropolitan of both churches. Bishops who traced their apostolic succession to the UAOC revived in 1942 or to the interwar Polish Orthodox Church led the three metropolitanates. That most Orthodox jurisdictions did not recognize the Ukrainian Orthodox Churches or admit their hierarchs to the Standing Conference of Orthodox Bishops (North America) merely served to reinforce their Ukrainian identity, since they were not drawn into discussions to abolish ethnic allegiances in the interests of Orthodox unity. In particular, Metropolitan Mstyslav remained dedicated to ensuring that the church in the West would be prepared for its mission in Ukraine. In his very person—as a nephew of Symon Petliura (the head of state of the Ukrainian People's Republic of 1919), as a participant in the struggle for Ukrainian independence from 1917 to 1921, as a political leader of Ukrainians in Poland in the interwar period, and as a bishop consecrated in Kyiv in 1942—Mstyslav embodied the strivings for Ukrainian religious and national rights.[19]

Perestroika and glasnost permitted the Ukrainian Orthodox Churches in the West to influence the religious situation in Ukraine. Visits and family contacts made more and more believers and clergy in Ukraine aware of these churches. The suspension of radio jamming permitted more of Ukraine's population to listen to the churches' religious programs. The end to seizures of religious literature by Ukrainian customs officers meant that a massive program of propaganda could be undertaken, in which the UOC of Canada dispatched thousands of books and pamphlets. As early as 1977 Father Vasyl' Romaniuk recognized the authority of Metropolitan Mstyslav, who held the title of metropolitan of Kyiv. When Bishop Ioan (Bodnarchuk) of Zhytomyr accepted the leadership of the autocephalists in the fall of 1989, he recognized the authority of Metropolitan Mstyslav. In June 1990 the first sobor of the UAOC elected Mstyslav "patriarch of Kyiv and all Ukraine," and in the autumn of that year the ninety-two-year old hierarch was finally granted a Soviet visa and was installed in Kyiv.

An important factor explaining the rapid rebirth of the UAOC was its ability to find mass support in Galicia. Before the Second World War only a few Orthodox parishes existed in that region. The

---

19. See "Biohrafiia sviatiishoho patriarkha kyïvs'koho i vsiieï Ukraïny Mstyslava," *Nasha vira pravoslav'ia* (Kyiv), no. 7 (October 1990).

forcible nature of Galicia's "conversion" to Orthodoxy in 1946 and the heroic struggle of the underground Ukrainian Greek Catholics there had led many western Ukrainians to assume that, with the end of persecution and the legalization of the church, almost all believers and parishes would return to the UGCC. Although the migration of eastern Ukrainians and Russians to western Ukraine after the Second World War meant that Eastern Christians in Galicia were no longer homogeneously western Ukrainians, the greater incidence of religious practice of the native Galicians ensured that they were the vast majority of believers and a majority of the clergy. Nevertheless, a considerable segment of the Galician population has chosen to remain Orthodox, and most of these have broken with the Moscow Patriarchate and joined the UAOC.[20]

Traditionally the UGCC had been divided between "Westernizers" and "Easternizers." The latter resisted the Latinization of the church, in part because it was associated with Polonization, and a segment had always been pro-Orthodox. In the decades after the Second World War some clergymen who had undergone forcible conversion in 1946 accepted their affiliation with Orthodoxy, in particular if they had traditionally been Easternizers. Their numbers increased as more and more of the clergy began studying at the Russian Orthodox seminaries of the Moscow Patriarchate. The Vatican's *Ostpolitik* under Pope Paul VI had profoundly disillusioned some believers, who consequently lost their devotion to the papacy. During the early 1980s the Soviet authorities had discussed the possibility of recognizing a UGCC that would break with Rome; and some believers, despairing of ever gaining recognition otherwise, had entertained this idea. In many ways the UAOC embodied this concept of a Ukrainian church not affiliated with the Moscow Patriarchate or with Rome. Also, because a faction of the underground church censured those who had attended the churches of the Moscow Patriarchate during the years of persecution, some clergy and believers found a return to the UGCC humiliating.

By 1989 the activities of the UGCC had greatly increased as it emerged from the underground and as the Soviet policy of denying religious freedom in western Ukraine became increasingly untenable

---

20. In the statistics of registered parishes as of 1 January 1990, published in "Über 10.000 staatlich registrierte Gemeinden," in Galicia the UAOC had 791 parishes, and the UOC had 734 parishes there. However, the number of UAOC parishes was undoubtedly higher, because some of the 128 UAOC parishes seeking registration must have been in Galicia.

for domestic and international reasons. Resentment against the Soviet regime and Russification surfaced powerfully in an area where the Moscow Patriarchate was viewed as intrinsically part of both. Facing the indifference and even hostility of the patriarchate and the exarchate to Ukrainian religious and national aspirations, those clergymen who wished to remain Orthodox and retain their congregations realized that only an autocephalous UOC could do so.[21]

The events and motivations of the establishment of the Ukrainian Autocephalous Orthodox Church in Galicia remain a subject of great controversy. Father Volodymyr Iarema and the parish of SS. Peter and Paul in Lviv declared their adherence to the UAOC on 19 August 1989, a few months before the Ukrainian Greek Catholics took control of the Church of the Transfiguration in the same city. Indeed, the clergy who began to declaring their allegiance to the UAOC were motivated by a desire to keep their congregations from passing over to the UGCC. Some Ukrainian Greek Catholics have claimed that the KGB had a hand in creating the UAOC as a means of hindering the UGCC and sowing discord in the Ukrainian national movement. In fact, some priests may have been compromised by the KGB and have realized that they had little future in the restored UGCC. Allegations centred on the person of Bishop (later Metropolitan) Ioan (Bodnarchuk), who took over the leadership of the nascent UAOC in late October 1989.

In 1990 the UAOC increased so rapidly in Galicia that by the end of the year about one thousand parishes had formed. This contrasts with the much slower growth of the church in other regions, where by early 1991 about 150 parishes existed.[22] With functioning parishes and church buildings, the UAOC in Galicia became the stronghold for religious and organizational activities. Seminaries were established in Lviv and Ternopil, and youth groups and church

---

21.   See Valerii Liubats'kyi's report in *News from Ukraine*, 1990, no. 37. The petitioners called for deposing Metropolitan Filaret and stated: "If the upper crust of the Russian Orthodox Church again displays its inability to make decisions for the benefit of Orthodoxy as it was before, we consider it our Christian and pastoral duty to decide independently." Father Viktor, church dean of Stryi, said: "We must be grateful, as we are still existing only due to autocephaly.... Autocephaly supporters save both us and the very idea of Orthodoxy."

22.   After his visit to Ukraine, Archpriest Stepan Iarmus' reported that of the 1,300 parishes of the UAOC, 250 were in eastern Ukraine. See his "Dukhovyi obraz narodu Ukraïny: Vrazhennia z vidvidyn Ukraïny 27 travnia–9 chervnia 1991," *Visnyk* (Winnipeg), 1991, no. 7: 3.

brotherhoods were organized in the three Galician eparchies.[23] Contacts with the Ukrainian Orthodox Churches abroad also assisted the UAOC in making inroads in Galicia, since the majority of Ukrainian Orthodox believers in Canada and at least a plurality in the United States are descended from Galician immigrants. The church also benefited from anti-Polish sentiments in western Ukraine, in particular suspicions of the Polish Roman Catholic Church and revanchist circles.[24] Here the attraction of the church was as much freedom from the Vatican led by a Polish pope as independence from Moscow.

By 1991 the UAOC had achieved sufficient stability as an institution to ensure that it would continue to play a major role in Ukrainian religious affairs. In addition to the patriarch, who was elected at the sobor of June 1990, the church had a metropolitan of Galicia in Lviv and bishops for Ternopil, Ivano-Frankivsk, Rivne (with an assistant in Dubno), Lutsk, Chernivtsi, Uzhhorod, Bila Tserkva, Sumy, Mykolaiv, Kamianets-Podilskyi, and Dnipropetrovsk. The most renowned of the bishops was Volodymyr of Bila Tserkva, formerly the political prisoner Father Vasyl' Romaniuk, who had responsibilities for mission work in central and eastern Ukraine. In Kyiv the church had four parishes and had established a central administration, although the patriarchal chancery was still housed in the Ukraina Hotel. The Galician eparchies had a considerable network of organizations. In other areas the Brotherhood of St. Andrew, with leadership provided by the Kyiv chapter, spearheaded missionary work. In 1991 over three hundred delegates from church brotherhoods throughout Ukraine attended the second congress of

---

23. On the activities of the Galician brotherhoods, see "Z zhyttia L'vivs'koho molodizhnoho bratstva," *Blahovisnyk vidrodzhennia Ukraïns'koï Avtokefal'noï Pravoslavnoï Tserkvy* (Chicago; hereafter *Blahovisnyk vidrodzhennia*), no. 15 (1 August 1991): 5-6. In March 1991 a conference of brotherhoods in Ivano-Frankivsk oblast drew 394 delegates. See *Blahovisnyk vidrodzhennia*, no. 7 (April 1991): 5.

24. The UAOC pointed out that numerous churches have been returned to the Poles in Galicia without securing similar action for the Ukrainians in Poland. See *Blahovisnyk vidrodzhennia*, no. 9 (1 May 1991): 7. Suspicion was also voiced in articles published in the West. Archpriest Stepan Iarmus' pointed to the subordination of the Roman Catholic hierarchy in Ukraine to Warsaw as the result of negotiations between John Paul II and Mikhail Gorbachev; he wrote that one must conclude that their policy is "Paralyze Galicia and western Ukraine and you simultaneously paralyze all Ukraine!" ("Dukhovyi obraz narodu Ukraïny").

the organization.[25] The UAOC had also established an active press, including newspapers, such as *Nasha vira pravoslav'ia* (with an initial press run of 10,000 copies), journals, such as *Tserkva i zhyttia*, and numerous local bulletins. Several Ukrainian intellectuals of note worked in the church as activists; among them was Ievhen Sverstiuk, a literary critic and former political prisoner, who served as editor of *Nasha vira pravoslav'ia*.

The great prominence that the church had assumed in Ukrainian civic and cultural life stemmed to a considerable degree from the active leadership of Patriarch Mstyslav. After his arrival in October 1990, despite his age he tirelessly travelled throughout Ukraine, from Lviv in the west to Kharkiv in the east. He paid great attention to pastoral affairs and ensuring that the church served at the numerous national and cultural commemorations that have become so common throughout Ukraine. Through his actions—such as meeting the material needs of the victims of the Chornobyl catastrophe; his press conference with Kyiv's Dynamo Soccer Club, which pledged to assist him in rebuilding the St. Michael's Monastery in the capital; and his appearance before hundreds of thousands gathered at Berestechko to commemorate the Cossacks who died there in 1651—Patriarch Mstyslav brought great visibility to the church, and with it recognition as a national institution.[26]

---

25.   On the brotherhood's activities, see Serhii Makarenko's speech at its second conference, held on 9–10 February 1991, in *Blahovisnyk vidrodzhennia*, no. 6 (17 March 1991): 3-4. For information on the conference, see Iaryna Tymoshenko, "Vidbulasia konferentsiia Vseukraïns'koho bratstva," *Ukraïns'ki visti* (Detroit), 24 February 1991.

26.   On Mstyslav's activities on behalf of the victims of the Chornobyl nuclear accident, see *Blahovisnyk vidrodzhennia*, no. 9 (1 May 1991), 2. On his plan to rebuild the ancient Ukrainian church destroyed by the Soviet authorities in 1934–35, and on his meeting with the soccer clubs, see *Blahovisnyk vidrodzhennia*, no. 11 (1 June 1991): 1–2. On the events at Berestechko, see Marta Kolomayets, "Battle of Berestechko: Glorious Kozak Legacy Recalled by Thousands," *The Ukrainian Weekly*, 30 June 1991. For an example of the respect in which Mstyslav was held by the Ukrainian intelligentsia, see the article on St. Andrew's Church by Oles' Bilodid and Larysa Kozlovs'ka, "Pervozvanna," *Ukraïna* (Kyiv), 1990, no. 48 (December): 12–13. The article describes Mstyslav's celebration of a Ukrainian-language liturgy in the church thus: "And is it not a good sign [that] the holy place is not empty? The word of God sounded there in the Ukrainian language from the lips of His Holiness Metropolitan Mstyslav, head of the Ukrainian Autocephalous [Orthodox] Church, a person of legendary fate, who underwent all the tortures and sufferings of the Ukrainian revolutionary

Despite the great achievements of the UAOC, it remained a very inchoate institution. Not only did the patriarch not obtain a permanent residence and administrative offices, he did not yet have a well-established chancery. The UOC and the Communist Party press tried to undermine his authority by charging that he had collaborated with the Germans during the Second World War. Lines of authority among the hierarchs were not clearly established, especially the powers of Metropolitan Ioan of Galicia (who went on leave for medical treatment in the United States) and Bishop Antonii (Masendych) of Rivne and Zhytomyr, who served as patriarchal exarch before Patriarch Mstyslav's arrival and continued to organize church activities in Kyiv. The division of functions between the Brotherhood of St. Andrew, which had played such a great role in the organization of the church in central and eastern Ukraine, and the hierarchy was not clear-cut. Outside Galicia the eparchies often had only a few parishes (e.g., the Rivne Eparchy had six parishes, but only four were registered in March 1991;[27] the Kamianets-Podilskyi Eparchy had three parishes as of June 1991).[28] The church also suffered from a critical shortage of clergy, and priests such as Father Iurii Boiko in Kyiv had to travel ceaselessly to provide services to the UAOC congregations and ensure that the church sanctified the numerous commemorations of the victims of the famine of 1932–33 and various Ukrainian cultural events.[29]

To a great degree the actions of the civil authorities determined the situation of the church. They registered congregations, disposed of church buildings, and controlled movement in and out of (and sometimes within) Ukraine. While political pluralism and assertion of the primacy of government institutions over Communist organizations came to many regions and levels of government in Ukraine, the hard-line Communist faction that opposed the UAOC still ruled substantial areas of the republic, particularly in the east

---

chaos, malevolence, and savagery and remained alive, because he had God in his heart and finally began to serve Him."

27. In March 1991 Bishop Antonii said that Rivne Eparchy had six parishes. He also gave statistics for Galicia that differed somewhat from other sources: Lviv oblast had four hundred parishes; Ivano-Frankivsk oblast, more than three hundred; and Ternopil oblast, two hundred. See "Rozum peremozhe emotsiï," Visti z Ukraïny (Kyiv), 1991, no. 13 (March).

28. Information provided by the bishop.

29. See the interview with Father Boiko in Blahovisnyk vidrodzhennia, no. 1991, nos. 14 (16 July 1991): 5–6 and 15 (1 August 1991): 7–8.

and in rural areas. In central and eastern Ukraine, only in large cities, such as Kyiv and Kharkiv, were there sufficient members of the democratic opposition and reform Communists to give the UAOC at least a hearing. Although Parliament also had significant similar factions, the registration of congregations and the assigning of buildings were settled at the oblast and municipality level. Patriarch Mstyslav's meetings with Chairman of the Supreme Soviet Leonid Kravchuk and Prime Minister Vitol'd Fokin at least signalled that after years of persecution, followed by harassment, the government of the republic viewed the UAOC as a legitimate institution. But at the local level the old-guard Communists fiercely opposed the UAOC, resorting to physical attacks, defamation, harassment, and overt preferential treatment of the UOC. Frequently groups organized jointly by the Communists and the UOC carried out violence and intimidation.[30] The triumph of Rukh (the Ukrainian popular front) and the democratic opposition in Galicia placed the UAOC in a much better position than in other areas. But certain elements of the new government were antagonistic to the UAOC and favoured the UGCC, although given a choice between the UAOC and the UOC their preference was the former.

The Moscow Patriarchate and the UOC were the major opponents of the UAOC. During his visit to Ukraine, Patriarch Aleksii even went so far as to counsel the municipal government of Zhytomyr against giving a church building to the UAOC.[31] Metropolitan Filaret and the hierarchs of the UOC launched an ongoing campaign against the UAOC, including attacks on the person of Patriarch Mstyslav and accusations that the UAOC is somehow Uniate. The UOC, with nineteen eparchies and more than five thousand parishes, was an imposing foe.[32] Although the number of parishes was

---

30. *Blahovisnyk vidrodzhennia* contains numerous reports of the persecution of the UAOC. See, for example, 1991, nos. 3 (3 February): 2 (from Chernihiv); 5 (3 March): 6–7 (Svitlovodsk); 10 (16 May): 2 (Zaporizhzhia); 12 (16 May): 3–4 (Chernihiv); 12 (16 May): 8 (Kirovohrad); and 13 (1 July): 4 (Kherson, Mykolaiv, Dnipropetrovsk, and Kirovohrad oblasts). For an account of the local authorities' campaign against the UAOC in the village of Mytkiv in Chernivtsi oblast, see "Repetytsiia pered referendumom," *Chas* (Chernivtsi), 15 February 1991.

31. See Valerii Liubats'kyi's account of Patriarch Aleksii's trip in *News from Ukraine*, 1990, no. 37.

32. At the time of the proclamation of the UOC's autonomy, nineteen hierarchs signed the statement. Only in southern and eastern Ukraine did the eparchies include more than one oblast (e.g., Kirovohrad and Mykolaiv,

somewhat inflated, because those parishes that it claimed in Galicia were virtually extinct—its believers having defected to the UAOC and the UGCC—the UOC expanded significantly in central and eastern Ukraine.[33] Indeed, the challenge of the UAOC has in some ways assisted the UOC in expanding, since the local authorities in such cities as Chernihiv and Dnipropetrovsk hastened to hand over closed churches to the UOC to avoid having to approve requests by the UAOC.[34] This was similar to the Communist authorities' policies in Galicia in 1988, when they handed over hundreds of closed churches to the ROC in order to prevent Ukrainian Catholics

---

Donetsk and Luhansk, and Odesa and Kherson). See *Pravoslavnyi visnyk*, 1991, no. 1: 9.

33. Of the 5,031 UOC parishes registered on 1 January 1991, 1,181 were in the traditional Uniate areas of Galicia and Transcarpathia. A further 1,160 were in Bukovyna and Volhynia, areas annexed to the Soviet Union during and after the Second World War. Of the 2,690 churches in pre-1939 Soviet Ukraine, 973 were in the three central Ukrainian oblasts of Zhytomyr, Vinnytsia, and Khmelnytskyi. The farther east and south, the fewer the registered religious communities were in general. The Crimea had only forty parishes, and Luhansk oblast had only ninety-two. Still, the UOC had greatly expanded its network of parishes in the pre-1939 Soviet Ukrainian territories and in Bukovyna and Volhynia. See "Über 10.000 staatlich registrierte religiöse Gemeinden". Despite the church's growth in the east, the losses in the west resulted in an actual decline in the number of parishes in the former exarchate from 5,700 in February 1990. See Archpriest Sozont Chobych, "I Tserkvy torknulasia perebudova," *Pravoslavnyi visnyk*, 1991, no. 2: 26.

34. In Chernihiv, in an oblast controlled by a particularly reactionary Communist Party organization, numerous historic churches were handed over to the UOC. The UOC removed the sarcophagus of Prince Mstyslav Volodymyrovych the Brave from the Transfiguration Cathedral. See Vasyl' Chepurnyi, "Chas rozkydaty kaminnia?" *Nasha vira pravoslav'ia* (Kyiv), 1991, no. 2 (10). The UAOC parish of Dnipropetrovsk had a history of attacks on its members, long-term refusal to register the community, and, after the community was registered, refusal to give it a church building, whereas the civil authorities gave a number of buildings to the UOC, which had nine churches in the city. The UAOC requested the Transfiguration Cathedral, which was being used to house a museum of religion. See *Blahovisnyk vidrodzhennia*, no. 15 (1 August 1991): 3–4. On the community's persecution and its campaign for that cathedral, see *Preobrazhens'kyi sobor: Vydannia Pravoslavnoï tserkvy Preobrazhens'koho katedral'noho soboru* (Dnipropetrovsk), no. 1 (April 1991). The Communist press in Dnipropetrovsk conducted a scurrilous campaign against the community and Patriarch Mstyslav. See "Chy vse sviate pid ianhol's'kymy krylamy?" *Zoria* (Dnipropetrovsk), 11 June 1991.

from using them.[35] Nevertheless, the dependence of the UOC on the Communist authorities made it vulnerable to accusations that it was "the Ukrainian [or Russian] Orthodox Church supporting the platform of the Communist Party of the Soviet Union." Given the growing anti-Communist feeling in Ukraine, the UOC was undermining its long-term position for short-term advantage.

In its competition with the UOC, the UAOC faced an opponent ever more conscious of its need to deal with Ukrainian issues. Well into 1990 the UAOC had great opportunities because it challenged a Russian, not a Ukrainian, Orthodox Church. With its change of name, the exarchate sought to adjust to the Ukrainian national and political revival, above all the declaration of sovereignty of 16 July 1990.[36] The UAOC's insistence on the continued Russian nature of what it frequently termed the "so-called UOC" testified to the exarchate's successes in partially defusing its alienation from Ukrainian aspirations. Initially the UAOC had no real competition in sanctifying events, such as commemorations of the famine of 1932–33 and celebrations of Cossack and national holidays, because the exarchate and later the UOC avoided what it saw as nationalist and anti-Soviet events. By 1991 the UOC ever more openly sought to take part in and even monopolize Ukrainian patriotic events. By May 1991 it not only took part in ceremonies honouring Taras Shevchenko, but also—with the compliance of the local Kaniv authorities—prevented Patriarch Mstyslav from conducting services at the monument in the city by holding services from 8:00 a.m. to 8:00 p.m.[37]

In this new role the UOC faced certain obstacles. As recently as 1989 its clergy had blessed the ceremonies celebrating the anniversary of the "Reunification of Ukraine with Russia," and in

---

35. Bohdan R. Bociurkiw estimated that over seven hundred closed, formerly Ukrainian Greek Catholic churches were handed over to the ROC beginning in the fall of 1988. See "The Ukrainian Catholic Church in the USSR under Gorbachev," 10.

36. For all its insistence that political factors should not determine religious affairs, the exarchate followed political changes in its policies. The Ukrainian language was introduced into the Odesa seminary as a reaction to the declaration of Ukrainian as the state language. See "Sozdan synod Ukrainskoi pravoslavnoi tserkvi," *Pravda Ukrainy* (Kyiv), 10 February 1990.

37. For the events at Kaniv on 22 May 1991, see Leonid Taniuk and Zinovii Duma, "Khto zh rozpaliuie vorozhnechu?" *Kul'tura i zhyttia*, 29 June 1991; and "Rosiis'ka Pravoslavna Tserkva ne dopustyla Patriiarkha Mstyslava do mohyly Shevchenka," *Ukraïns'ki visti*, 2 June 1991.

early 1991 its clergy had advocated voting "yes" on the all-Union treaty.[38] Consequently its sincerity in participating in Ukrainian events was questioned.[39] By the same token it possessed few nationally conscious and culturally educated cadres, and many of its clergy remained ardently Russian in language and worldview. The fact that the new seminary in Kyiv taught only one other subject in Ukrainian besides language and literature demonstrated how far the church's practices were from the goals of the Ukrainian national movement.[40] Numerous charges were made that the exarchate of the ROC, now the UOC, had destroyed Ukrainian art and desecrated monuments to Ukrainian national heroes in the churches it had been given.[41] The person and intentions of Metropolitan Filaret were especial objects of opprobrium and suspicion. Still, the church tried to make the necessary accommodations to the new situation. In 1991 it transferred the bishop of Chernivtsi to Russia because he did not

38.   See the account and photographs in *Visti z Ukraïny*, 1990, no. 6. Bishop Ionafan (Eletskikh) of Pereiaslav took part in this event, which was, in fact, a rally in support of the Union treaty. The exarchate of the ROC and the UOC have a tradition of supporting centralization and viewing the Russian Empire and the Soviet Union, not Ukraine, as the "fatherland." See, e.g., H. Chornomors'kyi's interview with Metropolitan Filaret, "'Ne ubyi' ne oznachaie 'ne zakhysty,'" 30.

39.   As late as 1990, Metropolitan Filaret still condemned the use of the Ukrainian national colours, blue and yellow. See "Ne sotvorit' goist' pepla," *Pravda Ukrainy*, 1 January 1990. In 1989 he maintained: "Speaking about our nation [*nash narod*], I have in mind all the nations of our country.... We must all care for our multinational culture" ("Liudyna povynna buty bezsmertnoiu," *Pam'iatnyky Ukraïny* (Kyiv), 1989, no. 2: 12). In general, the leaders of the UOC merely rejected the contention that the ROC promoted Russification. For one of the few admissions, albeit an apologetic one, see the interview with Bishop Ievfymii of Mukachiv and Uzhhorod in *Molod' Ukraïny* (Kyiv), 23 May 1991. He merely admits that in central and eastern Ukraine "The church fell under the pressure of Russification.... But one should not condemn the church—oppressed and persecuted."

40.   For an account of the Russian chauvinist atmosphere at the Kyiv Theological Seminary, see the open letter of 8 June 1990 by seven seminarians to Metropolitan Filaret in *Za vil'nu Ukraïnu*, 23 September 1990.

41.   A major debate surrounds the UOC's actions at the Kyivan Cave Monastery. See Iurii Horban', "Lavra b'ie na spolokh," *Nasha vira pravoslav'ia*, January 1991. For the church's actions in Chernihiv, see L. Fesenko, "Vidrodzhennia chy znyshchennia? Pro problemy zberezhennia kul'tovykh pam'iatok," *Robitnycha hazeta* (Kyiv), 23 January 1991. See also "Sim zapytan' mytropolytu Filaretu vid redaktsiï hazety 'Nasha vira pravoslav'ia,'" *Nasha vira pravoslav'ia*, December 1990.

speak Ukrainian.[42] Metropolitan Filaret tried to counter charges that the UOC was Russified by arguing that it uses two versions of Church Slavonic, a "Western" and an "Eastern" one, without mentioning that the "Eastern" version is identical with the Russian one.[43] The church adopted more Ukrainian elements, but it still insisted that it was linked to universal Orthodoxy through the Moscow patriarch, that the preservation of the Soviet Union was positive, and that the church in Ukraine was multiethnic.[44] In fact, it had to consider the consequences of any Ukrainianization because it feared losing Russian supporters who might defect to the ROC abroad.

The UAOC also faced a regional challenge in Galicia—the UGCC. In Galicia—everywhere but in the northeastern section of Ternopil oblast near the Pochaiv Monastery, which belonged to Volhynia before the Second World War—the UAOC was the predominant Orthodox group. In its initial phases the UAOC was primarily the creation of clergymen who wished to remain Orthodox and retain their parishes for Orthodoxy. Because the clergy were primarily western Ukrainians and the churches functioned as Ukrainian institutions with Ukrainian as the language of preaching, the Ukrainian version of Church Slavonic, and Ukrainian liturgical traditions, this shift could be accomplished merely by accepting Ukrainian as the liturgical language.

The formation of the UAOC entirely changed the religious situation in Galicia. The Orthodox-Catholic four-part commission, which was established by the Vatican and the Moscow Patriarchate in the fall of 1989 to adjudicate church properties, and which included representatives of the Vatican, the UGCC, the Moscow Patriarchate, and the Ukrainian Exarchate, quickly became irrelevant, partly because it did not include the major Orthodox group in the

---

42.   On the replacement of Bishop Antonii, see *Blahovisnyk vidrodzhennia*, no. 4 (17 February 1991), 8.

43.   Metropolitan Filaret proposed this theory during a press conference on 29 October 1990. See *Pravoslavnyi visnyk*, 1991, no. 1: 12. The UAOC and Ukrainian cultural groups frequently asserted that the UOC conducted services in Russian; in fact they were held in Church Slavonic with Russian pronunciation. In Filaret and the hierarchy's pastoral message, the metropolitan defended the primacy of Church Slavonic with the grudging comment that "There is no official document that would ban the use of the native language during the liturgy" (*Pravoslavnyi visnyk*, 1991, no. 1: 8).

44.   For a criticism of the lack of new thinking in the UOC, see "Mytropolyt Filaret poza chasom," *Nasha vira pravoslav'ia*, no. 7 (October 1990).

region. Although this somewhat simplified the position of the Vatican, which wished to maintain good relations with the Moscow Patriarchate, the situation gave the UAOC, which had been excluded from the commission, the occasion to maintain that the Vatican and the UGCC preferred to deal with the Moscow Patriarchate instead of the UAOC and that the UAOC could defend the religious interests of the Ukrainian people against foreign intrusions from Moscow and Rome better than the UGCC. The Vatican's lack of links to the UAOC made inter-group ecclesiastical relations primarily a matter of local UGCC and UAOC relations, in which the UGCC's clergy and intelligentsia bitterly condemned the UAOC as divisive and possibly KGB-inspired. In cities church buildings could be apportioned to the two churches, but in small towns and villages sharp conflicts emerged for the one edifice, with shared usage often increasing the friction, while withdrawal of the minority to erect a new church resulted in financial burdens for the community.[45] The UAOC was in a better situation than the UOC because the latter could be associated with the forcible dissolution of the UGCC in 1946 and with the Moscow Patriarchate's takeover of its buildings and properties. Still, Ukrainian Greek Catholics who believed that the UGCC should recover all the assets it possessed in 1946 expressed considerable resentment toward the UAOC.

Cultural, social, and personal issues often determined choices between two churches of similar liturgical practices and Ukrainian patriotic sentiments. Ukrainian Greek Catholics emphasized the patriotic activities of the UGCC in the nineteenth and twentieth centuries, the heroic struggle of the UGCC in the underground, and the identification of Orthodoxy with Russia as reasons for opting for the UGCC. Ukrainian Autocephalous Orthodox believers concentrated on Orthodoxy as the "Cossack faith," the use of force in organizing and propagating the church Union of Brest, the identification of Catholicism and the Union of Brest with Poland, and the advantages of the UAOC as an independent church under neither Rome nor Moscow.[46] In many cases attitudes toward the village priest, as well

---

45. On conflict in Galicia, see "Boli mizhkonfesiinoho konfliktu," *Blahovisnyk vidrodzhennia*, no. 9 (1 May 1991): 6–8. For UAOC protests against the government authorities, see *Za vil'nu Ukraïnu*, 21 July 1990. For a discussion of the conflicts and social divisions in Turka, see Iaroslav Hevrych, "Konflikty vynykaiut' postiino...," *Za vil'nu Ukraïnu*, 18 September 1990.

46. For the opposing visions of Ukrainian church history, see Ivan

as social and family allegiances, determined choices—particularly when villages were divided on the religious issue, and heated debate and violence took place. After the democratic opposition came to power in March 1990, the UAOC, the smaller of the institutions, charged that not only did it suffer violence from the Catholic majority, but also that it was discriminated against by the government.

By 1991 the religious conflict in Galicia seemed to be subsiding somewhat.[47] As opinion polls were taken and churches were assigned, factions had less reason to continue confrontation. The "losers" began directing their attention to finding other facilities and building churches. The Ukrainian Catholics came to realize that their vision of prewar Galicia, with a homogeneous Ukrainian Catholic society and possession of all church properties held in 1946, did not correspond to the reality of 1991. Being a religious minority, the UAOC's faithful understood that they had to come to an accommodation with the majority. The increasing activities of the UAOC outside Galicia won approval from Ukrainian patriots among the Uniates, who saw the development of the church in central and eastern Ukraine as positive for the Ukrainian cause. Supporters of the UAOC from outside Galicia, such as Ievhen Sverstiuk, strove to calm the religious strife. The commitment of the UGCC and the UAOC to Ukrainian culture and independence brought them together, if only for tactical reasons. Patriarch Mstyslav and Archbishop Major Liubachivs'kyi took over the leadership of the two churches, bringing with them the experience of the Ukrainian diaspora, where these churches had worked out a modus vivendi. But antagonism and frictions still existed. Despite professed declarations of their desire for a meeting, the leaders of the two churches did not meet in Ukraine.

One of the greatest problems that the UAOC faced was its relationship with the Orthodox world. The UAOC that had been established under the leadership of Metropolitan Vasyl' Lypkivs'kyi in 1921 could not be recognized by other Orthodox Churches

Paslavs'kyi, "Mizh skhodom i zakhodom," and Father Volodymyr Iarema, "Nasha ukraïns'ka Tserkva, abo chyï my dity," under the rubric "Boh i Ukraïna," *Dzvin* (Lviv), 1990, no. 10: 100–10.

47. For Ievhen Sverstiuk's role in calming the UGCC-UAOC conflict, see his "Kolonka redaktora," *Nasha vira pravoslav'ia*, 1991, no. 2. For Patriarch Mstyslav's attempts at calming the religious situation, see Anzhelika Tatomyr's interview with him, "Za dukhovnu iednist' Ukraïny," *Za vil'nu Ukraïnu*, 7 November 1990.

because of its radical canons, especially its consecration of bishops without the participation of existing bishops. The UAOC that had been formed in 1942 ensured that the church had bishops consecrated in the traditional manner, but in the short period that it existed in Ukraine it did not obtain recognition by other Orthodox Churches. The newly restored UAOC sought to secure recognition in the Orthodox Oecumene, but it faced formidable problems.

With its decentralized structure and lacking the elaborated procedures of the Catholic Church, the Orthodox Church does not have clearly established procedures for the institution of autocephaly or a patriarchate, as the modern history of the church in the Balkans has shown. Generally, political events have determined the evolution of ecclesiastical structures. Crucial to the situation of the church in Ukraine is the question of which Orthodox Church exercises legitimate ecclesiastical authority. The Moscow Patriarchate asserted that it had that right and that in its granting of autonomy to the UOC in 1990 it had full authority in its own ecclesiastical province. As recently as 1924, however, the Ecumenical Patriarchate had charged that the Moscow Patriarchate's absorption of the Kyiv Metropolitanate in 1685–86 was uncanonical, and thereby it claimed the continued subordination of that metropolitanate to the patriarch of Constantinople. The re-establishment of the UAOC must be placed in the context of the rivalry between Moscow and Constantinople. In recent times this tension resulted in Moscow's recognition of an autocephalous church in North America, an act that Constantinople views as illegitimate, and in the refusal of the patriarch of Constantinople to attend the Moscow celebrations of the millennium of Christianity in Rus'.

The UAOC asserted that the Moscow Patriarchate's claims to the Kyiv Metropolitanate are illegitimate because Kyiv is the mother church of Moscow and the acts of 1685–86 were uncanonical. Although the UAOC's leaders acted on their own in re-establishing their church, they hoped for recognition from Constantinople. The first parish of the UAOC, the Church of SS. Peter and Paul in Lviv, asked for Patriarch Demetrios's protection until a UAOC hierarchy could be established, and the sobor in Kyiv in June 1990 addressed an appeal to the Constantinople Patriarchate.

The Moscow Patriarchate and the UOC actively sought Constantinople's support against the autocephalists. While the diplomatic initiatives and the agreements are not fully public, the Moscow Patriarchate had considerable success. In early 1990 a delegation from Constantinople called the autocephalist issue an internal matter of the Moscow Patriarchate, and in early 1991 the Constantinople Patriarchate issued a statement censuring the autocephalist movement.[48] A delegation from the patriarch of Constantinople to Kyiv in July 1991 manifested support for the UOC by joint services and met with officials of the Ukrainian government.[49] No answers were issued to the UAOC's appeals. The Ecumenical Patriarchate, however, appeared not to be fully supportive of Moscow. It was rumoured to have chastised its 1990 delegation for going too far, and its statement of 1991 contained an ambiguous allusion to its recognition of the Moscow Patriarchate's authority on the basis of a council of 1593 that set borders excluding the Kyiv Metropolitanate.[50]

The situation of the Orthodox and Ukrainian diasporas, above all in North America, influenced the UAOC's relations with the rest of the Orthodox world.[51] In 1970 the Moscow Patriarchate recognized the Russian Orthodox Greek Catholic Metropolia as the Orthodox Church of America, basing its authority on the Russian church's mission to North America and its control over Orthodox believers until the Revolution of 1917. The Constantinople Patriarchate and other Eastern patriarchates condemned this act as illegitimate, with Constantinople arguing that canons gave it primary authority in lands where no fully constituted Orthodox Churches existed. Constantinople's dependence, above all financial, on the Greek Archdiocese of North and South America must have played a role in its adamant stance, as did the fact that the Greek church is the largest Orthodox group in North America. In practice this situation made Constantinople and the Greek Archdiocese allies of the UOC of the United States and the UOC of Canada, which favoured the retention of cultural traditions and historically opposed the Moscow

48. For Patriarch Demetrios II's letter of 10 January 1991 to Patriarch Aleksii condemning the "movement of autocephalists," see *Informator: Vydaie Students'ke t-vo Bohoslovs'koho fakul'tetu Kolegii Sv. Andreia* (Winnipeg), no. 5 (May–August 1991), 3.

49. TASS reported that on 26–7 July Metropolitan Bartholomew of Chalcedon led a delegation visiting Metropolitan Filaret and Prime Minister Vitol'd Fokin. For the UAOC's interpretation of the visit, see "RPTs vlashtovuie provokatsii," *Svoboda*, 6 August 1991.

50. This is the interpretation of the UOC of Canada; see *Informator*, no. 5 (May–August 1991): 3.

51. This problem is discussed in my article "The Ukrainian Orthodox Churches and the Ukrainian Diaspora," 22–4.

Patriarchate and the transformed Russian metropolia. Although the Constantinople Patriarchate and the Greek Archdiocese did not officially recognize the two Ukrainian churches and maintained a Ukrainian group (the UOC of America) under their direct authority, they lent a more sympathetic ear to the Ukrainians' aspirations and cultivated closer contacts. Metropolitan Mstyslav pursued this policy of rapprochement without conceding the principle of autocephaly for the UAOC in the West or the international unity of the Ukrainian Orthodox Churches.

Canada presented a special question, because the UOC of Canada was one of the largest and best organized Orthodox groups. Desiring to enter the general Orthodox community, the leaders of that church negotiated an agreement with the Constantinople Patriarchate that established intercommunion but maintained the church's traditional organization and autonomy. Although a Ukrainian Orthodox council in Canada approved the agreement in 1989, the exact nature of the relationship remained unclear.[52] In particular, just how the church was in intercommunion with Constantinople while retaining its links with its sister Ukrainian Orthodox metropolitanates and the UAOC in Ukraine, which it supported, remained uncertain. It would seem that the rebirth of the UAOC in Ukraine came unexpectedly, at a time when the Canadian church's negotiations with Constantinople were well advanced. With the increasing involvement of Ukrainian Canadians in their ancestral homeland and the rebirth of the UAOC, the Canadian church found its relations with Constantinople and Kyiv difficult to balance. On the other hand, the UOC of Canada could use its new relationship to secure Constantinople's support for Orthodox Ukrainians and argue the UAOC's case before the Ecumenical Patriarchate.[53]

---

52.   For the documents on the relationship between the Constantinople Patriarchate and the UOC of Canada, see *Ridna nyva: Kalendar na rik 1991* (Winnipeg), 115–19.

53.   The dean of St. Andrew's Seminary in Winnipeg, Father Tymofii Minenko, travelled to Ukraine, where he visited Patriarch Mstyslav and demonstrated support for the UAOC. UAOC circles criticized him for visiting Metropolitan Filaret. See *Blahovisnyk vidrodzhennia*, no. 15 (1 August 1991), 5. The UOC tried to exploit the Canadian situation to its advantage. In a distorted account of the situation, Metropolitan Filaret maintained: "Pay attention to the following fact—in Canada there exists a Ukrainian Greek Orthodox Church, which Metropolitan Vasyl' [Fedak] heads. Metropolitan Vasyl' does not have any spiritual contacts and Eucharistic communion with Mstyslav [Skrypnyk]. Why? Because he does not wish to soil his white robe

The UAOC faced great obstacles in obtaining recognition in the Orthodox world. As had been the experience of the UGCC at times when it sought the Vatican's support, the desire to maintain good relations with the large and powerful Moscow Patriarchate influenced the policies of churches outside the Soviet Union. The Eastern patriarchates and other autocephalous churches confronted even more difficult issues in choosing between the UAOC and the larger UOC. Adhering to the principle that the church should have only one bishop in one locality—a principle breached in many areas of the world—they viewed the existence of two hierarchies in Ukraine negatively. In addition, they were suspicious of the legacy of the UAOC, above all its break with traditional canons in 1921, as well as certain current practices of conciliar governance. Even the consecration of the present church hierarchy was questioned by some Orthodox.[54] Most Orthodox Churches looked askance at the UAOC's proclamation of a patriarchate. The Orthodox Churches were also extremely antagonistic to Uniates; hence, they viewed any co-operation between the UAOC and the UGCC negatively, even if such co-operation was solely for reasons of national unity. Nevertheless, resentment in the Orthodox world about many of the actions of the Moscow Patriarchate, as well as the traditional claims of the Constantinople Patriarchate to Ukraine, favoured a hearing for the UAOC.

Political and cultural factors also influenced the situation of the UAOC. The church was identified with the forces favouring real Ukrainian statehood. Relations between the UAOC and political groups were quite complex. The church generated considerable support in central and eastern Ukraine because it was associated with democratic and anti-Communist groups. The UAOC thus faced a quandary as it tried to set up an institutional structure under a Communist-dominated government. With the appearance of "sovereignty Communists" and the evolution of Leonid Kravchuk toward Ukrainian statist policies, the church faced a dilemma.

---

with an uncanonical link" (materials of the press conference of 28 October 1990, *Pravoslavnyi visnyk,* 1991, no. 1: 11).

54.   Before Patriarch Mstyslav's arrival, Bishop (later Metropolitan) Ioan, whom the ROC defrocked after he declared that he left its jurisdiction, joined with a bishop of a dissident ROC and an anonymous bishop of the Moscow Patriarchate to consecrate bishops. For an account of this issue by Bishop Antonii of Rivne, see the interview with him, "Rozum peremozhe emotsii."

Patriarch Mstyslav was involved in the difficult diplomacy of seeking the government's support, especially in changing the policies of hard-line Communist local governments against the UAOC. The "sovereignty Communists" sought legitimacy among Ukrainian patriots from the UAOC. At the commemoration of the Battle of Berestechko in June 1991, Patriarch Mstyslav went so far as to defend Kravchuk from protestors in the democratic camp, who viewed the presence of the former party ideologue as a desecration.[55] Therefore, the church had to tread a fine line of obtaining concessions from the government and supporting its movement toward sovereignty without alienating its core support from Rukh and the anticommunists.

Cultural change and the Ukrainian national revival also presented the UAOC with opportunities and challenges. The growth of Ukrainian national consciousness stimulated the rebirth of the church, especially in central and eastern Ukraine. In many areas the activists of the Society for the Ukrainian Language and the UAOC worked closely, and many members of the often secularized intelligentsia were drawn to the church as a preserver of Ukrainian spiritual and national traditions.[56] Yet as the national awakening broadened, especially as schools and government institutions propagated the Ukrainian language, the relative role of the church became less important.

The UAOC inherited an ecclesiastical tradition that both shaped the church and defined its strengths and weaknesses. The church of the 1920s had developed principles of autocephaly, Ukrainianization, separation of church and state, conciliar rule, and Christianization of life, which Bohdan Bociurkiw has described as a program for modernization.[57] In general, these traditions stood the church in

---

55. On the Berestechko celebrations, see Kolomayets, "Battle of Berestechko." The Communist press charged that the UAOC was merely an arm of Rukh. See "Pochemu miriane prishli k Sovminu," *Pravda Ukrainy*, 7 November 1990. See also "Patriiarkh Mstyslav zustrivsia z L. Kravchukom," *Ukraïns'ki visti*, 23 June 1991; and "Patriarch Mstyslav Meets with Ukrainian PM Vitold Fokin," *The Ukrainian Weekly*, 16 June 1991.

56. For an example of the co-operation of Ukrainian groups in Dnipropetrovsk, see "Rizdvo v Ukraïni," *Ukraïns'ke slovo* (Paris), 27 January 1991. Members of the UAOC, the Society for the Ukrainian Language, and Rukh joined to carol and to stage a *vertep* (Christmas pageant), including a version with political figures.

57. See his article "The Ukrainian Autocephalous Orthodox Church, 1920–1930: A Study in Religious Modernization," in *Religion and*

Ukraine in good stead during the early 1990s, for many of the characteristics of the ROC against which the Ukrainian church movement was formed at the beginning of the twentieth century still remained. Autocephaly and Ukrainianization obviously corresponded in the religious sphere to growing political and cultural movements in Ukraine. Conciliarism provided for the active involvement of the laity at a time when the bishops of the Moscow Patriarchate had compromised their hierarchically ruled church. Separation of church and state gave the UAOC a dynamism that was lacking in the Moscow Patriarchate and the UOC, which still hewed to the state as the proper protector of the church and executor of their decisions. Christianization of life mandated an active evangelization program in which the church engaged in cultural, social, and political movements.

But if the UAOC legacy left the church considerable strengths as an ecclesiastical entity, it also left it weaknesses. Some merely reflected the fact that the UAOC was able to develop in Ukraine only for short periods of time and could not resolve all problems. Not all liturgical books are available in Ukrainian, catechetical literature is insufficient, and theological works have rarely been translated. In the 1920s the UAOC was, above all, involved in the organization of parishes and local structures. This was once again the case in the years 1989–91, but with the establishment of seminaries and eparchial structures the UAOC had to develop further its own theological and ecclesiastical traditions. The relation of the UAOC to the Orthodox tradition and the existing Orthodox oecumene was an especially difficult issue. The UAOC declared its wish to adhere to these, but it had embarked on reforms that are not generally accepted. While the present UAOC did not go back to the radical canons of 1921, it also did not publicly criticize that church or its leader, Metropolitan Vasyl' Lypkivs'kyi. However, many UOC clergymen hesitated to join the UAOC unless it received full recognition by other Orthodox Churches.[58]

Modernization in the Soviet Union, ed. Dennis Dunn (Boulder, Colo., 1977), 310–47; repr. in his booklet *Ukrainian Churches under Soviet Rule: Two Case Studies* (Cambridge, Mass., 1984).

58.   On concern over the issue of canonicity, see Father Ihor Shvets''s letter of 11 January 1991 in *Visnyk*, 1991, no. 3: 6. For expressions of the strong desire to be in communion with other Orthodox Churches and the mother church of Constantinople, see Metropolitan Ioan's Christmas message in *Blahovisnyk vidrodzhennia*, 1991, no. 2 (20 January): 1–2.

The UAOC also faced the problem of whether it would define itself as the church of the Ukrainians or the territorial church of Ukraine. Certainly, the Orthodox world found the existence of two Orthodox Churches in an ancient Orthodox land troubling. If it wished to assume the role of a territorial church, the UAOC had to integrate the Russian population of Ukraine—a difficult task, given its specific Ukrainian character.[59]

The demise of Soviet totalitarianism and Communist ideology resulted in the re-emergence of long-suppressed political, cultural, and religious movements. In that context it was not unexpected that Ukraine, which has so long been a zone of competition between Uniatism and Orthodoxy and between Russian and Ukrainian Orthodoxy, should once again emerge as a region of conflict. Soviet policies decimated religious institutions and impeded the development of religious thought. However, as communism and Soviet rule were discredited, religion gained greater authority, and religious institutions became more prominent. In some cases, reassertion of cultural and national values contributed to this greater prominence of churches. In Ukraine Soviet rule had merely exacerbated religious conflicts. Through its support of Russian Orthodoxy against the UAOC and the UGCC, the Soviet government had left the Ukrainian churches bereft of institutions, but had given them a greater moral authority. The situation during the years 1989–91 also differed from that of earlier periods in that the Ukrainian lands were now almost all in one state and Ukrainians were more intermixed than they had ever been. Therefore the largely political divide between Orthodox and Uniate that existed from the late eighteenth century to the Second World War had broken down.

The breakdown of the Soviet order permitted the division of the Orthodox in Ukraine. The outcome of the religious competition was not yet decided when the proclamation of Ukrainian independence on 24 August 1991 created an entirely new political context for the religious situation. The rebirth of the UAOC had preceded the

---

59.   The ROC in Russia faced a similar problem as national consciousness rose among the Ukrainians, many of whom are settled in the Kuban, the Amur Basin, and Kazakhstan. Until now the ROC functioned entirely as a Russian national church, not even preaching in Ukrainian. UAOC parishes were organized as far away from Ukraine as Sakhalin. At Easter in 1991 members of the UAOC in Moscow gathered to listen to a recording of a service because they had neither a church nor a priest. See *Blahovisnyk vidrodzhennia*, 1991, no. 8 (16 April): 6.

emergence of Ukrainian independent statehood and had already split Orthodox believers before the political situation changed to favour some sort of autocephaly for Ukrainian Orthodox believers. For the new state this divide of Orthodox believers was a cause for concern because it engendered religious conflict and Ukrainian-Russian tension at a time when the government desired civic peace and support from religious believers. For the UAOC, the emergence of an independent Ukraine subject to significant, if not dominant, control by the old Communist elite meant that central and local authorities were often the former opponents of the UAOC and closely allied to the UOC. By challenging the established authorities, both ecclesiastical and secular, the reborn UAOC of 1989–91 created a complex crisis in the religious and political affairs of the new Ukrainian state.

Appendix

The failed coup of 19–21 August 1991 in the Soviet Union, the proclamation of Ukrainian independence on 24 August 1991, and the referendum of 1 December 1991, which brought international recognition of the Ukrainian state, considerably changed the religious situation. However, the shift of the former Communist Party apparat in Ukraine to a pro-independence position and the election of Leonid Kravchuk, the Party's former ideological secretary in Ukraine, as Ukraine's president meant that these changes were not as favourable to the UAOC as might be expected. As of 1 January 1992 the church had 1,619 parishes, of which 1,490 were officially registered. It still was much smaller than the UOC, which had 5,473 parishes; and it remained concentrated in Galicia, where 1,453 parishes existed. It was, however, gaining a greater institutional presence in oblasts near Galicia (Rivne, thirty-two parishes; Volyn, fourteen; Khmelnytskyi, twenty-eight; and Chernivtsi, fourteen). With a patriarch, fifteen eparchies, and four theological seminaries, the UAOC established the structures to become a major religious body throughout Ukraine.[60]

The new political situation influenced the UAOC and the UOC and their mutual relations. The continued absence of Patriarch Mstyslav for health and other reasons, as well as his age and unclear status as a foreign national, hindered the formation of clear lines of

---

60. Statistics from government materials for a new law on religious freedom provided by a private source.

authority in the church. In particular, conflicts with Metropolitan Ioan increased so much that Ioan was transferred to the Zhytomyr Eparchy. In March 1992 Ioan broke with Mstyslav and was expelled from the UAOC. The UAOC continued to seek acceptance in the Orthodox world, and in May it dispatched a delegation led by Mstyslav to Constantinople, where it secured a promise that the patriarch of Constantinople would send a delegation to investigate the status of the UAOC.

The UOC underwent ever greater change. In 1991 Bishop Ionafan (Eletskikh) of Pereiaslav, press secretary of the UOC, publicly denounced Metropolitan Filaret for leading an immoral life. The bishop was forced to recant, and the metropolitan then accused him of contacts with the UAOC and had him defrocked. Responding to the new political situation in Ukraine, on 1–3 November 1991 Filaret led a council of the UOC that requested autocephaly from the Moscow Patriarchate. Ultimately four bishops refused to sign this request, and the matter developed into a power struggle that centred on opposition to Filaret. In addition to requesting autocephaly, he antagonized the Moscow Patriarchate by seeking direct lines of contact with the Constantinople Patriarchate.

By the time a synod of ROC bishops met in Moscow on 1–3 April 1992 to consider the request for autocephaly, tensions had increased between Ukraine and Russia and the Ukrainian government had become more active in seeking religious support for Ukrainian statehood. The synod fully supported Filaret's opponents, and the metropolitan was forced to issue a statement that he would request the UOC synod to relieve him of his responsibilities and to elect a successor. The ROC hierarchs also tabled the issue of autocephaly to the next particular synod.[61]

On his return to Ukraine, Filaret announced that he would not abide by the promise that he had made under duress. He was called before an ecclesiastical court in Moscow and ultimately deprived of all episcopal and priestly functions. A synod of UOC bishops held in May in Kharkiv elected Volodymyr (Sabodan) of Rostov and Novocherkassk as his successor. Although Filaret received the support of the Ukrainian government, which refused to recognize the legality of a synod held without the metropolitan, he lost the support of almost all bishops and most of the clergy. As Filaret's

---

61. See my next article in this volume, "The Russian Sobor and the Rejection of Ukrainian Orthodox Autocephaly." No date was set for the synod's convocation.

position weakened, he sought accommodation with the UAOC. With government officials urging negotiation, the UAOC administrator, Metropolitan Antonii (Masendych), met with Filaret and his followers in June 1992. They formed by merger the Ukrainian Orthodox Church-Kyiv Patriarchate (UOC-KP), naming Mstyslav as patriarch and Filaret as deputy. Not a party to the talks, Mstyslav, though conciliatory, refused to bless the merger. In the ensuing confusion UAOC followers tended to view Filaret negatively, yet most clergy and UAOC bishops, except in Galicia, accepted the merger as a means of ensuring a viable autocephalous church.

At its October 1992 church council, which Mstyslav refused to attend, the UOC-KP found itself in the awkward position of recognizing Patriarch Mstyslav but suspending his administrative authority. Upon Mstyslav's death in June 1993, the UOC-KP declared Archbishop Volodymyr (Romaniuk) its *locum tenens* and called an all-UOC council for October 1993.

Whether the new UOC-KP could succeed the UAOC remained in doubt, as did the status of UAOC parishes rejecting the merger. Neither group had been recognized by other Orthodox Churches, and, except in Galicia, the UOC-Moscow Patriarchate remained the largest Orthodox Church in Ukraine.

Frank E. Sysyn

The Russian Sobor and the Rejection of Ukrainian Orthodox Autocephaly[*]

When the archiepiscopal sobor of the Russian Orthodox Church (ROC) met on 1–4 April 1992, it refused to affirm the request for autocephaly made on 1–3 November 1991 by the synod of the Ukrainian Orthodox Church (UOC). Although the sobor's official statement delayed the issue to the next local sobor, the forced resignation of Metropolitan Filaret (Denysenko) of Kyiv, who had brought forth the request, showed how adamantly the ninety-seven hierarchs opposed the issue. Metropolitan Filaret, who subsequently retracted his promise to resign, called his situation at the sobor a personal Golgotha over the autocephaly issue and described the atmosphere as one guided by the spirit of "one and indivisible Russia."

Indeed, Metropolitan Filaret arrived at the sobor in a relatively weak position. During his twenty-five-year tenure, he had opposed any Ukrainian tendencies in the church. However, in the year and a half that he had led the UOC, which was given autonomy after the proclamation of Ukrainian sovereignty in July 1990, Filaret had faced religious and political changes that made autocephaly the only solution for the problems of the church he headed.

Not only had the Ukrainian Greek Catholic Church re-emerged strongly in the three Galician oblasts, but the Ukrainian Autocephalous Orthodox Church (UAOC) had taken over the vast majority of parishes in that region that wished to remain Orthodox. While the UAOC made much slower progress in other areas of Ukraine, over four hundred parishes had been registered by 1 January 1992.

The adherence of elements of the Ukrainian intelligentsia to the UAOC and its high profile, thanks to the proclamation of a patriarchate and participation in activities of the Ukrainian national revival, made the autocephalist challenge more serious than their mere numbers would warrant, particularly in the capital, Kyiv.

---

[*]   This article originally appeared in *The Ukrainian Weekly*, 26 July 1992, 8–9. It has been revised.

The proclamation of Ukrainian independence on 24 August 1991 and its affirmation by more than ninety percent of the electorate on 1 December 1991 further complicated the church's status. In many areas the local authorities who had backed the church against the autocephalist challenge either lost power or swung around to support Ukrainian independence. Most important, the new Ukrainian president, Leonid Kravchuk, pursued a policy of establishing a fully independent Ukrainian state and looked to the UOC to support his actions. Suddenly, a church that had curried favour by its advocacy of Soviet statehood and its condemnation of Ukrainian nationalism found itself markedly out of tune.

Meanwhile Metropolitan Filaret found that his personal authority in the church was openly questioned. Universally assumed to be living with a woman and his children, he could no longer suppress charges about his personal life. This situation became intertwined with dissatisfaction about Filaret's management of the church and his stand on ecclesiastical issues.

In 1991 this resulted in the public denunciation of Filaret by Ionafan (Eletskikh), Filaret's vicar (bishop) and liaison with the press. Ionafan then recanted, but still he was deprived of his episcopal rank. It is unclear whether he initially acted in collusion with ecclesiastical circles in Moscow. In the serpentine world of Ukrainian church politics, even though Ionafan is a Russian newly arrived in Ukraine, Filaret's charge that he negotiated to join the UAOC when his cause was lost cannot be lightly dismissed. Even the influential Moscow magazine *Ogonek* could not fully explain the affair, although it gave additional evidence about Filaret's personal life.

Dissension within the UAOC also stimulated Metropolitan Filaret to consider autocephaly a solution to his church's problems. Questions over whether the UAOC was fully canonical and why it was not recognized by other Orthodox Churches continued to plague it. In central and eastern Ukraine, where the UAOC's followers were few and the church had limited chances of winning over parishes from the deeply entrenched UOC (still frequently backed by remnants of the old Communist elite), the hierarchs and clergy of the UAOC could hope to achieve their goal by convincing the official church to obtain autocephaly and then reuniting with it.

In addition, personal conflicts intervened. Metropolitan (then archbishop) Ioan (Bodnarchuk), who had left Filaret's jurisdiction in late 1989 to head the parishes of the UAOC, had never been fully accepted by many believers or by Patriarch Mstyslav, in part because of allegations of KGB links. A year's stay in North America for health reasons did not resolve this issue. Indeed, Ioan spent considerable time in Canada, where the UOC of Canada has accepted the jurisdiction of the patriarch of Constantinople, thereby implicitly questioning the status of the UAOC in Ukraine and the UOC in the United States, which is also led by Patriarch Mstyslav.

Upon his return to Ukraine, Ioan entered into negotiations with Filaret. The presence of seven UAOC bishops at a meeting of the UOC synod without Patriarch Mstyslav's participation shows how advanced contacts had become. Resistance within the UAOC to these negotiations remained strong. Ioan's demotion from the populous Galician metropolitanate to his former eparchy of Zhytomyr seemed a recognition of the breach with the UAOC. In March 1992, however, he announced his break with the UAOC and his return to Filaret's jurisdiction, thereby signalling that his intermediary role was being rejected in the UAOC.

Meanwhile Metropolitan Filaret was facing resistance to his own authority and policies. It is not known whether the question of autocephaly was the original cause of disagreement, but ultimately Filaret's opponents resisted autocephaly. The metropolitan tried to banish his opponents by sending them to the UOC's "Siberia"—Ivano-Frankivsk Eparchy, where only eight parishes remained.

Filaret initially replaced Archbishop Feodosii (Dykun) of Ivano-Frankivsk with Metropolitan Agafangel (Savvin) of Vinnytsia. But Agafangel chose to retire instead. Filaret then transferred Bishop Onufrii (Berezovs'kyi) of Chernivtsi to Ivano-Frankivsk. But Onufrii and his supporters refused to turn over properties and offices to his successor, Ilarion (Shukalo). In the midst of these internal struggles, Filaret was unable to obtain the signatures of four of the twenty-one bishops on the request for autocephaly. How many signed under duress is unknown.

The Moscow Patriarchate's Position

The full details of the ROC sobor's meeting on autocephaly are not yet available. The April issue of *Moskovskii tserkovnyi vestnik* (*MTsV*) contains the official account after the decisions not to grant autocephaly and to force Filaret to resign had been taken. Therefore it presents the views that the Moscow Patriarchate wishes to communicate to its faithful. Several points are indicative: only a fragment of Metropolitan Filaret's discourse requesting autocephaly was printed; it appears after the decision, not before; and it is considerably shorter than the first item printed, a speech by Bishop Vasylii of Kirovohrad calling for rejection of the request.

In the fragment of Metropolitan Filaret's request for autocephaly, four grounds are mentioned. First, he argues that it is in the interest of Orthodoxy to allow the church to combat autocephalist and Catholic challenges, thereby bringing about harmony among antagonistic confessions and the consolidation of all nationalities in Ukraine and contributing to the unity of the Ukrainian people. Second, he asserts that the religious situation resulting from Ukrainian independence requires autocephaly. Third, he maintains that the UOC meets all of the requirements for autocephaly—it has 24 eparchies, 5,478 parishes, 32 monasteries, and about 36 million faithful. Fourth, he says that autocephaly is desired by the clergy and believers. Therefore he characterizes autocephaly as "justified and historically inevitable."

What is lacking in the fragment, however, is any discussion of the historical development of the Ukrainian Orthodox tradition and the development of strivings for autocephaly. Even less is there any questioning of the relationship between the Kyiv Metropolitanate and the Moscow Patriarchate in historical terms (the annexation of 1685–86) or criticism of the ROC's treatment of Ukrainian autocephalist strivings in the twentieth century. Whatever the participants of the sobor heard, the readers of *MTsV* could not know that the issue had any substance before the recent political changes.

Hierarchs' Comments

In presenting the case for rejection, the editors chose comments by eight hierarchs—four from Ukraine, two from Russia, and two from other former republics of the USSR. It is instructive to begin with the non-Ukrainian choices to see the perspective of the ROC that would remain if Ukrainian autocephaly were granted.

The participation of the archbishops of Almaty in Kazakhstan and Vilnius in Lithuania underlines that while the breakup of the Soviet Union has presented the ROC with a major problem in Ukraine, all the independent states may question the control of Moscow in the future. Only Ukraine and Belarus have semi-autonomous churches at present. The participation by a bishop from the Baltic states who speaks out against autocephaly highlights that although these countries are decisively asserting their independence, their substantial Orthodox populations (primarily Russians and Belarusians in Lithuania, but both Russians and Latvians in Latvia and Russians and Estonians in Estonia) remain fully integrated into the Moscow Patriarchate.

The problem of the patriarchate's unity, despite the formation of independent states, was most directly addressed by Archbishop

Aleksii (Kutepov) of Almaty, who read out the decisions of his eparchial council of 6 March 1992. As a state with an almost evenly matched population of Muslims and Orthodox and a substantial Ukrainian segment among the Orthodox, Kazakhstan faces an extremely delicate religious and national situation. Aleksii urged the church not to mix political affairs and personal ambitions with church issues, and he called for the unity of the ROC. He asserted that the granting of autocephaly to the UOC would lead to schisms in the Moscow Patriarchate along national lines. He maintained that if the Ukrainian church were independent, Orthodox Ukrainians on the territory of Kazakhstan would have every reason to create their own parishes, thereby leading to inter-ethnic conflicts.

While Aleksii's fears that Ukrainians might wish to form their own parishes might be justified, linking this to granting autocephaly to the UOC seems spurious. First, it indicates how deeply the church in Kazakhstan is Russified, since one might assume that otherwise parishes in which Ukrainian was the primary language of sermons and church life might already exist in areas of Ukrainian settlement. Rather than facing this pastoral need, the archbishop saw the independence of the UOC as dangerously justifying these aspirations. Yet the UOC was merely seeking autocephaly as a territorial church of Ukraine. It would seem much more likely that the existing UAOC would form parishes in Kazakhstan, and that the granting of autocephaly to the UOC, thereby facilitating the merger of the UOC and the UAOC, might avert such a process.

The two Russian bishops came from eparchies bordering on Ukraine. The archbishop of Krasnodar and the Kuban is merely quoted as saying that "only the unity of Orthodoxy among the fraternal Slavic nations—the Russians, the Ukrainians, [and] the Belarusians—could allow them to survive all the trials the Lord had sent," and that the ROC, as earlier, should unite "our peoples" and bring about the "flourishing of Orthodoxy in Rus'."

This usual cliché of Soviet and imperial Russian ideology does not even take into consideration the UOC's existence. Of course, coming as he is from an area with a considerable Ukrainian population, the archbishop might have reason to worry about a breakdown of unity if his Ukrainian flock seeks to use its native language in sermons or is attracted by an autocephalous UOC across the border.

Metropolitan Mefodii (Nemtsov) of Voronezh goes even further in propagating a political ideology, albeit in the guise of condemning political influences in the churches. Ignoring the independence of Ukraine, he says these phenomena exist "not only in Ukraine—they occur in our country [the former USSR] as a whole." He states that on foreign radio he had heard a politician claim that as foreign politicians had succeeded in destroying the political structure, so they sought to divide the ROC. In sum, the Russian bishops regret Ukrainian independence and the breakup of the Soviet Union.

The four Ukrainian bishops came from the Vinnytsia, Odesa, Kirovohrad, and Volhynia eparchies, with only the last supporting autocephaly. The bishops of Vinnytsia and Odesa served earlier in western Ukrainian eparchies that have been almost totally lost to the UAOC and the Ukrainian Greek Catholic Church. Archbishop Feodosii (Dykun) of Vinnytsia (formerly of Ivano-Frankivsk) describes the situation as "horrifying, difficult," while Archbishop Lazar (Shvets') of Odesa (formerly of Ternopil) calls it a hell where one is beaten up for saying a single word in Russian. Lazar makes no recommendation on autocephaly, while Feodosii says that although he formerly supported autocephaly, he sees that ninety percent of the priests and faithful of his eparchy are opposed.

The remarks of Bishop Vasylii of Kirovohrad are the first published and most sweeping indictment of autocephaly. He argues mainly that in a time of troubles (*smuta*), of the collapse of the political unity of the state, the church should remain united. He maintains that "ecclesiastical unity ought and can be the basis of spiritual and political unity of the nations of our country." He argues for the church as preserving a feeling of spiritual kinship between Russians and Ukrainians. Not only does Vasylii implicitly see the establishment of a Ukrainian state as negative, but he sees the spirituality of Ukraine as deficient without Russian Orthodoxy. He maintains that it is not the fault of the Moscow Patriarchate that the church in Ukraine does not deal effectively with difficulties, but rather the fault of the Ukrainian church. He argues that a church can be autocephalous only when it is spiritually self-sufficient, and maintains that the Ukrainian church does not possess this quality.

It falls to Bishop Varfolomii (Vashchuk) of Volhynia to present the autocephalist position. Yet, in political and cultural terms he does not differ greatly from the other hierarchs. He warns his colleagues that the situation is changing "and it is not changing in our interest. The union has fallen apart: Today in Ukraine, on the borders with all fraternal republics—Belarus, Russia, Moldova—customs offices stand." He admits that the separation of Ukraine "is painful for our whole church" and asserts that he would be for the unity of the church, but in the given situation this unity is dangerous for Orthodoxy in Ukraine. Even though the UOC has approved the use of Ukrainian in liturgies, he cites the use of Church Slavonic in the area of his eparchy bordering on the Lviv Eparchy as a sign of devotion to Orthodoxy.

Varfolomii does, however, characterize the pressure toward autocephaly. He reports that the UAOC has five parishes and twenty-eight registered communities in his eparchy. He informs his colleagues that eighteen parishes in his flock have refused to register the new church statute because they are unsure to which church they will belong, that one hundred parishes refuse to mention the patriarch of Moscow in their prayers, and that two hundred parishes in southern Volhynia are awaiting a "wise" decision of the sobor on autocephaly. He cites a UAOC statement that time is working for the autocephalists as correct, and warns that what is occurring in western Ukraine will occur someday elsewhere in Ukraine as well if the UOC does not obtain autocephaly. Unlike the other bishops who say that their faithful oppose autocephaly and that political interests distant from the church favour it, Varfolomii says that a "mass of believing people" are for it.

Loyalty to the ROC

These fragments do not include the opinions of the majority of the bishops of the UOC. But even if they are selected by the editors of the *MTsV*, they display attitudes current among some hierarchs. They regret the break-up of the Soviet Union, remain loyal to the ROC, and see the current situation in Ukraine as negative. Bishop Feodosii of Vinnytsia goes so far as to say, "We find ourselves in a more difficult situation than in 1937. Then our enemies were external; then we had martyrs. Today they wish to rip us apart from within; they wish to show us as Judases."

For at least part of the hierarchy, Bishop Vasylii's contention that the church in Ukraine lacks spiritual self-sufficiency seems quite correct. Brought up in a spirit of Russian Orthodoxy, these bishops cannot conceive of Ukraine's having its own church or spirituality. The question remains whether, after the departure to the UAOC of so many clergy and believers who conceived of a Ukrainian Orthodox tradition, a sufficient Ukrainian element exists in the UOC to make it a particular church. Even the proclamation of Ukrainian independence and the chance to unite with the UAOC did not convince some bishops of the UOC to adopt this position.

If all the hierarchs within the UOC do not accept the political and religious changes in Ukraine, it is no surprise that the hierarchs of the ROC do not. They hold to the conception of Russian Orthodoxy as a force favouring the maintenance of the old empire, which, to their minds, is a natural unity. They see their loyalty to the Russian language and Russian traditions as somehow supranational. For them, of course, recognition of Ukrainian autocephaly would merely begin a process that would inevitably reach the major groups of Orthodox believers in the Baltic states, Belarus, Moldova, and Kazakhstan.

The sobor took a decision to postpone the autocephaly issues until the convocation of the local sobor of the patriarchate, and Patriarch Aleksii II wrote a pastoral to the faithful in Ukraine and one to President Kravchuk. In the first he maintained that while the idea of autocephaly was viewed positively in the western eparchies, it was rejected by the majority of the faithful and clergy in the others—a statement difficult to verify at worst, and questionable at best.

More importantly, without explaining Metropolitan Filaret's reasons, Aleksii announced that the sobor had taken into account Filaret's announcement that he would put in a request to resign before the next archiepiscopal sobor of the UOC. In his pastoral letter he called for calm and the avoidance of schism, even addressing remarks to the UAOC.

Most difficult to write was a letter in response to President Kravchuk's letter supporting autocephaly. Here we find the only remarks in the whole discussion favourable to Ukrainian independence. Aleksii announces Filaret's resignation and calls on President Kravchuk to support his successor's attempt at bringing calm to the Orthodox and improve relationships with other confessions. He calls for adherence to principles of religious freedom in Ukraine.

The ROC's response to the Ukrainian request for autocephaly and the forced resignation of Metropolitan Filaret set the stage for the present religious turmoil in Ukraine. The tenacity of allegiance to "one and indivisible" empire and church permeates the thinking of the Orthodox leadership in Russia and in the UOC. In essence, they have not yet accepted the existence of a Ukrainian church or state.

Serhii Plokhy

Ukrainian Orthodox Autocephaly and Metropolitan Filaret[*]

The dynamic and tragic dimensions of the events that enveloped the Ukrainian Orthodox Church (UOC) in the spring of 1992 are reminiscent of the turmoil it underwent in the late sixteenth to mid-seventeenth centuries. At its archiepiscopal sobor, which took place in April 1992, the Russian Orthodox Church (ROC) effectively refused the UOC's request to be granted canonical independence, or status as an autocephalous church, and deferred any decision on the matter to the next local sobor. The date for the next such assembly has not been determined, although it is to take place within the next three years.

The Moscow Patriarchate obviously shares the view of certain leading Russian politicians that Ukraine will "recover from the illness" of independence and return to the Russian yoke. For the moment, the patriarchate has affirmed the concept of a single and indivisible church, if not state. Moscow could not issue an outright refusal, because Ukraine has been granted international recognition as an independent state and the issue of Ukrainian autocephaly has entered the global arena. As a result, Moscow decided to delay and to use the hiatus to its own advantage.

The first blow to the UOC's autocephalous movement was struck at this sobor. Its target was Metropolitan Filaret (Denysenko), primate of the UOC, an extraordinarily controversial figure and an easy mark for attacks and accusations. Already in 1991, prior to the declaration of Ukrainian independence and before his change of policy from backing a united Russian church to the support of Ukrainian autocephaly, Filaret found himself under strong attack from within and without the UOC.

The first accusation was made by Ionafan (Eletskikh), then bishop of Pereiaslav-Khmelnytskyi. He charged that Filaret was guilty of

---

*   Translated from the Ukrainian by Andrij Wynnyckyj. This article originally appeared in *The Ukrainian Weekly*, 2 August 1992. It has been revised.

breaking his monastic vows. According to Ionafan's information, supported by a number of rumours circulating in Kyiv and later by the testimonies of other bishops, Filaret has a family and children, whom he made no effort to conceal because he was so confident of his position. The second accusation appeared in the Moscow press. Filaret was charged with long-standing collaboration with the KGB and organizing a series of provocations against the Ukrainian Greek Catholic Church.

Characteristically, the Moscow sobor, seeking a pretext to punish Filaret for his demands for autocephaly, referred to these charges only unofficially. In official documents completely different arguments were presented. The reasons for such a game are fairly obvious. For a time, the patriarchate supported Filaret against Ionafan and sanctioned the latter's removal as bishop. As far as the charges of collaboration with the KGB are concerned, similar allegations were also made in the press about Patriarch Aleksii II himself and about the entire Holy Synod of the ROC. Therefore using this argument against Filaret would have failed. According to a document issued in the mid-1970s by the Council for Religious Affairs (CRA) of the Council of Ministers of the USSR, Filaret belonged to that group of ROC hierarchs who collaborated with the Soviet authorities even though they had certain reservations. Some of them who now wished to judge him, including Aleksii II, according to the same document, were in the category of those who unquestioningly carried out the directives of the regime.

At the April sobor in Moscow, Filaret was officially charged with leading the church toward schism.[1] It was also stated that he had "lost the trust of the majority of the Ukrainian episcopate and can no longer be the servant and the symbol of church unity." This was a reference to the conflict between Filaret and a few UOC bishops who had refused to back him in his search for autocephaly. On the whole, these were hierarchs who were most closely bound by personal or

---

1.   During my interview with him on 24 September 1997, Patriarch Filaret told me that members of the ROC's Holy Synod had accused him of causing a church schism so that he could become a patriarch in Ukraine. He allegedly responded by declaring that if he wanted to be a patriarch he would become one in Moscow with the help of the head of the CRA, Konstantin Kharchev, who had promised Filaret his support in this matter. According to Filaret, in late 1988 Kharchev was about to remove the future Patriarch Aleksii II and a number of other metropolitans from the Holy Synod, but Filaret saved Aleksii by siding with the other metropolitans against Kharchev, thereby making Kharchev's removal from office possible in June 1989.

official ties with the Moscow Patriarchate. One of them, Alipii (Pohrebniak), had just been consecrated in October 1991 as bishop of Donetsk. After graduating from the theological seminary and academy in Moscow, he served as personal assistant to the archimandrite of the Trinity-St. Sergei Monastery, as the custodian of the patriarch's chambers, and then as overseer of the Trinity Cathedral. The other two members of the anti-Filaret group were Bishops Onufrii (Berezovs'kyi) of Chernivtsi and Serhii (Hensyts'kyi) of Ternopil, both of whom had personal contacts with the ruling elite in Moscow.

According to the Ukrainian press, the clerical careers of Onufrii and Serhii, both of whom were from Bukovyna, were marked by their financial dealings while they were based at the Pochaiv Monastery. There Onufrii served as vicar, and Serhii as accountant. Funds from the monastery, including those converted into U.S. currency, were transferred directly to Moscow. Particularly suspicious in that respect was the affair concerning the consecration of Bishop Serhii, whose patron in Moscow was the director of the Moscow Patriarchate's external-relations department, Metropolitan Kirill (Gundiaev) of Smolensk. Serhii was elevated to his post without any theological training or having served as a hegumen or an archimandrite. It is difficult to determine the accuracy of press reports dealing with this issue. Equally uncertain is how much more morally upstanding the other hierarchs of the UOC were. But there is no doubt about the close personal contacts of Onufrii, Serhii, and Alipii with Moscow or that these contacts were a significant factor in their anti-Filaret positions.

Filaret's reaction to the refusal of the three bishops to back him in his efforts to secure autocephaly was sharp, though much more cautious than his response to Ionafan's attacks. To be sure, the bishops were removed from their eparchies, but they were offered other positions. At the synod of the UOC on 23 January it was decided to transfer Onufrii to the Ivano-Frankivsk Eparchy, where only a handful of UOC parishes remained, while Serhii was assigned to Pereiaslav-Khmelnytskyi and named a vicar of the Kyiv Eparchy. In other words, he was placed under Filaret's direct control. An analogous decision was made with regard to Alipii, who submitted a written request to be released from the Donetsk Eparchy. He was installed as the bishop of Cherkasy and also given a vicarship in Kyiv. The synod renewed its request to Moscow for autocephaly.

Onufrii demonstrated the most active opposition to the synod's decisions. He organized some of the laity, who allegedly confined him to his residence in Chernivtsi against his will. Rumours even began circulating that a metropolitanate independent of Kyiv had been established in Bukovyna. Onufrii also brought his supporters to Moscow, where they staged a demonstration during a session of the archiepiscopal sobor of the ROC in April 1992. At the sobor Filaret was forced to promise to resign, but he was to step down only after his return to Ukraine, during an archiepiscopal sobor of the UOC. According to information provided by the Moscow Patriarchate, he swore to do so on a holy cross and a gospel and was given the sobor's blessing to serve as bishop at one of the UOC's cathedrals.[2]

Subsequent reports in the Ukrainian press suggest that the initial intention of the congress's organizers was to remove Filaret in Moscow, convene a sobor of Ukrainian bishops on the spot, and elect Volodymyr (Sabodan), the metropolitan of Rostov and Novocherkassk, as the new metropolitan of Kyiv. Filaret's promise to step down delayed his ouster. When Filaret returned to Ukraine, he refused to vacate the Kyivan see. At a press conference he held in Kyiv, he declared that he had endured a "Golgotha" in Moscow. He then blocked the appointment of "Moscow's designate" as the head of the UOC and asserted that he could not leave his post at this crucial juncture. In other words, he refused to resign. Judging by the wide currency given to Filaret's declaration by the official mass media, the Ukrainian government supported his stand. Prior to the archiepiscopal sobor in Moscow, President Leonid Kravchuk had sent a special letter to the Moscow patriarch in which he expressed his support for the UOC's request for autocephaly issued in November 1991. The sobor's decision gave a clear indication of Moscow's position in this regard.

In the meantime, the Moscow Patriarchate, taking advantage of its rights as the overseer of the Orthodox Church's administrative centre, took the offensive and organized an unprecedented campaign against Filaret's supporters through its representatives in Ukraine. Particularly indicative were the events that took place in the Odesa Eparchy. For many decades it had been considered the "Crimea" of the Moscow Patriarchate. The summer residence of the patriarch, the Dormition Monastery near Odesa, was the site of the ROC's sole

---

2. According to what one participant in the Moscow sobor, Metropolitan Filaret (Vakhromeev) of Minsk, told me during my interview with him in June 1997, the possibility of transferring Metropolitan Filaret (Denysenko) to Siberia and creating a Siberian exarchate of the ROC for that purpose was discussed during the sobor.

theological seminary outside Russia. Moscow's position here is stronger than anywhere else in Ukraine, all the more since elsewhere numerous educational institutions of the Ukrainian Greek Catholic Church and the Ukrainian Autocephalous Orthodox Church (UAOC) had been established and were attracting nationally conscious youth who no longer wished to attend seminaries affiliated with the Moscow Patriarchate. Regardless of the eparchy's evident leanings toward Moscow, Archbishop Lazar (Shvets') of Odesa did not oppose Filaret's position on autocephaly at the archiepiscopal sobor in Moscow. As a result, upon his return, Lazar was forced out of his residence. A written appeal on behalf of the clergy requesting that the eparchy and the Dormition Monastery be placed under Moscow's direct authority was forwarded to Patriarch Aleksii II.

On 30 April a congress of bishops, clergy, and laity of the UOC was held in Zhytomyr. There resolutions expressing no confidence in Filaret and demanding his resignation were adopted. On 7 May a meeting of the Holy Synod of the ROC took place. There Filaret, who was not present, was ordered to call an archiepiscopal sobor of the UOC by 15 May and to resign. He was also forbidden to act as a representative of any church, and all of the sanctions or interdictions he had imposed were declared invalid. Filaret was told that he would face a tribunal of the archiepiscopal sobor of the ROC if he did not comply with this edict.

Filaret refused to submit, and Moscow made good on its threat. On 12 June he was accused of flagrant insubordination to church authorities, brutal treatment of the bishops in his jurisdiction, the creation of a church schism, and personal conduct unworthy of a hierarch. He was stripped of his rank and demoted to the status of a simple monk. The latter decision was strange, since the "personal conduct" referred to was his relationship with his family. The Russian sobor's decision made it seem that while a metropolitan was not permitted to have a family life, it was entirely permissible for a monk.

The decisions adopted by the archiepiscopal sobor of the ROC completely reversed its own previous resolution granting religious and administrative independence to the UOC. As the course of events has demonstrated, the original ROC decision was obviously just a tactical concession and a game of words. Like Mikhail Gorbachev in 1990–91, Aleksii II was initially in favour of "independence," "autonomy" and "sovereignty" as long as there was no actual change in the status quo. The Moscow patriarch was the head of the UOC; he remains so in practice and manipulates it primarily in the best interests of Moscow.

In May Aleksii handed over the functions of overseer of the UOC to Metropolitan Nykodym (Rusnak) of Kharkiv, who convened a bishops' sobor in Kharkiv on 27 May. As planned in Moscow in April, the sobor elected Metropolitan Volodymyr, a Ukrainian from the Khmelnytskyi region who had long served as a hierarch in Ukraine but whose most recent posting had been in Russia, as the new head of the UOC. The sobor's choice received the Moscow patriarch's blessing.[3]

Volodymyr was supported by the majority of Ukrainian bishops, including the administration of the Kyivan Cave Monastery. Filaret's authority now extended only to his own residence. Security for the grounds was assumed by a nationalist paramilitary group. One of its commanders, Dmytro Korchyns'kyi, commented on the decision: "At the moment, Filaret, notwithstanding his moral failings, has been promoting the interests of Ukraine and he stands against Moscow."

The CRA of the Cabinet of Ministers of Ukraine passed a resolution in defence of Filaret and rejected the decisions made at the Kharkiv sobor. It was noted that the sobor had taken place with considerable deviations from the statutes of the UOC, which had been registered with Ukraine's government agencies. Among the many violations was the selection of a UOC head who was serving outside the territory of Ukraine. Thus, Volodymyr's election was not recognized by the Ukrainian government.

* * *

At this point, we must depart from a strictly chronological account of events in the Ukrainian-Russian conflict so as to examine the factors that produced the Moscow Patriarchate's impressive victory. One of the principal factors was the person of Metropolitan Filaret himself. Until 1991 he was widely known as an opponent of everything Ukrainian in church life. By some accounts, Filaret had even berated his future opponent, Metropolitan Volodymyr, when the latter was the rector of the Moscow Theological Academy, for agreeing to conduct oral examinations of Ukrainian candidates in their native language. This accusation is quite plausible, for Filaret's drastic change in attitude was forced by the proclamation of Ukrainian independence in August 1991.

---

3.   According to a priest who visited Metropolitan Kirill (Gundiaev) in his Moscow office at the time of the Kharkiv sobor and agreed to talk to me if he remained anonymous, Kirill was constantly on the phone "co-ordinating" the proceedings of the sobor in Ukraine.

The Ukrainian government and most leaders of the opposition in Parliament unquestioningly supported Filaret in order to defend autocephaly, even though his character not only threw a shadow on the cause but also complicated it immensely. A hierarch with a family would inevitably have met with insubordination in the new atmosphere, and as such Filaret was an easy target for the church elite. Quite a few Ukrainian bishops detested Filaret for his arbitrary and autocratic rule. According to some hierarchs, the church was actually led by two individuals—"Sister" Ievheniia Rodionova, the mother of Filaret's children and his de facto wife, whose hand the hierarchs of the UOC were forced to kiss at church celebrations; and the layman Iurii M. Pinkus. Obviously the bishops whom Filaret had intimidated and humiliated were waiting for an opportunity to restore fairness in church life.

The intentions of the Moscow Patriarchate leave no room for doubt. It clearly wishes to retain control over the UOC and can deceive few with its contention that it seeks to remove Filaret not because of his support of autocephaly, but for his other actions. It is no coincidence that foreign journalists present at a press conference in Moscow were curious to learn why questions about Filaret's amorality arose only after he began issuing demands for Ukrainian Orthodox autocephaly. They did not receive a satisfactory reply.

The new Ukrainian administration continues to support Filaret's cause. According to reports in the Ukrainian media, a UOC-UAOC sobor was held in Kyiv on 25–26 June. There the unification of the two churches was announced, as was the establishment of a single church organization to be known as the Ukrainian Orthodox Church—Kyiv Patriarchate. The higher sobor of this new organization included the parliamentarians Oles' Shevchenko, Vasyl' Chervonii, and Mykola Porovs'kyi (the latter two are from Volhynia), which demonstrates the support for this action in Ukraine's political circles.

In the light of recent events, the joint sobor's action appears to be a last-ditch effort to save Filaret. He was chosen as Patriarch Mstyslav's deputy even though he brought little to the unified church besides the church's funds and his personal residence, which was secured by a nationalist paramilitary group and Bishop Iakiv, who had recently been expelled from the Pochaiv Eparchy. The sobor took place unbeknownst to the head of the UAOC, Mstyslav, and was not endorsed by the western Ukrainian eparchies of the UAOC. In other words, it brought the UAOC to the brink of schism. It is difficult to say whether the sobor, having given Filaret hope he would remain in church affairs at the highest level, has presented a new threat to the cause of Ukrainian Orthodox autocephaly.

It is equally instructive for the government to listen to the voices of the Ukrainian bishops who opposed Filaret. The Kharkiv sobor affirmed the episcopate's demand for "canonical autocephaly." The new leader of the UOC, Metropolitan Volodymyr, has made similar demands. Of course, it is difficult to believe in the sincerity of such strivings by certain hierarchs, but it is certain that the Ukrainian government will support them in this area.

The history of the Orthodox Church has demonstrated that the attainment of autocephaly is an extraordinary difficult and complex process. It will not be easy for the UOC to achieve this goal. Indeed, it will be impossible without the support of the majority of the UOC episcopate.

Serhii Plokhy

Kyiv vs. Moscow: The Autocephalous Movement in Independent Ukraine[*]

Centuries of Confrontation

Kyiv is often regarded in the West as one of the centres of historic, if not contemporary, Russia. This especially pertains to the area of church tradition. Indeed, Kyiv occupies an exceptionally important place in the history of Russian Orthodoxy: it is linked with Moscow by spiritual traditions and church histories that have much in common. At the same time, as events of the past century—especially those of the past few years—have shown, Orthodox Kyiv has found itself in a fairly sharp confrontation with Orthodox Moscow.

This confrontation between the two Orthodox capitals became especially noticeable during and after the celebration of the millennium of Christianity in Rus'. But it began much earlier and has a centuries-long history. In 1988, when a dramatic change in church-state relations was taking place in the USSR, Mikhail Gorbachev's government decided to make the celebration of the millennium of the baptism of Kyivan Rus' an official state commemoration. Moscow, the capital of the Russian Orthodox patriarchate, was made the centre of the celebrations, while Kyiv, the city from which Christianity spread throughout Rus', was assigned a secondary role by the organizers of the celebrations. Moscow openly enjoyed the glory of the "Third Rome"—the capital of Slavic, if not world, Orthodoxy. The concept of Moscow as the Third Rome was first formulated in the sixteenth century. It presented Moscow as the last bulwark of the true faith after the fall of the "Second Rome"—Constantinople. This concept was accepted and has existed for some time along with another introduced by Muscovite scribes—the theory that presented Moscow as the "Third Kyiv." This theory was based on the transfer of the centre of princely power from Kyiv, first to Vladimir on the Kliazma and then to Moscow.

* This article originally appeared in *The Harriman Review* 9, nos. 1–2 (Spring 1996): 32–7, and was translated from the Ukrainian by Mary Ann Szporluk. It has been revised.

Until the middle of the fifteenth century, Orthodox metropolitans who resided in Moscow continued to use the title "metropolitan of all Rus'," and they asserted—successfully for the most part—their right to exercise authority over all of Rus'. From the second half of the fifteenth to the first half of the seventeenth century, the Kyiv Metropolitanate existed completely independently of Moscow.

Only the annexation of Left-Bank Ukraine by Muscovy and the subordination of the Kyiv Metropolitanate to the Moscow Patriarchate in the second half of the seventeenth century again brought Moscow and Kyiv together within the framework of one church jurisdiction. Kyivan scribes of that period sought to raise the status of Kyiv in the common church organization, and for their own purposes they invoked the old Muscovite theory that proclaimed Moscow's state power had been transferred from Kyiv.

The reforms of Peter I—namely, the liquidation of the patriarchate, the transfer of the imperial capital from Moscow to St. Petersburg, and the concentration of all church authority in the hands of the Petersburg synod—weakened the confrontation between Kyiv and Moscow and made it less relevant. The appointment of Kyivan hierarchs to Russian sees by Peter and his successors promoted a considerable "Kyivization" of the Russian Orthodox Church (ROC) and a unification of church practices in the Russian Empire. From the time of Catherine II, this "Kyivization" was replaced by the obvious Russification of church life in the Kyiv Metropolitanate. This state of affairs lasted throughout the entire "synodal" period in the history of the ROC, i.e., until the revolution of 1917.

The Moscow Patriarchate was restored in 1917. But it was weakened by the non-Russian national movements and the actions of the atheistic Soviet government and was unable to maintain control over many lands of the former empire, including Ukraine. During the course of the revolution, the Kyiv Metropolitanate, which had been reduced to the status of an ordinary metropolitan see, extended its authority over the Orthodox Church throughout Ukraine. In 1921 the Ukrainian Autocephalous Orthodox Church (UAOC) declared its independence from Moscow and created its own metropolitan cathedral in Kyiv. Its example of independence (autocephaly) was then imitated by the Ukrainian "renovationists" (*obnovlentsy*). Both of these churches rejected the authority and jurisdiction of Moscow on the grounds of Kyiv's primacy as the capital of Rus' Christianity.[1]

---

1.   According to legend, Kyiv had been visited by the apostle Andrew and was the place where Prince Volodymyr the Great first baptized Rus'.

The government's liquidation of the autocephalous churches in Ukraine in the 1930s and the alliance formed between Stalin and the Moscow Patriarchate during the Second World War resulted in the consolidation of the Moscow Patriarchate's complete ecclesiastical control over Kyiv. That control was only reinforced when yet another branch of Kyivan Christianity—the Ukrainian Greek Catholic Church (UGCC) in Galicia and Transcarpathia—was forced to join with Moscow soon after the war ended.

Moscow's control was so complete that only in the mid-1960s was an ethnic Ukrainian, Metropolitan Filaret (Denysenko), appointed to the Kyivan see for the first time in more than 150 years. Later, in the 1980s, with the coming of glasnost and the liberalization of official Soviet religious policy, Moscow's authority was challenged, first by the surviving UGCC and then by a revived UAOC. The UAOC held its sobor in June 1990 in Kyiv, where it elected as its own first patriarch the metropolitan of the Ukrainian Orthodox Church (UOC) in the United States, Mstyslav (Skrypnyk). In this way, for the first time it unilaterally raised the status of the Kyivan see to that of a patriarchate, i.e., made it equal to the Moscow see.

With the breakup of the USSR, both the secular and Orthodox elites of Ukraine supported the movement for the independence of Ukrainian (Kyivan) Orthodoxy from Moscow. The age-old ecclesiastical rivalry between Kyiv and Moscow acquired new resonance in the context of official Kyiv's struggle with official Moscow for the affirmation of Ukraine's national independence.

Official Attempts at Autocephaly: The Ukrainian Orthodox Church-Moscow Patriarchate

By early 1990 there were three large church organizations in Ukraine in place of the former Ukrainian Exarchate of the ROC: the UOC under the jurisdiction of the Moscow Patriarchate (UOC-MP), the UGCC, and the UAOC. The leadership of the Communist Party of Ukraine and the local authorities in eastern and southern Ukraine were allied with the UOC-MP, headed by Metropolitan Filaret; the local authorities in Galicia actively supported the UGCC; and a group of deputies in Ukraine's Supreme Soviet (later Supreme Rada) and the pro-Ukrainian urban intelligentsia supported the UAOC. The latter church was persecuted by local authorities both in Galicia and in eastern Ukraine. This situation forced the leaders of the Supreme Soviet, headed by Leonid Kravchuk, to engage in a balancing act among different political factions and churches. The August 1991 putsch in Moscow, the banning of the Communist

Party, and the declaration of Ukrainian independence gave the Supreme Rada the political upper hand. From that time on the Rada leadership's manoeuvering among the different churches gave way to a specific religious policy. The main theme became the idea of autocephaly for the largest Orthodox Church in Ukraine—the UOC-MP, which the Moscow Patriarchate had granted "independence and self-government" in early 1990.

On the question of autocephaly, official circles placed their main hopes on Metropolitan Filaret. In November 1991, shortly before the December referendum on Ukraine's independence, Filaret called together a synod of bishops, who resolved to ask the patriarch of Moscow to grant autocephaly to the UOC. Although there was not full unanimity among the bishops, the synod's decision could rightly be considered a success for the government's policy on this issue.

Within a short time, however, the government's plans suffered a setback. It came from Moscow—which had been expected, though no one knew when—but also from the bishops under Filaret, which had not been expected at all. In April 1992 the synod of ROC bishops conducted what was, in fact, a trial of Filaret and forced him to promise that he would resign from the Kyivan see. When Filaret refused to do so after returning to Kyiv, the ROC synod forbade him to perform his clerical duties. In May 1992 a synod of UOC-MP bishops was held in Kharkiv. It removed Filaret and elected in his place a hierarch of the ROC, Metropolitan Volodymyr (Sabodan).

This interference by Moscow in the affairs of an "independent and self-governing" UOC became possible largely owing to the opposition to Filaret by bishops of his own church. Filaret was accused of having a family while holding the post of metropolitan. Because he also behaved autocratically and intimidated bishops under his authority, many bishops decided to take advantage of Filaret's tenuous situation to rid themselves of the detested metropolitan.

Ukraine's secular authorities reacted to the Kharkiv synod's decisions with open hostility, for the latter signalled that the government had suffered a serious defeat in its pursuit of autocephaly for the Ukrainian church. Not only had Moscow postponed dealing with the issue for several years and thereby manifested its opposition to autocephaly, but a majority of Ukraine's episcopate had also declared itself against government policy. Official Kyiv had acted on the issue according to the old, Soviet method of administering matters involving church-state relations. In keeping with principles hitherto developed, the bishops were supposed to support government policy, for which Filaret was the spokesman, unconditionally. This time, however, the old ideas and old policies did not work. Perestroika had loosened the state's control over the church, and the widespread fear created by Stalin's repressions had vanished. On the one hand, the bishops who were dissatisfied with Filaret and the prospects of his gaining more power were incited by Moscow and given full support by Patriarch Aleksii II. On the other hand, their policy was also fully supported by their old ally—the Communist elites of southern and eastern Ukraine, who not only remained in power despite Ukrainian independence, but had even strengthened their influence in local affairs.

Government Attempts at Autocephaly: The Ukrainian Orthodox Church-Kyiv Patriarchate

The government's "defeat" by the Kharkiv synod did not lead to a change in the goals or tactics of official religious policy. Metropolitan Filaret remained the symbol of this policy. The idea of creating a state church, however, was transferred from the UOC, whose episcopate Moscow had made into rebels, to the UAOC. The government had previously neglected this church, some of whose bishops had long been seeking government support and aspired to become leaders of a state church.

Inasmuch as the government trusted Filaret and did not have faith in Patriarch Mstyslav, the legal head of the UAOC, in June 1992 Filaret joined the UAOC—a church he had persecuted in the past—without the patriarch's knowledge. The synod of the UAOC, convened at short notice under pressure from government circles, created a new church, the Ukrainian Orthodox Church-Kyiv Patriarchate (UOC-KP). The synod also elected Filaret the patriarch's deputy. Because Mstyslav visited Ukraine only occasionally, it was thus Filaret who took over the leadership the UOC-KP, a de facto state church enjoying the central government's support.

In this connection, certain personnel changes occurred within the government. The experienced apparatchik Mykola Kolisnyk, who had long headed the Ukrainian Council for Religious Affairs (CRA), was replaced by a supporter of Ukrainian autocephaly, Arsen Zinchenko. Under Zinchenko the CRA's support for the UOC-KP was completely open, and Zinchenko himself lectured at the theological academy established by that church. A slogan that had been popularized by Oleksander Lotots'kyi when he was a minister in the Hetman government of 1918—"An independent state must have an independent church"—became current once again in government circles. But government policy was far from monolithic. Certain influential persons in the presidential administration spoke out against unconditionally supporting Filaret and in favour of normalizing relations with the UOC-MP.

As a result of the CRA's policy, the UOC-KP finally expanded its influence beyond Galicia and established itself in Kyiv and Volyn oblasts. But at the same time it lost support in Lviv oblast. The parishes that joined that church did so because of the active official interference in church affairs at the expense of the UOC-MP, while losses occurred because the new UAOC had been created by Filaret's opponents with Patriarch Mstyslav's support.

The small membership of the newly established UOC-KP, while not causing the government to end its support of this church, prevented it from considering the issue of autocephaly resolved. For this reason, in the summer of 1993, in connection with the death of Patriarch Mstyslav while he was abroad, the government conducted an intensive campaign for the unification of all three Ukrainian Orthodox Churches under the patriarch of Kyiv. This campaign did not have positive results: the UOC-KP and the UAOC elected their own patriarchs in place of Mstyslav, thus deepening already existing divisions, while the largest church, the UOC-MP headed by Metropolitan Volodymyr, remained under Moscow's jurisdiction. This signified a new defeat for the government on the issue of autocephaly. President Kravchuk made several appeals to the patriarchs of Moscow and Constantinople to grant autocephaly to the UOC-KP, but these also did not produce desired results.

In fact, on the eve of the 1994 presidential elections, the government admitted the failure of its policy of giving unconditional support to the UOC-KP and of its undeclared war with the UOC-MP when President Kravchuk met with Metropolitan Volodymyr to seek his support. Soon after, in one of his first decrees, the new president, Leonid Kuchma, abolished the CRA and transferred its functions to the newly created Ministry of Nationalities, Migration, and [Religious] Cults. As far as religious issues were concerned, the key posts in that ministry were given to opponents of the previous administration's pro-Filaret policy.

Holy Places and the Kyivan Heritage

Informal support for the UOC-MP and the refusal to support the UOC-KP became features of the Kuchma administration's church policy. This sharpened the existing competition between these two churches for possession of holy places in Kyiv. The fierce struggle has been carried out not so much for buildings as for sacred sites—the symbols of Kyivan Christianity—i.e., for the spiritual heritage of Kyiv and, accordingly, for the legitimacy of this or that jurisdiction. Among the holy places that are revered both in Ukraine and in Russia are, above all, the Kyivan Cave Monastery and the St. Sophia Cathedral, built during the reign of Grand Prince Iaroslav the Wise. The Kyivan Cave Monastery—to be more precise, that part of it that was handed over to Orthodox believers during the celebration of the millennium of the baptism of Rus'—ended up in the hands of the UOC-MP as early as 1992, and Filaret's attempts at getting it back for his own church with the help of paramilitary nationalist units ended in failure. Meanwhile, the St. Sophia Cathedral remains a museum fully at the disposal of the government; all ecclesiastical claims to the cathedral have been rejected, and the government may relinquish control of it only when and if unification of the three Ukrainian Orthodox Churches occurs.

Another, fourth, potential claimant to the St. Sophia Cathedral is the UGCC, whose late patriarch, Iosyf Cardinal Slipyi, had requested in his will to be buried there. In the fall of 1993 members of a new denomination, the White Brotherhood, headed by their "living god Maria Devi Khrystos" (Maryna Tsvyhun), tried to seize the cathedral. But the main battle for that sacred shrine has been between Ukrainian autocephaly and the Moscow Patriarchate. The first stage of the struggle occurred in the fall of 1990, when supporters of autocephaly tried to prevent Patriarch Aleksii II of Moscow from entering the cathedral. At that time bloodshed was avoided, and Aleksii managed to enter the cathedral through a side entrance. In the summer of 1995, however, it proved impossible to prevent bloodshed. On 18 July, a day that came to be known as Black Tuesday, government units dispersed the funeral procession of UOC-KP supporters while the latter tried to bury their newly deceased patriarch, Volodymyr (Romaniuk), on the grounds of the cathedral and thus gain control of it for their church.

Even though the Kyiv Patriarchate has encountered serious problems with securing its rights to the Kyivan heritage in Kyiv itself, its hierarchs have succeeded in presenting a serious challenge to Moscow beyond the borders of Ukraine. They reject as absurd the assertion that Kyiv, the mother church of the Eastern Slavs, should ask its "daughter," the Moscow Patriarchate, to grant it independence. On the contrary, they make claims to Kyiv's supremacy over certain Orthodox parishes in Russia and in certain countries where emigrants from the former Russian Empire have settled. In 1993 the title "patriarch of Kyiv" was changed to "patriarch of Kyiv and all Ukraine-Rus'," which reflects not only the Kyiv's claims to the heritage of Kyivan Rus' but also to the East Slavic lands beyond Ukraine.

In recent years the UOC-KP has created several of its own eparchies on the territory of the Russian Federation. In Moscow, Tula, Kursk, and Voronezh oblasts there are "patriarchal parishes" of the UOC-KP administered by the bishop of Sicheslav (Dnipropetrovsk), Adrian (Staryna), who resides in Noginsk near Moscow. The Kyiv Patriarchate has also put under its supreme authority several Orthodox Churches whose canonical status, like its own, is not recognized by world Orthodoxy. Among such acquisitions are a few parishes in Europe and North America headed by the metropolitan of Milan, Eulogius, as well as parishes of one of the Ukrainian Orthodox Churches in the United States. According to some reports, there have been negotiations about extending Kyiv's jurisdiction to Orthodox communities in Azerbaijan and Japan.

Although in a practical sense the achievements of the UOC-KP outside the borders of Ukraine are modest at best—the foreign parishes attached to it are neither large nor strong—one must not underestimate the ideological significance of the challenge that Orthodox Kyiv has presented to Orthodox Moscow. The UOC-KP leaders' claims to Kyiv's primacy in the East Slavic Orthodox world are being supported and developed in a purely political sense by that church's closest political partner—the ultra-nationalist Ukrainian National Assembly-Ukrainian National Self-Defence (UNA-UNSO), which advocates the creation of an East Slavic state in which Ukraine would play a dominant role and whose capital would be Kyiv. Recently these Ukrainian nationalist sentiments have been encouraged in Russia by Vladimir Zhirinovskii, who has declared that if Ukraine does not want to join Russia, Russia might join Ukraine.

Leaving aside these extravagant declarations and the daring challenge posed to Orthodox Moscow, Kyiv is now the loser in its confrontation with Moscow even on the territory of Ukraine. The government's support for autocephaly has not led to any significant changes in this regard. Ukrainian Orthodoxy remains divided among three mercilessly competing factions, the largest of which remains under Moscow's jurisdiction.

Church Policies in Post-Communist Society

The years of enforced atheism during the Soviet period turned the majority of the Ukrainian population into either passive atheists or independent believers not affiliated with the institutions of any organized religion. In many respects the significance that the government attributed to the cause of Orthodox autocephaly far exceeds the limits of the church's real influence on the society and political life of the country. For an explanation of this phenomenon one clearly needs to look at the role that religion has begun to play in public life in many post-Communist countries. While this role has increased little in the private sphere, in the public sphere religion and nationalism have fully replaced the bankrupt Communist ideology. The church has become one of the institutions affirming the legitimacy of newly created governments. For many national elites the struggle for an independent state church has fallen clearly into the sphere of political interests. Ukraine is no exception in this respect.

The policies of Ukraine's governing circles, whose leitmotif has been the attempt at establishing the UOC as a de facto state church, were in many respects influenced by the examples of Ukraine's neighbours. Post-Communist Poland's and post-Communist Russia's governments have co-operated with their respective traditional churches, the Roman Catholic and the Orthodox, and there these churches have acquired the de facto status of state churches. The ROC has also taken upon itself the role of preserving and restoring Russian influences beyond Russia's borders and thus become an instrument for advocates of the restoration of a Russian empire. The experience of Ukraine's neighbours and the pressure from Russia have unquestionably prompted the Ukrainian leadership to establish its own state church.

In Ukraine there is a conflict between two concepts of autocephaly. Although the CRA's policies (which supported the discredited Metropolitan Filaret and removed from the scene the unpredictable but nonetheless authoritative Patriarch Mstyslav) furthered the breakup of the movement for autocephaly, the intellectual grounds of the conflict must be sought in the confrontation between these two differing concepts.

The first of these concepts was originally enacted in a law declared by the government of the Directory of the Ukrainian People's Republic on 1 January 1919 with the aim of establishing a Ukrainian autocephalous church on the territorial principle. The UOC-KP was asked to implement this idea of territorial autocephaly, which would not have required the immediate Ukrainianization of church life and would have been open to all Orthodox believers in Ukraine irrespective of their ethnic or national identity.

The second concept of autocephaly, which viewed the Orthodox Church first of all as a Ukrainian national church and required Ukrainianization of all spheres church life, was fully formulated in the 1920s by the metropolitan of the original UAOC, Vasyl' Lypkivs'kyi. The policy pursued by the future Metropolitan Ilarion (Ivan Ohiienko) was, by and large, the same as the one he formulated when he was the minister for religious affairs in the government of the Directory that resided in Kamianets-Podilskyi. In 1919 and 1920 Ohiienko tried to restore the Ukrainian church's national character in the Podillia region, which had been virtually untouched by Russification. This concept of national-cultural autocephaly was supported by the Ukrainian Orthodox Churches in the West and by the UAOC in Ukraine before and after the synod that approved the union with Metropolitan Filaret.

In multiethnic and heavily Russified eastern and southern Ukraine, a church built on the principle of national-cultural, rather than territorial, autocephaly had no chance to succeed. This fact obviously became one of the reasons why the Ukrainian government has supported the territorial idea of autocephaly, i.e., the UOC-KP. The 1991 model of independent Ukraine was based precisely on the territorial and not the national-cultural principle. In the context sketched out above, one can clearly understand why the government of a country built on the principles of territoriality would support a church based on the same principles. However, this policy did not take into account other factors that have influenced organized church life, and because of this it ended in failure.

The common church tradition in Ukraine and Russia, which was not only reflected in the centuries-long domination of the metropolitan see of Kyiv by Moscow and St. Petersburg, but also in the significant contribution by Kyivan clergymen to the creation of Russian Orthodoxy, has in our time proved to be a serious rival to the national movements that destroyed the USSR. In comparison with secular institutions, the Orthodox Church has always shown a more conservative attitude toward changes in the world. At the same time, as the history of Orthodox countries has shown, sooner or later the church accepts the conditions of a new political division of the world. This is the normal way in which new autocephalies are formed, and it is primarily this path that Orthodox Kyiv is now following, slowly but ever more surely.

Serhii Plokhy

Between Moscow and Rome: The Struggle for a Ukrainian Catholic Patriarchate[*]

When Kiril Lakota, the main character of the award-winning film based on Morris West's bestseller, *The Shoes of the Fisherman*, was released from the Soviet Gulag and came to Rome, he was elected pope. When Iosyf Slipyi (1892–1984), the metropolitan archbishop of the Ukrainian Greek Catholic Church (UGCC) and the prototype of Lakota, was released from the Gulag by Nikita Khrushchev in 1963, he came to Rome to proclaim himself patriarch of Kyiv and Halych.[1]

The idea of a Kyiv Patriarchate under the jurisdiction of Rome first appeared in the 1580s, on the eve of the ecclesiastical union of the Orthodox Kyiv Metropolitanate with Rome.[2] The union was

---

[*]   This article originally appeared under the title "Between Moscow and Rome: The Struggle for a Greek Catholic Patriarchate in Ukraine" in the *Journal of Church and State* 37, no. 4 (Autumn 1995): 849–67. It has been revised.

1.   According to the publisher, William Morrow and Company, Morris L. West's *Shoes of the Fisherman* (New York, 1963) was written between March 1961 and August 1962, before Archbishop Slipyi's release from Soviet imprisonment in January 1963. The name of the central figure of West's book, Kiril Lakota, is derived from Hryhorii Lakota (1883–1950), the Greek Catholic auxiliary bishop of Przemyśl (Peremyshl), who was imprisoned in 1946 and died in the Gulag. See *Martyrolohiia ukraïns'kykh Tserkov u chotyr'okh tomakh*, vol. 2, *Ukraïns'ka Katolyts'ka Tserkva: Dokumenty, materiialy, khrystyians'kyi samvydav Ukraïny*, comp. and ed. Osyp Zinkevych and the Rev. Taras Lonchyna (Toronto and Baltimore, 1985), 105, 325–31. On Slipyi's arrival in the West in 1963 and the reaction of the world press to his release from the Gulag, see Milena Rudnyts'ka, *Nevydymi styhmaty* (Rome, Munich, and Philadelphia, 1971.) On his activities, see Jaroslav Pelikan, *Confessor Between East and West: A Portrait of Ukrainian Cardinal Josyf Slipyj* (Grand Rapids, Mich., 1990).

2.   On the history of the idea of the patriarchate in early modern Ukraine, see Oscar Halecki, *From Florence to Brest (1439–1596)*, 2d ed. (Hamden, Conn., 1968), 215–18; Jan Krajcar, "The Ruthenian Patriarchate: Some Remarks on the Project for Its Establishment in the 17th Century," *Orientalia*

concluded in Rome in 1595, and the resulting Uniate Church, founded at its Council in Brest in 1596, later became known as the Ukrainian Greek Catholic (UGCC) or Ukrainian Catholic Church. Although the idea of a Greek Catholic patriarchate has existed since the sixteenth century, it has never been realized. The forcible liquidation of the church by the Soviet authorities after the Second World War, which left approximately one million Ukrainian Catholics in the Western diaspora without their traditional religious centre and their hierarchs without their titular territory, was a major setback for this idea in the twentieth century.[3] Nevertheless, the 1960s and 1970s witnessed a growing movement in the Ukrainian diaspora for the creation of a Ukrainian Catholic patriarchate.

In 1963 Archbishop Slipyi raised the issue of the Ukrainian patriarchate in his speech at the Second Vatican Council. Subsequently he built a strong movement in support of patriarchal status for the church among his flock. A number of factors contributed to the success of Slipyi's propaganda. First, the nationalistically minded Ukrainian diaspora wanted its dispersed eparchies to be united into one national Catholic Church. Secondly, Vatican II recognized the right of the Eastern-rite Catholic Churches to preserve their distinct character, and the Ukrainian Catholic diaspora, with more than a million faithful, felt discriminated against without a patriarchate of its own, given that significantly smaller Eastern-rite Catholic Churches, such as the Coptic, the Syrian, and the Armenian, had their own patriarchates.[4]

Christiana Periodica 30 (1964): 65–84; D. Tanczuk, "Questio patriarchatus Kioviensis tempore conaminum Unionis Ruthenorum (1582-1632)," *Analecta Ordinis S. Basilii Magni*, 1949, no. 1 (7): 128–46; and Hryhor M. Luznycky, "The Quest for the Patriarchate in the Past of the Ukrainian Church," in *The Quest for an Ukrainian Catholic Patriarchate*, ed. Victor J. Pospishil and Hryhor M. Luznycky (Philadelphia, 1971), 32–43.

3.   On the liquidation of the UGCC, see Bohdan Rostyslav Bociurkiw, *The Ukrainian Greek Catholic Church and the Soviet State (1939–1950)* (Edmonton and Toronto, 1996); Denis Dirscherl, "The Soviet Destruction of the Greek Catholic Church," *Journal of Church and State* 12 (Autumn 1970): 421–39; and my article "In the Shadow of Yalta: International Politics and the Soviet Liquidation of the Greek Catholic Church" in this volume.

4.   On the issue of the patriarchate, see Victor J. Pospishil's articles "An Autonomous Ukrainian Catholic Church," "Towards a Ukrainian Catholic Patriarchate," "In the Wake of a Rejection," and "A Summary View of the Problem of the Ukrainian Catholic Church in the Light of the Principles of Canon Law," in *The Quest for an Ukrainian Catholic Patriarchate*, 7–31 and

Archbishop Slipyi proclaimed himself patriarch of Kyiv and Halych in 1974. Although he never achieved his ultimate goal—the recognition of his patriarchate by Rome—his devotion to the cause brought results.[5] In 1980 Pope John Paul II recognized the Synod of Ukrainian Bishops, created by Slipyi as part of the patriarchal structure, as a legitimate body. This move by the new pope provoked a strong negative reaction by the Moscow Patriarchate; it not only threatened the ecumenical dialogue that the Vatican was trying to establish with Moscow, but also made Vatican-Soviet relations even more difficult and unpredictable.[6]

The Challenge of the National Idea

The restoration of the independent Ukrainian state in 1991 gave impetus to both the Ukrainian Catholic patriarchal movement and the autocephalous movement in the Ukrainian Orthodox Church. Both movements had been inspired by the development of Ukrainian national ideology throughout the twentieth century. Thus the achievement of the main goal of the national movement—the creation of an independent state—inevitably brought to the church's agenda the task of achieving maximum independence in church affairs as well. In the case of the Orthodox Church, such independence could be accomplished by granting autocephaly to the church. In the case of the UGCC, so long as it was not beyond

43–74; Johannes Madey, *Das Zweite Vatikanische Konzil und die Revision des Rechtes der Ostkirchen* (Rome, 1978); J. Madey, *Le patriarchat ukrainien vers la perfection de l'état juridique actuel* (Rome, 1971); George A. Maloney, S.J., "The Present Canonical Status of the Ukrainian Catholic Church and Its Future," in *Archiepiscopal and Patriarchal Autonomy*, ed. Thomas E. Bird and Eva Piddubcheshen (New York, 1972), 44–56; and Meletius Michael Wojnar, OSBM, "Proiekt konstytutsiï Patriiarkhatu ukraïns'koi Tserkvy," *Bohosloviia* 34 (1970): 5–39.

5.   On Slipyi's struggle for recognition of his patriarchate, see Pelikan, *Confessor between East and West*, 190–215; and the Rev. Russel P. Moroziuk, *Politics of a Church Union* (Montreal, 1983).

6.   On the role of the "Uniate" factor in Vatican-Moscow relations, see Hansjakob Stehle, *Eastern Politics, of the Vatican, 1917–1979* (Athens, Ohio, 1981); the Rev. Russel P. Moroziuk, *Politicized Ecumenism: Rome, Moscow and the Ukrainian Church* (Montreal, 1984); Alexis U. Floridi, S.J., "The Role of Ukraine in Recent Soviet-Vatican Diplomacy," in *Archiepiscopal and Patriarchal Autonomy*, ed. Bird and Piddubcheshen, 61–70; Ivan Hvat, *The Catacomb Church and Pope John Paul II* (Cambridge, Mass., 1985); and Bohdan R. Bociurkiw, "The Ukrainian Catholic Church in the USSR under Gorbachev," *Problems of Communism*, November–December 1990, 1–19.

Rome's jurisdiction the creation of an Eastern-rite Catholic patriarchate in Ukraine has been viewed as a possible solution.

At the time of its liquidation by the Soviet authorities in 1945–46, the UGCC was closely linked to the Ukrainian national movement. The legal restoration of that church in 1989 was also closely connected to the acceleration of the Ukrainian national movement during the perestroika years. Nevertheless, very soon the UGCC's national character was severely challenged by its newly emerged rival—the Ukrainian Autocephalous Orthodox Church (UAOC). The latter's adherents emphasized the complete independence of their church at a time when, by contrast, Ukrainian Greek Catholics were subject to Rome's decisions. They also argued that the 1596 Union of Brest was introduced and imposed by force in Ukraine in the sixteenth and seventeenth centuries and that the highly praised Zaporozhian Cossacks defended Orthodoxy against the Uniate offensive. The proclamation of the UAOC's patriarchal status in June 1990 undermined the UGCC's claim to be the only truly national church. The UGCC has since found itself on the defensive, and it has been forced to accelerate its struggle for the recognition of its patriarchal status.

The struggle for a Ukrainian Greek Catholic patriarchate in Ukraine has been significantly influenced by three major factors: the development of a patriarchal movement within the church, the Vatican's attitude toward the idea of a Ukrainian patriarchate and, last but not least, the state's policy toward Ukrainian Greek Catholics in an independent Ukraine.

The Lviv Synod of 1992

The legalization of the UGCC that took place in Ukraine in late 1989 with significant support from the Vatican, especially John Paul II, strengthened the pro-patriarchal faction within that church. The main canonical obstacle on the road to the establishment of a Greek Catholic patriarchate—the absence of any titular territory under the jurisdiction of the patriarch—ceased to exist with the restoration of church structures in Ukraine.

The patriotic sentiments of the UGCC's adherents in Ukraine, who view the church as the vehicle of Ukrainian national ideology and who desire to strengthen the church's national image, found legitimacy in the patriarchal movement that was born and shaped in the Ukrainian diaspora. Two currents, one coming from Ukraine and the other from abroad, converged in the desire to create the patriarchal structures of the UGCC.

In May 1992 a unique opportunity to demonstrate the strength of the patriarchal movement came with the convening of the Synod of the UGCC for the first time in Ukraine. It took place in Lviv, the titular city of the metropolitan. The synod, which was attended by the Vatican's first nuncio in Ukraine, Archbishop Antonio Franco, created the main bodies of the patriarchate, including the patriarchal Curia and the Permanent Synod of Bishops, and requested that the Vatican not so much create the patriarchate as recognize the patriarchal structures that already existed.[7]

Besides the question of the patriarchate, the synod made other decisions that were of special importance for the church. The synod requested that the Greek Catholic eparchy of Przemyśl (Peremyshl) in Poland be put under the jurisdiction of the Ukrainian Greek Catholic patriarch and that the Greek Catholic eparchy in Transcarpathia be subordinated to the Lviv see. There were also proposals to create Greek Catholic eparchies in central and eastern Ukraine and in Russia. Not all of the synod's requests have been made public, but the program of the patriarchal faction of the church has been expressed by its members on a number of occasions. One of them, the Rev. Dr. Mykhailo Dymyd, believes that the Kyiv-Halych Patriarchate should be comprised of four metropolitanates (Kyiv, Lviv, Peremyshl, and Uzhhorod) and seven exarchates, three of them in Ukraine (Kharkiv, Odesa, Donetsk) and four elsewhere on the territory of the former USSR (Belarusian, Russian, Siberian, and Asian).[8] The synod also presented candidates for consecration as bishops and submitted all of its requests and proposals to Rome for approval.[9]

Rome's reluctance to provide answers to the requests of the synod provoked a negative reaction on the part of the UGCC and forced its head, Myroslav Ivan Cardinal Liubachivs'kyi, to issue a special statement on the matter. In the "Appeal to the Greek Catholics of Ukraine and the Settlements" of 15 February 1993, he called his flock to pray that the decisions of the Lviv Synod, especially the one concerning the Kyiv-Halych Patriarchate, be promulgated and confirmed by the Vatican authorities. He also criticized those who considered the very existence of the UGCC to be an obstacle to improving Orthodox-Catholic relations. He expressed his

---

7.   See the press releases of the St. Sophia Religious Association of Ukrainian Catholics in Canada, 27 May and 2 June 1992.

8.   Mykhailo Dymyd, "Hreko-katolyky: Stanovlennia pislia katakomb," *Holos Ukraïny*, 3 November 1992.

9.   Press release of the St. Sophia Religious Association, 27 May 1992.

deep concern about the latest developments in the Vatican's Eastern policy and rebuked those influential Vatican circles that supported the spread of Roman Catholicism in Ukraine and limited the UGCC's jurisdiction to Galicia. He complained that the UGCC had been put in an unfavourable position by having to prove its right to create eparchies in Ukraine, while Roman Catholics had no such problems. He stressed that his church's jurisdiction had to be expanded to encompass not only Transcarpathia and central and eastern Ukraine, but also reach far beyond Ukraine to all the territories of the former USSR where Ukrainian Greek Catholics had been resettled.[10]

There is little doubt that Cardinal Liubachivs'kyi, who has been generally known for his loyalty to the Vatican and personal allegiance to Pope John-Paul II, was forced by his flock's growing discontent to express his dissatisfaction with the Vatican's policy of delay. Two scandals that shocked the church in early 1993 have shown the degree to which tensions exist within it. One of these scandals took place in Ukraine and concerned the leader of Soviet-era clandestine UGCC, Archbishop Volodymyr Sterniuk; the other occurred in Canada and was caused by the Vatican's appointment of an apostolic administrator for the Toronto Eparchy.

Discontent in Ukraine

The scandal that involved Archbishop Sterniuk arose in January 1993 after the newspaper News from Ukraine published an article by Nestor Hodovany-Stone, a former Ukrainian Greek Catholic priest who had converted to Orthodoxy. In his article the Rev. Hodovany-Stone claimed that Archbishop Sterniuk, the former leader of the clandestine UGCC in Soviet Ukraine and a martyr for the faith, was under the surveillance of the people who had come from Rome together with Cardinal Liubachivs'kyi; and that Sterniuk was, in fact, a prisoner of the Vatican in the metropolitan's residence on St. George's Hill in Lviv. Sterniuk had reportedly dictated to Hodovany-Stone a statement to the Ukrainian people in which he expressed his desire for unity with the UAOC: "If my brother Orthodox Metropolitans in Kyiv unite, I would be willing to unite with them to form one Ukrainian Church of Christ under one pastor. By this I understand not a Uniate Church, but a Unity of churches in one general, Holy, Apostolic Orthodox Church."[11]

---

10. Cardinal Liubachivs'kyi's appeal was published in Svoboda, 2 April 1992.

11. The Rev. Nestor Hodovany-Stone, "A Prisoner of Mount St. George," News from Ukraine, January 1993.

Although the UGCC's leadership had long proclaimed unity with the Orthodox Church as the UGCC's ultimate goal, their reaction to this article was very sharp. The chancellor of the Lviv Archeparchy, the Rev. Ivan Dats'ko, met with journalists to publicize Metropolitan Sterniuk's denial that he had ever been "the prisoner of St. George's Hill" and confirmation of his loyalty to Cardinal Liubachivs'kyi and the pope.[12]

Metropolitan Sterniuk had likely been forced to make this new statement, for he did not take part in the press conference and never denied a single word of his original statement. Moreover, in a statement that was sent to the editor of *News from Ukraine*, Sterniuk quoted from a 1942 letter by Metropolitan Andrei Sheptyts'kyi, the unchallenged authority for all Ukrainian Catholics, where Sheptyts'kyi expressed the view that the metropolitan of Kyiv should be elected from among the Autocephalous Orthodox bishops or priests and that once there is unity between the metropolitan of Kyiv and the universal church, Greek Catholics should recognize that metropolitan's authority.[13]

Because the word "Orthodox" was used to define the Catholic Church in the first six centuries after Christ, and because both churches define themselves as catholic (universal) and orthodox (true), the use of the words "union," "unity," "universal," "Catholic," and "Orthodox" in different combinations gives the Greek Catholic clergy the opportunity to preserve their formal loyalty to the Vatican and at the same time to rebel against its authority.

The publication of Metropolitan Sterniuk's proclamation provoked a strong reaction on the part of the church authorities, owing chiefly to the growing tensions between the different factions within the UGCC. This was not the first time that the archbishop had created problems for the church authorities and the Vatican. The first instance occurred in 1990, during the proceedings of the quadri-partite commission of Vatican, Moscow, Ukrainian Orthodox, and UGCC representatives in Lviv. At that time Sterniuk left one of the proceedings in protest against Vatican representatives' attempts at concluding a deal with Moscow at the expense of the UGCC.

---

12. Iaroslav Mel'nychuk, "Ia vnov zaiavliaiu o svoei vernosti Ioannu Pavlu II, pape rimskomu," *Pravda Ukrainy*, 25 February 1993.

13. *Visti z Ukraïny*, 25 February–3 March 1993. On Metropolitan Sheptyts'kyi's life and activities, see Cyrille Korolevskij, *Métropolite André Szeptyckyj, 1865–1944* (Rome, 1964); and *Morality and Reality: The Life and Times of Andrei Sheptytsky*, ed. Paul R. Magocsi with the assistance of Andrii Krawchuk (Edmonton, 1989).

For many believers Archbishop Sterniuk serves as a symbol of the most radical UGCC members—the clandestine bishops, priests, and monks, whose struggle for the legalization of the church during Soviet rule was closely connected to the struggle for the liberation of Ukraine, and who see in the UGCC's patriarchal structure the fulfilment of not only their religious but also their national aspirations. Their position has the support of a substantial number of politically active lay persons. It was despite their protests that the Vatican forced Sterniuk to resign in 1991, and it was these activists who disseminated leaflets throughout Lviv stating "Our Patriarch is Volodymyr Sterniuk" during the May 1992 church synod.[14]

By the beginning of 1993 the UGCC in Ukraine had approximately five hundred priests who had operated in the underground before 1990; another four hundred who had converted from Orthodoxy after the legalization of the UGCC; and forty who had come to Ukraine from the West.[15] The latter have occupied leading positions in the church's administration; they have also dominated its scholarly structures and kept all links with the Vatican in their hands. Many formerly clandestine priests who had not received proper theological training and were extremely nationalistic have often come into conflict with both the clerics from abroad and the former Orthodox priests.

In Lviv in February 1994, during the second UGCC synod, tensions mounted between the attending diasporic clergy, who refused to accept Ukrainian citizenship, and the native priests. A group of Ukrainian Catholic faithful demonstrated near the walls of St. George's Cathedral, where the synod was taking place. Protesting against foreign control of church affairs, they shouted out: "Lviv is for Galicians, not for dealers from overseas."[16]

Rebellion in the Diaspora

The pressure on the UGCC's leadership regarding matters concerning their church's patriarchal status has increased as a result of events outside Ukraine—in Australia and in Canada, where

---

14.   Press release of the St. Sophia Religious Association, 27 May 1992. ·

15.   Rev. Ivan Dats'ko, "Suchasnyi stan Ukraïns'koï Hreko-Katolyts'koï Tserkvy," *Ukraïns'ka dumka*, 4 February 1993.

16.   See Kost' Chavaga, "Synod UHKTs," *Shliakh peremohy*, 6 March 1994; and Klymentyna Darmohrai, "Druhyi synod u L'vovi vidbuvsia u nezatyshnii obstanovtsi," *Ukraïna i svit*, 2–8 March 1994.

priests and lay persons in the Toronto Eparchy have sharply expressed their dissatisfaction with the Vatican's interference in the eparchy's affairs. The Vatican had introduced a law on the retirement of Catholic bishops upon reaching the age of seventy-five. As far as the Ukrainian Catholic Church was concerned, this law affected the Australian Exarchate, the Winnipeg Archeparchy, and the Toronto Eparchy. In Winnipeg and Melbourne the replacement of retirement-age bishops took place almost smoothly. But this was not the case in Toronto. There the eparchy's bishop, Isidore Borecky, refused to resign. His stand was supported by the majority of the eparchy's clergy and lay activists. For decades, under Borecky the Toronto Eparchy has been known as a stronghold of the Ukrainian Catholic patriarchal movement; the bishop also championed the preservation of Eastern traditions in his eparchy and continued ordaining married men as Ukrainian Catholic priests despite the Vatican's wishes to the contrary.[17]

The Lviv synod of 1992, taking into account the Vatican's law on retirement, requested that the Vatican appoint an auxiliary bishop to help Borecky in his eparchy. Instead, on 29 December 1992 the Vatican appointed an apostolic administrator. A wave of discontent arose partly because Rome's appointee, the Rev. Roman Danyliak, was known for his negative attitude toward the patriarchal movement. "The person who has been named to this appointment, moreover, is one who is widely regarded within the Ukrainian Catholic community as one who himself does not respect the integrity and particularity of the Ukrainian Greek Catholic Church", stressed a May 1992 statement by the Etobicoke Group Coalition of Concerned Canadian Catholics.[18] Tensions in the eparchy appeared to be so acute that Rome was forced to dispatch Bishop Michael Hrynchyshyn, the exarch of the Ukrainian Catholics in France, Belgium, and the Netherlands, to help implement the Vatican's will in the Toronto Eparchy.[19] Thus the Vatican's move against Bishop Borecky, a well-known advocate of patriarchal status for the Ukrainian Catholic Church, achieved the opposite result: the

---

17. Andrij Wynnyckyj, "Furor Erupts in Toronto Eparchy as Rome Makes Move against Bishop," *The Ukrainian Weekly*, 31 January 1993.

18. Press release of the St. Sophia Religious Association, 5 May 1993.

19. See Andrij Wynnyckyj's interviews "Bishop Hrynchyshyn Speaks on the Controversy in Toronto," *The Ukrainian Weekly*, 4 April 1993; and "Bishop Hrynchyshyn on Dangers Facing Ukrainian Catholic Church," *The Ukrainian Weekly*, 11 April 1993.

activities of the patriarchal movement intensified in both Canada and the United States, where the Ukrainian Patriarchal Society vocally protested against the Vatican's policy. Angry anti-Vatican articles and statements appeared in the North American Ukrainian-language press. "It's time to consider an independent Ukrainian Church," declared the author of a letter quoted in an editorial in the respected *Ukrainian Weekly*.[20]

The crisis in the Toronto Eparchy was exacerbated by a rumour Vatican authorities had made a decision to limit the UGCC's jurisdiction to the three Galician oblasts—Lviv, Ivano-Frankivsk, and Ternopil; to elevate the Mukachiv Eparchy to a metropolitanate and place it under the direct jurisdiction of Rome; to place the UGCC parishes outside Galicia under the jurisdiction of Roman Catholic bishops; and, finally, to prohibit the ordination of married men.[21]

In September 1993 the *New Catholic Times* informed its readers that Bishop Borecky had visited Bartholomew I, the ecumenical patriarch of Constantinople; it reported that the patriarch supported the creation of a Ukrainian Catholic patriarchate and that he promised to raise the issue of Borecky's removal as bishop of the Toronto Eparchy in his talks with the pope.[22] Bartholomew's desire "to be much closer to the Ukrainian Orthodox and the Greek Catholics in Ukraine," which he had allegedly expressed during his meeting with Borecky, contained a potential threat to both Moscow and Rome. Borecky had managed to introduce a new player onto the scene—the Constantinople Patriarchate, which has been involved in a centuries-long conflict with Moscow about who has jurisdiction over the Kyiv Metropolitanate and who should lead the entire Orthodox world.[23]

---

20. Editorial, "The Ukrainian Catholic Church Must Listen to Its Own Voice," *The Ukrainian Weekly*, 7 March 1993; see also an article by Myron Kuropas, a former aide to U.S. President Gerald Ford, "Rome Just Doesn't Get It," *The Ukrainian Weekly*, 14 March 1993.

21. On the character of the rumours, see Andrij Wynnyckyj's interviews with Bishop Hrynchyshyn in *The Ukrainian Weekly*, 4 and 11 April 1993; and the appeal of the Ukrainian Patriarchal Society in the United States in *The Ukrainian Weekly*, 21 March 1993.

22. See Louise Slobodian, "Ukrainian Catholic Bishop Brings Toronto Struggle to Istanbul," *Pravoslavnyi visnyk*, November 1993.

23. In his concluding remarks at the meeting, the patriarch reportedly said, "I wish you to always remember if you wish to return to the Church from whence you came, you will always be welcome and if you wish to

Vatican Politics

During his trip to the United States in May 1991, Archbishop
Sterniuk spoke about the need to consecrate Ukrainian Greek
Catholic bishops for Belarus and Russia.[24] Very soon, however, the
initial optimism of the leader of the clandestine UGCC gave way to
deep concern over the future of his church, especially after the pope
ordained not Greek Catholic but Roman Catholic bishops not only
for Russia and the other former Soviet republics, but also for central
and eastern Ukraine. Furthermore, the UGCC parishes in Poland
have continued to remain under the jurisdiction of the Polish Roman
Catholic primate, and the question of the subordination of the
Ukrainian Greek Catholic eparchy in Transcarpathia to the Lviv
metropolitan see has not been resolved.

Many of the current problems in relations between the Vatican
and the Ukrainian Catholics have their origins in conflicts and
misunderstandings dating back to the 1960s and 1970s. Today, as in
the past, the issues of the recognition of a Ukrainian Catholic
patriarchate and the preservation of the UGCC's Eastern-rite
traditions largely depend on the Vatican's policy toward Moscow.[25]

---

remain where you are, we wish to be your good friends, as we respect and
love you" (Slobodian, "Ukrainian Catholic Bishop").

On the rivalry between Constantinople and Moscow over the Kyiv
Metropolitanate, see Nicholas Chubaty, "Moscow and the Ukrainian Church
after 1654," *The Ukrainian Quarterly*, 1954, no. 10: 60–71; S. Ternovskii,
"Issledovanie o podchinenii Kievskoi mitropolii Moskovskomu
patriarkhatu," *Arkhiv Iugo-Zapadnoi Rossii* (Kyiv), part 1, vol. 5 (1872): 1–172;
H. Udod, *Pryiednannia Ukraïns'koï Tserkvy do Moskovs'koho patriiarkhatu 1686
roku* (Winnipeg, 1972); M. Zajikyn, *Autokefalia i zasady jej zastosowania*
(Warsaw, 1931); and Suzanne Gwen Hruby, Leslie Laszlo, and Stephan K.
Pawlowitch, "Minor Orthodox Churches of Eastern Europe," in *Eastern
Christianity and Politics in the Twentieth Century*, ed. Pedro Ramet (Durham,
N.C., 1988), 321–30.

The issue of the Toronto Eparchy was discussed at the UGCC synod
held in Lviv in February 1994. The synod reportedly recommended that
Bishop Borecky resign and Bishop Danyliak be moved to another eparchy.
It seems that both bishops ignored these recommendations. See Darmohrai,
"Druhyi synod u L'vovi."

24. Roma Hadzevych, "Archbishop Volodymyr Sterniuk Describes Legal
Status of Ukrainian Catholic Church," *The Ukrainian Weekly*, 9 May 1991.

25. See Bohdan R. Bociurkiw, "Politics and Religion in Ukraine: The
Orthodox and Greek Catholics," in *The Politics of Religion in Russia and the
New States of Eurasia*, ed. Michael Bourdeaux (Armonk, N.Y., 1995), 143–54.

While the restoration of Ukrainian independence in 1991 brought about many changes in world politics, it had little or no effect on the Vatican's approach to ecumenical dialogue. It has been understood in the Vatican that Ukraine is no longer a part of the USSR and that issues of vital importance for both the Roman Catholic Church in Ukraine and the UGCC must be decided not in Moscow but in Kyiv. At the same time, however, the Vatican has shown little understanding of the Moscow Patriarchate's loss of almost all of its parishes in western Ukraine. The Vatican should be concerned more with Ukrainian Orthodox autocephaly than with the Ukrainian Greek Catholic threat in Galicia.

Even before the formal legalization of the UGCC in Ukraine, in the course of negotiations between the Vatican and the Moscow Patriarchate in January 1989 both sides agreed that the church union could not be considered an appropriate form of Christian unity and that they should make way for ecumenical dialogue between the two churches.[26] This approach has long been promoted by the Pontifical Council for Christian Unity, and it was probably no accident that the Vatican's delegation at the negotiations in Moscow was comprised mostly of that council's representatives.[27]

The restoration of the UGCC in Ukraine has caused serious problems for the Vatican's relations with Moscow. There is little doubt that the latter agreed to the legalization of the UGCC and to deliberations with the Vatican only under pressure from the Gorbachev administration. The Moscow Patriarchate was forced to accept the main provisions of the Soviet government's policy toward the UGCC, but it struck back with the accusation that the Vatican was aggressively proselytizing in Ukraine. It viewed the "corporate [church] union," of which the UGCC had been the main product, as the major threat to Orthodoxy on the territory of the former USSR.

Faced with the deterioration of Orthodox-Catholic relations, some influential Roman Catholic politicians in the Council for the Promotion of Church Unity accused Ukrainian Greek Catholics of causing problems for the Catholic-Orthodox dialogue. Consequently the atmosphere in the Vatican changed to one that was very

---

26. *Pravoslavnyi visnyk*, 1990, no. 4: 13–16.

27. For the composition of the delegation to Moscow, see ibid., 13. On the Ukrainian Catholic reaction to the activity of the Joint International Commission for Theological Dialogue between the Roman Catholic and the Orthodox Church, see the Rev. Peter Galadza, "Good News from Balamand," *Logos: A Journal of Eastern Christian Studies* 34 (1993): 352–4.

unfavourable to Ukrainian Catholics. In September 1991, after the proclamation of Ukrainian independence, Edward Idris Cardinal Cassidy, the prefect of the pope's Council for Church Union, reportedly stated that the emergence of an independent Ukraine would threaten the ecumenical dialogue.[28]

The Moscow Patriarchate managed to mobilize the world Orthodox community, including the Eastern patriarchs, against the Vatican. The ordination of Roman Catholic bishops for Russia brought the ecumenical dialogue between Moscow and the Vatican to the brink of collapse. The Moscow Patriarchate claims almost the entire Russian population in the former Soviet Union as Orthodox believers and does not want any significant Catholic presence there.

Under these circumstances, the leaders of the UGCC have placed their hopes more and more on the personal support of Pope John-Paul II. In April 1993, in his statement on the intention to build a patriarchal cathedral in Kyiv, Cardinal Liubachivs'kyi, asserted: "I remind you all that the Holy Father, John Paul II Pope of Rome, himself stated, in the presence of the 28 bishops of our Ukrainian Greek Catholic Church, 'I no longer see any obstacle to the proclamation of a Patriarchate.'"[29] The same confidence in the pope's support was expressed by the Vatican's emissary to the Toronto Eparchy, Bishop Michael Hrynchyshyn, who stated in an interview that "The Pope has repeatedly come out in our defence—many times. I'm sure he hasn't changed his mind. There might have been some statements made, but that is certainly not what the Holy Father thinks." According to Hrynchyshyn, the pope has been inclined to extend the powers of the Lviv metropolitan outside Ukraine so that he could also exercise them over the UGCC eparchies elsewhere in Europe and in the Americas and Australia.[30]

The interdicasterial Commission for the Church in Eastern Europe, created by the pope on 15 January 1993 to co-ordinate Catholic activities in that part of the world, was also charged with co-ordinating the activities of the UGCC and the Roman Catholic Church in Ukraine. According to the Rev. Dr. Andriy Chirovsky,

28. For the Ukrainian reaction to the cardinal's statement, see *Svoboda*, 5 November 1991. It should be noted here that the Vatican was the 103d state to recognize independent Ukraine.
29. For the Ukrainian text of the statement, see *Novyi shliakh* (Toronto), 15 May 1993; for the English translation, see the press release of the St. Sophia Religious Association, 6 May 1993.
30. *The Ukrainian Weekly*, 11 April 1993.

there have been three main tendencies in the Vatican's policy toward the UGCC. The first is connected with the desire of certain circles in Rome to support the UGCC, which is highly respected for its struggle for survival under the Communist regime. The two other tendencies are linked to the activity of two groups within the Vatican leadership, the "ecumenists" and the "centralists." Both groups are hostile to the idea of a Ukrainian patriarchate. The "ecumenists" are mainly preoccupied with a dialogue with Moscow, and the "centralists" oppose any move toward the decentralization of world Catholicism. These forces refuse to consider the theological and historical arguments of the proponents of a Ukrainian patriarchate, which are based on the widespread idea of the ancient tradition of the Kyivan church as an intermediary between East and West.[31]

There can be little doubt that the Vatican and the proponents of a Ukrainian patriarchate, though building their respective arguments on the decisions of the Second Vatican Ecumenical Council, see the legacy of the council from a different perspective.

Church-State Relations

The re-emergence of the Ukrainian state has created a new environment for the activity of the UGCC. The main goals of Ukrainian government policy toward the Ukrainian Catholics have been made public on a number of occasions by officials in Lviv and Kyiv. In May 1992, in his statement to the synod of the UGCC, Mykola Horyn, then the head of the Lviv Oblast Council, strongly supported the idea of a Ukrainian Catholic patriarchate: "Today's synod is being held in circumstances that greatly differ from all the situations in the long history of the Ukrainian Greek Catholic Church. For the first time it is being held in an independent state. And therefore the question of a Patriarchate and Patriarch is immensely important as a certain symbol of an independent country, and as the way to ecumenism among all Ukrainian Christians."[32]

Horyn's statement reflects the position of the Galician authorities and of the Greek Catholic lay intelligentsia, who were extremely active in the fight for Ukrainian independence.[33] Kyiv's official

---

31. The Rev. Chirovsky, director of the Metropolitan Andrei Sheptytsky Institute of Eastern Christian Studies, St. Paul University, Ottawa, expressed these opinions during my interview with him on 4 June 1993.

32. Press release of the St. Sophia Religious Association, 27 May 1992.

33. Mykola Horyn comes from a Galician family whose members were active in the Soviet Ukrainian dissident movement of the 1960s, 1970s, and

position was expressed for the first time in August 1992 by none
other than President Leonid Kravchuk. In his speech on the occasion
of the transfer of the remains of Cardinal Iosyf Slipyi from Rome to
Lviv, Kravchuk called for the unity of all Christian Ukrainians. He
did not address the issue of the patriarchate, but he did stress that
the church in independent Ukraine should be free from foreign
intervention and severely criticized foreign religious centres'
attempts at interfering in Ukraine's religious affairs.[34]

Although President Kravchuk's statement came at a time of
severe crisis in relations between Kyiv and Moscow over the issue
of Ukrainian Orthodox autocephaly, no signals that the general
approach to the problem of church-state relations did not relate to
the UGCC were sent out. Later a UGCC official even complained
that such an approach could create certain problems.[35] Partly
responding to such concerns, President Kravchuk mentioned in his
1993 Easter greetings to Ukraine's Christians that there was no such
thing as "our" (i.e., a national) or "not our" (a foreign) church and
that the government treats all confessions equally.[36]

In fact, however, there are two levels of decision-making
regarding church-state relations in Ukraine. While the central
authorities, who are generally supportive of the national movements
within all of the nation's churches, declare their support for the
UGCC, on the local level there is no unity on official policy toward
that church. While the authorities in Galicia are definitely
pro-UGCC, the local administrations in central and eastern Ukraine
support either the Ukrainian Orthodox Church-Kyiv Patriarchate or
the Ukrainian Orthodox Church-Moscow Patriarchate.

Thus, the local authorities in Kyiv have demonstrated negative
attitudes toward the UGCC. In Ukraine's capital that church had to
abandon its hopes of obtaining a church building in the central part
of the city from the state, and subsequently it announced plans to

---

1980s. His brothers Bohdan, a scholar of art and literature, and Mykhailo,
a psychologist and a former leader of the Ukrainian Republican Party, were
imprisoned for "anti-Soviet agitation and propaganda." See their short
biographies in the *Encyclopedia of Ukraine*, vol. 2, ed. Volodymyr Kubijovyč
(Toronto, 1988), 229.

34. "Vystup Prezydenta Ukraïny Leonida Kravchuka na sviatochnii
akademiï u pam'iat' Patriarkha Iosypa kardynala Slipoho," *Holos Ukraïny*, 24
September 1992.

35. Dats'ko, "Suchasnyi stan Ukraïns'koï Hreko-Katolyts'koï Tserkvy."

36. *Ukraïns'ke slovo*, 16 April 1993.

build a cathedral on its own. The lack of understanding between the municipal authorities and the church led two Western diplomats in Ukraine in 1992—the American ambassador Roman Popadiuk and the Canadian chargé d'affaires Nestor Gayowsky, both of whom are Ukrainian Catholics—to participate in Sunday services of the local UGCC community in front of the locked church.[37]

Despite all of the UGCC leaders' and activists' efforts at influencing the central authorities in Kyiv to rise to the defence of that church in its conflict with the Vatican and to support the idea of a Ukrainian Catholic patriarchate, President Kravchuk never intervened in this matter. In fact, the UGCC was left to its own devices in its struggle with the Vatican. The state has never exhibited the same degree of support for the creation of a Ukrainian Catholic patriarchate that it gave to the cause of Ukrainian Orthodox autocephaly, on whose behalf President Kravchuk wrote a letter of support to the patriarchs of Moscow and Constantinople.[38]

The main goals of Ukrainian government policy toward the UGCC and Ukrainian-Vatican relations were formulated by Kravchuk's successor, President Leonid Kuchma, during his meeting with the papal nuncio, Archbishop Antonio Franco, in early January 1995. Kuchma reportedly told the nuncio: "We would like help from the Vatican in integrating into Europe ... [and] we're interested in help from the Vatican to integrate the churches in Ukraine."[39] On 2 May 1995 Kuchma visited the pope in Rome and discussed with him the prospects for opening a Ukrainian embassy at the Vatican, the return of former UGCC property confiscated by the Soviet state in the years 1939–46, and the Vatican's support for Ukraine's efforts at joining the Council of Europe. Both sides agreed that if the pope visited Ukraine in the near future, Orthodox-Catholic relations in the country would be harmed.[40]

Because the Ukrainian authorities have been more preoccupied with securing the pope's support in the international arena than

---

37. Myroslav Ivan Cardinal Liubachivs'kyi, "Za suttiu — vselenska, za formoiu — natsional'na," *Kul'tura i zhyttia,* 15 August 1992; and Myroslav Levyts'kyi, "Svitlo i tini mizhkonfesiinoho spivisnuvannia," *Nashe slovo,* 18 April 1993.

38. On the Ukrainian government's policy toward the Orthodox Church, see Bociurkiw, "Politics and Religion in Ukraine."

39. See the Reuters report from Kyiv, 3 January 1995.

40. See "Ukrainian President Received by Pope," *OMRI Daily Reports,* 3 May 1995; and the Reuters report on that issue from Vatican City, 2 May 1995.

with the fate of the UGCC in central and eastern Ukraine, it appears that once again they have left the UGCC to sort out its relations with the Vatican on its own. Meanwhile the Vatican seems interested only in the return of former UGCC property in Galicia to that church.

Both Rome and Kyiv have demonstrated little, if any, support for Lviv's attempts at establishing a Ukrainian Catholic patriarchate. Nevertheless, in view of the main provisions of Ukraine's religious policy, the Vatican's efforts at limiting the territory under the jurisdiction of the Lviv see may come into conflict with the interests of the state. Certainly there are some aspects of current Vatican-Lviv relations that are of special concern to independent Ukraine. The first of them pertains to the jurisdiction of the Mukachiv Eparchy in Transcarpathia and touches on the issue of the territorial integrity of the Ukrainian state; the second, to the jurisdiction of the UGCC's Przemyśl (Peremyshl) Eparchy in Poland, which affects the development of Ukrainian-Polish relations.

"Our Capital City of Kyiv"

In 15 February 1993, shortly after the creation, in January 1993, of the interdicasterial Commission for the Church in Eastern Europe by the pope, Cardinal Liubachivs'kyi issued a statement in which he recognized the problems that exist in Vatican-Ukrainian relations over the issues of territorial jurisdiction and the UGCC's role in the ecumenical process. On the one hand the statement showed to the cardinal's flock that he shared their concern over the Vatican's Eastern policy, and on the other it sent a signal to the Vatican that the tensions within the UGCC were so high that he could not keep the situation under control. On 27 April 1993 Liubachivs'kyi came forward with another statement in which he announced his plan to build a Ukrainian Greek Catholic cathedral in Kyiv. The move was calculated to accelerate the confirmation of the UGCC's patriarchal structure by the Vatican. The erection of a cathedral in Kyiv would also justify the UGCC's desire to name its patriarchate that of Kyiv and Halych and to support its claims to jurisdiction over the territories of eastern Ukraine. In unveiling the plan to build a cathedral in Kyiv, Cardinal Liubachivs'kyi stated:

> Bearing in mind the Patriarchal structure of the Kiev-Halych Patriarchate of our Church and the decision of the Lviv synod to revive the Eparchy of Chernihiv-Vyshhorod with its seat in Kiev (the see responsible for all our parishes in Eastern, Central and Southern Ukraine), we intend to build a Patriarchal Sobor [cathedral] for the Ukrainian Greek Catholic Church in our capital city of Kiev.

As the head of the Ukrainian Greek Catholic Church, with the help of God, I dare to head this holy and essential Action of our people of God in the name of the existence and development of our Church throughout the sovereign territory of the independent Ukrainian State and the territories of settlement.[41]

Because the UGCC did not manage to obtain an existing church building in central Kyiv to serve as their cathedral, the decision to build a cathedral provided a solution to the problem. In the broader context, the issue of that cathedral helps us understand the way in which the UGCC has been trying to respond to its major challenge in the twentieth century—that of the national idea.

The Ukrainian national idea that occupied the minds of the Galician intelligentsia at the turn of the twentieth century eventually resulted in the UGCC serving as one of the major vehicles of Ukrainian nation building. The nationalists in Galicia, who accepted the notion of an independent Ukraine from the Carpathian Mountains in the west to the Don River in the east, wanted their church to respond to the nation-building agenda and to overcome that church's regional, strictly Galician character. An ongoing dialogue with an autocephalous Orthodox Church in central and eastern Ukraine was one of the goals of Metropolitan Andrei Sheptyts'kyi's activity. It was developed further by his successor, Cardinal Iosyf Slipyi.

The conflict between the local (regional) character of the UGCC and the all-Ukrainian aspirations of its adherents has also been reflected in the UGCC's official approach to ecumenical problems. In this area the church's goal has been viewed as a return to the times of St. Volodymyr, the prince who Christianized Kyivan Rus' in 988. At that time, it is claimed, the Kyivan (Ukrainian) church comprised part of the universal church that was not yet divided between East and West. Thus, a unified Ukrainian church, which should be comprised of both Ukrainian Greek Catholics and Ukrainian Orthodox and should be in communion with both East and West, has been presented as the UGCC's main aspiration. As was stated by the chancellor of the Lviv Metropolitanate, the Rev. Ivan Dats'ko, the process of the unification of Ukraine's three Orthodox Churches and the UGCC depends on the position of the "Three Romes"—the Vatican, Constantinople, and Moscow. According to Dats'ko, if those religious centres pursued the goal of

---

41. Press release of the St. Sophia Religious Association, 6 May 1993.

Christian unity, the prospects for church unity in Ukraine would improve considerably.[42]

Though the idea of a unified Ukrainian church does not contradict the Vatican's views on the provisions of church unity in the future, a strong Ukrainian church uniting the Orthodox and the Greek Catholics would be inconvenient for those Vatican ecumenists who have placed all of their hopes on Moscow, as well as for those Vatican centralists who do not want to see strong autonomous local churches.

Conclusion

The restoration of Ukrainian independence after the December 1991 referendum created a new environment for religious activity in the country. The most dramatic changes took place within the Orthodox Church in Ukraine, which eventually split into three competing churches, two of them with autocephalous status and one remaining under the jurisdiction of the Moscow Patriarchate. In the UGCC, the movement for patriarchal status has intensified under the influence of the victorious national ideology.

In the twentieth century the UGCC has sustained two major losses caused as a result of the advance of Ukrainian national ideology. The first was the mass conversion of Greek Catholics to Orthodoxy in the 1920s in the United States and Canada; the second was the refusal of a significant part of formerly Greek Catholic parishes to reconvert to Ukrainian Catholicism after the legalization of the UGCC in Ukraine in 1989. In both cases, former Ukrainian Catholics preferred the more nationalistic autocephalous churches. After the proclamation of an Orthodox patriarchate in Ukraine, the UGCC authorities faced new challenges from the Ukrainian national ideology and were strongly encouraged to go forward with the idea of a Ukrainian Catholic patriarchate.

The UGCC's legalization during perestroika and glasnost under Gorbachev provoked a sharp anti-Catholic reaction from the Moscow

---

42. Rev. Ivan Dats'ko, "Spivvidnoshennia UHKTserkvy z inshymy konfesiiamy Ukraïny," *Ukraïns'ke slovo*, 28 February 1993. The dissatisfaction of Greek Catholics in Ukraine with the Vatican's actions is reflected in the results of a poll conducted in Ukraine in 1994. Of the respondents, 72.7 percent claimed to be Orthodox, 16.7 percent recognized Cardinal Liubachivs'kyi as their spiritual leader, and only 14.6 percent recognized the pope. Among Greek Catholics, 56.3 percent favoured the creation of one national Church in Ukraine. See Oleksii Shuba, "Iedyna natsional'na tserkva: Mit chy diisnist'?" *Ukraïns'ka dumka*, 12 May 1994.

Patriarchate. The conflict in Vatican-Moscow relations that emerged after the collapse of the USSR has been extremely deep and difficult to overcome. The Joint International Commission for Theological Dialogue between the Roman Catholic Church and the Orthodox Church, which allowed Eastern Catholics to participate in the Orthodox-Catholic dialogue, nevertheless condemned "uniatism" as an inappropriate form of Christian unity.

After its legalization the UGCC found itself under constant attack from the Christian East and with little support from the Christian West. The Ukrainian government has shown little understanding of church problems, even though the UGCC proved itself an ardent supporter and promoter of Ukrainian independence. During President Kuchma's visit to the Vatican in May 1995, the pope agreed to turn down the UGCC's invitation to visit Ukraine in 1996 to mark that church's four hundredth anniversary. He also assured the president that the celebrations in Ukraine would be held "in the spirit of church unity."

Under these circumstances, Rome refused to make use of the anniversary to recognize the Kyiv-Halych Patriarchate proclaimed by Cardinal Slipyi. It is much more likely that if a Ukrainian Greek Catholic patriarchate is to be recognized by Rome in the near future, its territory will be limited mainly to Galicia. On the eve of its four hundredth anniversary, after its triumphant restoration in the late 1980s following decades of suffering under the atheistic Soviet regime, the UGCC is struggling again, this time to prove that its existence is not the consequence of a mistake that Rome committed in the late sixteenth century.

Serhii Plokhy

Church, State, and Nation in Ukraine*

Much of the current discussion concerning the future of independent
Ukraine has centred on the issue of nation building. Two models of
the Ukrainian state—the national (the state of the "Ukrainian
people") and the multiethnic (the state of "the people of
Ukraine")—usually serve as starting points for scholarly discussion.[1]
    It is quite obvious that the future of church-state relations in
Ukraine will depend heavily on the choice made by the newly
independent state in its nation-building strategy. It is equally true that
the religious policy of the government and the response to it on the
part of organized religion will influence the process of nation building.
In the area of church-state relations, current Ukrainian governments
face the dilemma of either forging an alliance with the traditional
(national) churches or allowing "all flowers to bloom," with consequent
equal treatment of all denominations, including those closely linked to
neighbouring states (especially Russia and Poland).
    For contemporary analysts of church-state relations, the concepts of
freedom of conscience (religious belief) and the separation of church
and state are closely associated with each other. Historically, both
concepts are identified primarily with the United States, where the
first—freedom of belief—is firmly based on the second—separation of
church and state. But the so-called liberal model, which provides for

---

*   Translated, except for the concluding section, from the Ukrainian by
Myroslav Yurkevich. This article originally appeared in Religion in Eastern
Europe 19, no. 5 (October 1999): 1–28. It has been revised.
1.   For a discussion of nation building in post-1991 Ukraine, see
Alexander J. Motyl, Dilemmas of Independence: Ukraine after Totalitarianism
(New York, 1993); Dominique Arel, "Ukraine: The Temptation of the
Nationalizing State," in Politics, Culture and Civil Society in Russia and the New
States of Eurasia, ed. Vladimir Tismaneanu (Armonk, N.Y., 1995), 157–88;
Andrew Wilson, Ukrainian Nationalism in the 1990s: A Minority Faith
(Cambridge, 1997); and Frank E. Sysyn, "Ukrainian 'Nationalism': A
Minority Faith?" Harriman Review 10, no. 2 (Summer 1997): 12–20. On
church-state relations in post-Soviet Ukraine, see my article "Nezalezhna
Ukraïna: Derzhavna tserkva chy hromadians'ka relihiia?" Pam'iatky Ukraïny,
1992, nos. 2–3: 3–6.

the maximum feasible separation of church and state, has been fully implemented only in the land of its origin, the United States. In Western Europe, on the other hand, models often far removed from the American one have proved successful; i.e., the principle of freedom of conscience is protected concurrently with the functioning of state churches or various degrees of state "interference" in church affairs.

Contemporary Ukraine has yet to make a clear choice between the American and the European models of guaranteeing freedom of conscience. Purely geographic considerations would suggest that Ukraine follow the examples of its European neighbours, but from the historical viewpoint, Ukrainian society, like that of North America, is a product of colonization and an "advancing frontier" more closely resembling the American model than the European.

In Ukraine, the discussion of which road to take—whether to Ukrainianize the traditional churches (the Orthodox and the UGCC) and make them into state bodies or to abandon all hope in their nation-building potential and throw open the doors to Protestantism and its attendant spirit of capitalism—was begun more than a century ago by Mykhailo Drahomanov.[2] That discussion is by no means over, but its subject has already entered current political debate.

The present article concerns the formation of religious policy in Ukraine between 1991 and 1999 and examines the ways in which it was influenced by the nation-building agenda of the newly independent state. The traditions that independent Ukraine inherited in the area of church-state relations will also be considered. The following discussion will be restricted to twentieth-century traditions, which comprise two dominant influences—that of the brief period of Ukrainian statehood in the years 1917–20 and that of the Soviet period.

The Religious Policies of the Ukrainian Governments of 1917–20

The period of Ukrainian sovereignty and independence after the Revolution of 1917 and during the Ukrainian-Soviet (1918–21) and Ukrainian-Polish (1918–19) wars created a legacy of four religious policies—those of the Central Rada of the Ukrainian People's

---

2.   On the place of Protestantism in Mykhailo Drahomanov's political plans, see Ivan L. Rudnytsky, "Drahomanov as a Political Theorist," in his *Essays in Modern Ukrainian History* (Edmonton, 1987), 212–14; Ukrainian translation: Ivan Lysiak-Rudnyts'kyi, "Drahomanov iak politychnyi teoretyk," in his *Istorychni ese*, vol. 1 (Kyiv, 1994), 308–9.

Republic (UNR), the Ukrainian State of Hetman Pavlo Skoropads'kyi, the Directory of the UNR, and the Western Ukrainian People's Republic (ZUNR). The leading figures of the Central Rada, most of whom were socialists, proceeded from the principle of the separation of church and state, but left very little by way of a legacy in that sphere.[3] As for the ZUNR's religious policy, it was not declared in practice, although the Ukrainian Greek Catholic Church (UGCC) actually functioned as a state church, and the Ukrainian-Polish War was marked by distinct confessional features. The ZUNR government guaranteed all its citizens equal rights regardless of their religion or nationality, but such guarantees were standard fare in all the new states of Eastern Europe.[4]

An analysis of the religious policies of the Ukrainian State of 1918 and of the Directory of the UNR in 1918 and 1919 holds considerably more interest for a student of church-state relations. Beginning virtually from the first weeks of its existence, Hetman Skoropads'kyi's administration conducted an active religious policy. The "Laws on the Provisional State Order of Ukraine" (29 April 1918) proclaimed freedom of religious belief, but also asserted that "the Orthodox Christian faith is the leading faith in the Ukrainian State." The basic legislative provisions of the Hetman government's religious policy clearly replicated the fundamental principles of the Russian Provisional Government's religious policy in 1917, which proclaimed the Orthodox Church to be de facto a state church.[5]

With regard to the Orthodox Church, the two Hetman governments followed a rather consistent policy based on the principle that a

---

3.   On the Central Rada's policy regarding church-state relations, see Ivan Vlasovs'kyi, *Narys istoriï Ukraïns'koï Pravoslavnoï Tserkvy*, vol. 4, pt. 1 (New York and Bound Brook, N. J., 1961), 20–4; and Bohdan R. Bociurkiw, *The Politics of Religion in the Ukraine: The Orthodox Church and the Ukrainian Revolution, 1917–1919*, Kennan Institute for Advanced Russian Studies Occasional Paper, no. 202: 10–13. The latest study of the topic, based on extensive archival research, is Vasyl' Ul'ianovs'kyi, *Tserkva v Ukraïns'kii derzhavi, 1917–1920 (Doba Tsentral'noï Rady)* (Kyiv, 1997).

4.   See the text of the declaration of the Ukrainian People's Council of 1 November 1918 in *Politolohiia: Kinets' XIX-persha polovyna XX st. Khrestomatiia*, ed. Ostap Semkiv (Lviv, 1996), 768.

5.   See the somewhat different versions of the Hetman government's law "On [Religious] Faith" in *Politolohiia*, ed. Semkiv, 766; and in *Martyrolohiia ukraïns'kykh Tserkov u chotyr'okh tomakh*, vol. 1, *Ukraïns'ka Pravoslavna Tserkva: Dokumenty, materiialy, khrystyians'kyi samvydav Ukraïny*, comp. and ed. Osyp Zinkevych and Oleksander Voronyn (Toronto and Baltimore, 1987), 40.

sovereign state required an independent church. This idea was first expressed at the All-Ukrainian Orthodox Sobor in January 1918 after the proclamation of the Fourth Universal of the Central Rada. The minister for religious affairs in the first Hetman government, Vasyl' Zinkivs'kyi, worked resolutely with the sobor's leadership and delegates to proclaim the autocephaly of the Ukrainian Orthodox Church (UOC). It was expected that the first step toward the achievement of that goal would be the establishment of a UOC made up of the Ukrainian eparchies of the Russian Orthodox Church (ROC) and headed by the metropolitan of Kyiv, and the winning of autonomous status for that church within the framework of the Moscow Patriarchate. Zinkivs'kyi managed to attain that intermediate goal. Under government pressure, the sobor's members appealed to the patriarch of Moscow to grant autonomy. This Moscow did, amending the conditions of the grant to its own advantage.[6]

The minister for religious affairs in the second Hetman government, Oleksander Lotots'kyi, was now in a position to pose the question of the UOC's autocephaly in absolutely unequivocal terms for the UOC to those attending the sobor. His argument was based precisely on the idea that a sovereign state required an independent church. Most participants in the sobor were nevertheless hostile to Lotots'kyi's attitude. The hetman's agreement to Ukraine's federal union with Russia, the withdrawal of the Germans, the anti-hetman coup, and the termination of the sobor's activity ended the efforts of the Ukrainian government to reach an understanding with the church leadership on the question of autocephaly.[7]

The autocephaly of Ukrainian Orthodoxy was enacted on 1 January 1919 by the Directory of the UNR, the government that replaced Hetman Skoropads'kyi's rule. The possibility of a government proclamation of autocephaly was first discussed during the Hetman's regime and was to have been implemented in the

---

6. On the Hetman government's religious policy, see Vlasovs'kyi, *Narys*, 4, pt. 1: 43–59. For a new interpretation, based on previously unpublished documents, of Zinkivs'kyi's activities, see Vasyl' Ul'ianovs'kyi, *Tserkva v ukraïns'kii derzhavi 1917–1920 rr. (Doba het'manatu Pavla Skoropads'koho* (Kyiv, 1997).

7. Oleksander Lotots'kyi's activity as minister of religious affairs in the Hetman government is described in his memoirs, *Storinky mynuloho*, 4 vols. (Warsaw, 1932–9; repr. 1966). Bohdan R. Bociurkiw provides a survey of the Hetman government's religious policy in "The Politics of Religion in the Ukraine," 20–32. The most recent work on Lotots'kyi's life and work is André Partykevich's *Between Kyiv and Constantinople: Oleksander Lototsky and the Quest for Ukrainian Autocephaly* (Edmonton, 1998).

event that the pro-Russian episcopate of the church refused to co-operate with the government on the matter. The impossibility of a compromise with Metropolitan Antonii (Khrapovitskii) of Kyiv and his followers became obvious with the Directory's takeover of power. This impasse was also apparently responsible for the government's choice of a synodal form of administration for the new church. It was based on the Erastian model of church-state relations, introduced into the Russian Empire by Peter I, in which the church played the role of a virtual department of state. Under the new law, a Ukrainian synod financed by the state and meeting in the presence of a government representative was to become the governing body of the UOC.[8]

The proclamation of the Act of Union of the UNR and the ZUNR confronted Ukrainian leaders with the fact of the co-existence of the two traditional Ukrainian churches, the Orthodox and the Greek Catholic, within one state. As a practical measure, the Directory reacted by establishing a Ukrainian diplomatic mission at the Vatican.[9] On the theoretical plane, the possibility was considered of electing the Greek Catholic metropolitan of Lviv, Andrei Sheptyts'kyi, to the Kyiv Metropolitanate, followed by acceptance of the church union by the Orthodox and the pope's subsequent proclamation of a Ukrainian patriarchate. One of the reputed authors of that idea, the prominent writer and statesman Volodymyr Vynnychenko, saw it as a means of separating Ukraine from both Poland and Russia in denominational terms.[10]

Wartime conditions did not permit the Directory to implement fully the autocephaly proclaimed by law, to say nothing of Vynnychenko's more controversial ideas. It was only in exile that the supreme otaman (head of state) of the UNR, Symon Petliura, expressed the idea of establishing a Ukrainian Orthodox patriarchate.[11]

Of the policies adopted by the Ukrainian governments of 1918–19, the only fully successful one was the Hetman administration's

---

8. See the Directory's law on the autocephaly of the Orthodox Church in Ukraine in *Martyrolohiia ukraïns'kykh Tserkov*, 1: 50.

9. On relations between Ukraine and the Vatican during the Ukrainian-Soviet War, see Ivan Khoma, "Ukraïns'ke posol'stvo pry Apostol's'komu Prestoli, 1919–1921," *Bohosloviia* 45 (1981): 3–65.

10. See L'onhyn Tsehel's'kyi, *Vid legendy do pravdy: Spomyny pro podiï v Ukraïni zv'iazani z pershym lystopada 1918 r.* (New York and Philadelphia, 1960), 192–5.

11. See the excerpts of Petliura's 19 December 1921 letter to Ivan Ohiienko, then the UNR's minister of religious affairs, in *Symon Petliura: Statti, lysty, dokumenty*, vol. 1 (New York, 1956), 400–3.

compromise plan to create an autonomous Orthodox Church in Ukraine. It was in those years that the problems of Ukrainian Orthodox autocephaly and of Orthodox-Greek Catholic relations were first brought forward as matters of state policy. As will be seen below, some approaches to the solution of those problems were to exert considerable influence on the church policy of independent Ukraine after 1991.

The Soviet Legacy

The influence of Soviet religious policy on the practice of church-state relations in independent Ukraine can scarcely be exaggerated. All the major actors in the reform of church-state relations in Ukraine after 1991 were products of the Soviet era, including the first president of post-Soviet independent Ukraine, Leonid Kravchuk, who, to quote his own ironic formulation, had played the role of the "first atheist" of Ukraine in the 1980s.[12]

Soviet religious policy originated with the adoption of Lenin's well-known decree on the separation of church and state and of school and church (January 1918). Its general features conform to the "anti-church" model of church-state relations. Soviet religious policy may be divided into two major periods. The first, encompassing the 1920s and 1930s, was characterized by an overtly anti-religious posture on the part of the state, which fought the church with every means at its disposal. Most notably, those means included direct pressure and repression, sowing division in the ecclesiastical milieu, and setting one church against another. It was in this period, between 1921 and 1930, that the authorities permitted the existence of the Ukrainian Autocephalous Orthodox Church (UAOC) as a temporary measure in order to undermine the status of the Moscow Patriarchate.

The second period began in 1943, when the government permitted the appointment of a patriarch in Moscow. The enfeebled ROC was then transformed into a disciplined instrument of state, and official policy toward the church began to acquire a number of features characteristic of the Erastian model of church-state relations. Early in this period, between 1946 and 1949, the ROC was exploited by the state as an effective tool for the liquidation of the UGCC, which was thoroughly Ukrainian in spirit, in Galicia and Transcarpathia.[13]

---

12. For Kravchuk's comments on his attitude toward religion, see Valentyn Chemerys, *Prezydent* (Kyiv, 1994), 85.

13. For a detailed history of the suppression of the UGCC, see Bohdan Rostyslav Bociurkiw, *The Ukrainian Greek Catholic Church and the Soviet State (1939–1950)* (Edmonton and Toronto, 1996).

The religious policy of the Soviet leaders Nikita Khrushchev and Mikhail Gorbachev should be considered as belonging to this period. During the Khrushchev administration, religious policy consisted mainly of repression, while the Gorbachev years were notable in Ukraine for successful efforts to set one denomination against another. But in both cases the government tried to treat the church above all as an instrument of its foreign policy.[14]

In general, the legacy of the Soviet period in church-state relations was one of legal and illegal state surveillance of religious life and active intervention of the state authorities in church affairs. In the USSR the gradual transformation of the church into a tool of the atheist regime fostered the development of more or less stable alliances between the ecclesiastical and Communist elites at both the local and republican levels. In Kyiv this took the form of an alliance between the Communist authorities and the hierarchy of the Ukrainian exarchate of the ROC, which joined forces in 1988, 1989, and 1990 to combat the renaissance of the UGCC and the UAOC.

In the latter half of the 1980s, during the administration of the first secretary of the Communist Party of Ukraine (CPU), Volodymyr Shcherbyts'kyi, the republican authorities in Kyiv, heedless of Moscow's overtly liberal line, sought to prevent the legalization of the UGCC at all costs. They colluded in the mass transfer of former UGCC churches to the Moscow Patriarchate and tolerated the autocephalist movement in Galicia as anti-Catholic even as they combated it in central and eastern Ukraine.[15] The religious conflict that independent Ukraine inherited from the former Soviet Union was inflamed with the active participation of the state apparat at the oblast and republican levels. After 1991 it was up to that same apparat not to fan the flames of conflict, but to eliminate it in the interests of independent Ukraine. At that historical juncture and within the personalities of those individuals, the Soviet experience had its contradictory encounter with the tradition of the religious

---

14.   For recent surveys of Soviet religious policy, see John Anderson, *Religion, State and Politics in the Soviet Union and Successor States* (Cambridge, 1994); Nathaniel Davis, *A Long Walk to Church: A Contemporary History of Russian Orthodoxy* (Boulder, Colo., 1995); and Jane Ellis, *The Russian Orthodox Church: Triumphalism and Defensiveness* (Oxford, 1996).

15.   Patriarch Filaret (Denysenko) of the UOC-Kyiv Patriarchate stated during my interview with him on 24 September 1997 that the official policy toward the UGCC and the UAOC in Galicia was based on the precedent of the revival of the UGCC in Slovakia in 1968.

policies of the Ukrainian governments of 1917–20. The old Soviet tradition was represented by the virtually intact Soviet apparatus. The renaissance of the independentist tradition was led by the new head of the Council for Religious Affairs (CRA), the historian Arsen Zinchenko, and his associate, the Ukrainian Republican Party activist Artur Hubar. The religious policy of the Kravchuk administration was in no small measure a product of the encounter of those traditions.

The Religious Policy of the Kravchuk Administration (1991–94)

In 1991 the Supreme Rada (Parliament) of Ukraine adopted a law on religious associations that, like the old, Soviet legislation, proclaimed the complete separation of church and state. But it was much more democratic than the Soviet laws previously in force. In many respects, this law could be termed a declaration of intent on the part of the state, while everyday political circumstances and the historical tradition inherited by society impelled state functionaries toward active intervention in church affairs.[16] By August 1991, when Ukraine declared its independence, the Ukrainian churches had become deeply involved in political conflict. Each of them had its political sponsors, who in turn enjoyed church support in election campaigns, political activity, and so on.

Probably the last serious decision that Moscow made in the area of church-state affairs in Ukraine was the legalization of the UGCC. After that the management of church-state relations and the settlement of denominational conflicts in the republic came increasingly under the authority of Kyiv. At the same time, however, Kyiv's power over church-state relations was rather illusory. The Kyiv leadership proved incapable of effectively concentrating in its hands the power that had slipped from Moscow's grasp. The dissolution of power that had begun in Moscow was not halted at the level of Kyiv, but went on apace. That process was intensified by the division of power in Kyiv—the struggle between the Supreme Rada, headed by Leonid Kravchuk, and the Central Committee of

---

16.   See the text of the law "On Freedom of Conscience and Religious Organizations" in *Vidomosti Verkhovnoï Rady Ukraïns'koï RSR*, 1991, vyp. 25. For English translations of the USSR and Russian RSFSR laws on freedom of conscience, see Igor Troianovsky, *Religion in the Soviet Republics: A Guide to Christianity, Judaism, Islam, Buddhism and Other Religions* (San Francisco, 1991), 19–37.

the CPU, led by Stanislav Hurenko—as well as the growing influence of regional elites and local councils elected in the spring of 1990.[17]

The failure of the August 1991 coup in Moscow thrust political initiative into the hands of the Supreme Rada in Kyiv. The proclamation of Ukraine's independence and election of Leonid Kravchuk as the first president of Ukraine in December 1991 in turn established the presidential administration as the main generator of ideas in the realm of church-state relations. Like the Hetman government before it, the administration of President Kravchuk staked the achievement of autocephaly not on a rather inconsiderable pro-Ukrainian church organization (the Brotherhood of SS. Cyril and Methodius in 1918 and the UAOC in 1991), but on a powerful Orthodox Church with a large following subordinated to the Moscow Patriarchate. In this respect, the Ukrainian administration found itself more or less at the terminus reached by the government of Hetman Skoropads'kyi in 1918: the UOC, the largest in Ukraine, was an autonomous body within the framework of the Moscow Patriarchate. True, the terms of autonomy were now considerably more generous: the UOC was granted "liberty and independence of administration." Even though the Kravchuk administration, unlike the Hetman government, did not proclaim Orthodoxy the "leading faith," all of its activity in the area of church-state relations was directed toward the establishment of a de facto state church of the Ukrainian Orthodox denomination.

The government found a devoted supporter and executor of its plans in the head of the UOC, Metropolitan Filaret (Denysenko), who had held the Kyiv Metropolitanate since 1966 and was well known for his anti-Uniate and anti-autocephalist views. Compared with the fruitless efforts of the Hetmanate to win over Metropolitan Antonii (Khrapovitskii), this was an unqualified success for the Kravchuk administration. It was based on the previously noted alliance between the Orthodox hierarchy and the CPU elite during the Soviet period. Moscow managed, however, to exploit tensions within the church in Ukraine, particularly the Ukrainian episcopate's dissatisfaction with Filaret, in order to remove him from the church leadership in the spring of 1992. In June of that year, with the support of the government, Filaret became one of the leaders of the

---

17. On the political situation in Ukraine in late 1990 and early 1991, see Volodymyr Lytvyn, *Politychna arena Ukraïny: Diiovi osoby ta vykonavtsi* (Kyiv, 1994), 218–68.

UAOC, which he had once persecuted, and which was now renamed the Ukrainian Orthodox Church-Kyiv Patriarchate (UOC-KP). This new church enjoyed substantial support from the government during the administration of President Kravchuk.[18] The establishment of a state church, which the CRA was in fact bringing about, involved inter alia the defence of the UOC-KP not only against its Orthodox competitors, but also against those of other denominations as well. Its main Orthodox rival was the Ukrainian Orthodox Church that remained under the jurisdiction of the Moscow Patriarchate, the Ukrainian Orthodox Church-Moscow Patriarchate (UOC-MP). Kyiv's policy toward another national church, the UGCC, remained largely undefined during the Kravchuk administration. One of the signs of this was the lack of Ukrainian representation at the Vatican. Even the government of the Directory of the UNR had proceeded to establish its mission at the Holy See in 1919.

Another symptom of indecision was the central government's complete passivity in the matter of winning recognition of a UGCC patriarchate. Even though several prominent representatives of the Ukrainian diaspora made personal appeals to President Kravchuk, arguing that the establishment of a patriarchate would serve the purposes of state policy as concerned the need for an independent church in a sovereign state, the government remained entirely passive on the question. This passivity is particularly striking when compared with the government's active support for Orthodox autocephaly and the Orthodox Kyiv Patriarchate. In a certain sense, President Kravchuk's religious policy even favoured Roman Catholics over Greek Catholics, according in that respect with the Vatican's official line. Thus one national church, the UGCC, was denied support, while another, the UOC-KP, was generously showered with it.[19]

18.　See Bohdan R. Bociurkiw, "The Politics of Religion in Ukraine: The Orthodox and the Greek Catholics," in *The Politics of Religion in Russia and the New States of Eurasia,* ed. Michael Bourdeaux (Armonk, N.Y., and London, 1995), 144–50. On developments within the Orthodox Church in Ukraine at the time, see, in the present volume, Frank Sysyn's essay "The Russian Sobor and the Rejection of Ukrainian Orthodox Autocephaly" and my essay "Ukrainian Orthodox Autocephaly and Metropolitan Filaret."

19.　On the issue of the Greek Catholic patriarchate, see my article "Between Moscow and Rome: The Struggle for a Ukrainian Catholic Patriarchate" in this volume.

The roots of that policy should be sought in the close alliance between the authorities and the Orthodox hierarchy, especially Metropolitan Filaret, who (not without reason) regarded the Greek Catholics as his competitors; in the traditional suspicion with which Uniates had been treated in the Russian Empire and the Soviet Union; and in the official policy of the creation of a state church that was to be exclusively Orthodox.

The government's semi-official attitude of support for an independent church in a sovereign state also served to define the main lines of official policy toward Protestants and representatives of other non-traditional churches in Ukraine. On the one hand, the government tried to make the administrative centres of those churches independent of Moscow, a goal that it more or less effectively achieved;[20] on the other hand, it was open to pressure from the Orthodox hierarchs who were its allies and demanded resolute measures against the flood of missionaries entering Ukraine from the West.

The Moscow Patriarchate requested similar measures from the government of Russia. Because of international public protests against changes in Russian legislation, measures to limit the activity of foreign missionaries in Russia were blocked. In Ukraine, however, such legislative changes were made almost invisibly. There was virtually no protest against them, as the amendments were adopted by Parliament following the White Brotherhood's efforts at seizing the St. Sophia Cathedral in the autumn of 1993, which was widely featured in the media.[21] It was generally considered that the discriminatory changes in legislation were directed against Russia, whence most of the "brothers" had come to Ukraine, and they did not lead to any noticeable restrictions on the activity of Western

---

20.   On the status of the Protestant Churches in Ukraine, see Vasyl Markus, "Politics and Religion in Ukraine: In Search of a New Pluralistic Dimension," in *The Politics of Religion*, 169–77.

21.   Amendments and addenda to Ukraine's law "On Freedom of Conscience and Religious Organizations" were introduced by the Supreme Rada's resolution of 23 December 1993. On the activity of the White Brotherhood and the "living god" Maryna Tsvyhun, see Oleksandr Skoryna, "Zhyttia v borh i zhyttia na znyshchennia," *Ukraïns'ka hazeta*, 1993, nos. 19–20; and Vladimir Skachko, "Boginia rodilas' v Donetske, a mozhet sest' v Kieve," *Zerkalo nedeli*, 11 March 1995. The brotherhood's attempts at seizing the St. Sophia Cathedral and the arrest of its leaders were also reported in the foreign press; see, e.g., Malcolm Gray, "Kiev's Cult of Doom," *Maclean's* (Toronto), 22 November 1993, 32–3.

missionaries. As in the past, those missionaries could preach freely in Ukraine and buy time on radio and television, competing only with the officially supported UOC-KP in terms of hours of air time.

The Religious Policy of the Kuchma Administration

In July 1994 almost all the newspapers in Ukraine and some foreign publications carried a photograph showing the new Ukrainian president, Leonid Kuchma, taking the oath of office in Parliament. During this ceremony the president's hand rested on the Peresopnytsia Gospel, a sixteenth-century Ukrainian manuscript codex.[22] Taking the oath on that ancient tome meant simultaneously swearing an oath before God (who in this instance might be considered Orthodox, given the provenance of that gospel) and Ukraine (since the manuscript is considered one of the most hallowed relics of Ukrainian culture).

By swearing his oath on the Peresopnytsia Gospel, President Kuchma was in effect continuing the tradition begun by his predecessor, Leonid Kravchuk, who had taken his oath on the same gospel following his election in 1991. But this was the only instance in which Kuchma imitated Kravchuk in the area of church-state relations. All of his subsequent actions in that area were intended more to contradict than to continue what his predecessor had done in almost every respect.

The new government's decision to support the UOC-MP fully corresponded to the broader policy of the presidential administration on questions of nationality, culture, and language. That policy was determined by the basic postulates of Kuchma's electoral program and the circumstances of his struggle for the presidency. The organizers of the Kravchuk campaign, seeking to distract voter attention from economic problems and government inaction on economic reform, staked their fortunes on the national question. During that campaign Kravchuk was represented as the sole guarantor of Ukrainian independence, which would be surrendered to Moscow in the event of Kuchma's coming to power.

Leonid Kuchma sought electoral support primarily among the culturally Russified electorate of southern and eastern Ukraine, often playing up to the pro-Russian attitudes of a portion of that electorate. Echoes of his campaign rhetoric were also apparent in the

---

22. This popular photograph found its way onto the covers of several books in Ukraine; see, e.g., Lytvyn, *Politychna arena Ukraïny*.

text of Kuchma's inaugural address, in which he promised to fight for the granting of official status to the Russian language and employed Russian, especially Eurasian, political terminology to identify the strategic position and foreign-policy interests of Ukraine.[23]

President Kuchma had to devote attention to the "church question" during his first days in office. It is worth noting here that his decree on the abolition of the CRA—the symbol of active state intervention in the affairs of religious associations—was signed on the same day (26 July 1994) as his decree appointing the head of the presidential administration. The CRA was replaced by the awkwardly named Ministry for Nationalities, Migration, and Cults.[24] The date of the signing of the decree and the poorly conceived name of the new ministry (an observer, commenting on the word "cults," noted that at least "superstitions" had not been used instead) testify to the hastiness of the decision and the new administration's desire to dissociate itself from the policy of its predecessor.[25]

The direction of President Kuchma's new policy became apparent with the autumn 1994 appointment of Vasyl' Sereda, until then an advisor in the presidential administration and an opponent of the former CRA leadership, as the deputy minister for nationalities, migration, and cults with responsibility for religious affairs. When the Kravchuk administration was in office, Sereda had come out against state support for the UOC-KP and in favour of ending the government's "cold war" with the UOC-MP. Now, having become the country's leading official responsible for shaping church-state relations, he was able to deprive the UOC-KP of official favour and provide tacit support for the UOC-MP.[26]

Kuchma's coming to power, the dissolution of the pro-Filaret CRA, and the administration's new course in the area of church-state relations greatly worsened relations between the state and the UOC-KP, creating a strained and volatile situation in that area. The

---

23. For a survey of the electoral campaign, see Lytvyn, *Polytychna arena Ukraïny*, 450–76.

24. Radio Liberty, 28 July 1994.

25. On "church question's" role in the presidential election, see Viktor Ielens'kyi, "Tserkva i derzhava: Seredyna 1994 r.," *Ukraïna i svit* (Toronto), 20–6 July 1994.

26. Information provided by Artur Hubar, a former official of the disbanded CRA, during my interview with him in September 1994. On the CRA's activity, see the article by its former deputy head, H. Kutsenko, in *Narodna hazeta*, 1994, no. 43 (November).

incident that sparked the transformation of this cold war into a hot one was the dispute between the government and the UOC-KP over the place of interment of its patriarch, Volodymyr (Romaniuk), on 18 July 1995. In fact, the incident was provoked by the ongoing rivalry between the UOC-KP and the UOC-MP for control over Kyiv's sacred buildings and sites, the most notable of which were under state ownership.[27]

The Moscow Patriarchate had retained control of the Kyivan Cave Monastery, while the UOC-KP had taken tenuous hold of part of the less prestigious Vydubychi Monastery. But the ecclesiastical jewel in Kyiv, the St. Sophia Cathedral, remained under the complete control of the state. Rumours circulated in Kyiv about the government's readiness to hand over St. Cyril's Church, St. Andrew's Church, and a number of other churches in the city to the UOC-MP. Given that situation, the UOC-KP decided to stake everything on an attempt at burying its patriarch on the grounds of the St. Sophia Cathedral, thereby staking a claim to the greatest shrine of East Slavic Christendom.[28]

The government, under pressure from its new ally, the UOC-MP, opposed the interment of Patriarch Volodymyr on the grounds of the St. Sophia Cathedral or the Kyivan Cave or Vydubychi monasteries. Instead it granted permission to bury him only in the Baikove Cemetery or on the grounds of St. Volodymyr's Cathedral. The question of the patriarch's burial site remained unresolved until the very day of his funeral. It was in this situation that Metropolitan Filaret, yielding to the demands of the paramilitary Ukrainian National Assembly-Ukrainian National Self-Defence (UNA-UNSO) and numerous members of the Supreme Rada who took part in the funeral together with the former patron of the UOC-KP, ex-president Leonid Kravchuk, led the funeral procession to the St. Sophia Cathedral.

The police had removed the cordon it had initially put up along the funeral-procession route, but a special police unit set up

---

27. On the Orthodox Churches' struggle for control of Kyiv's sacred sites, see my article "Kyiv vs. Moscow: The Autocephalous Movement in Independent Ukraine" in this volume.

28. Preparations for the transfer of St. Cyril's Church to the UOC-MP, the confiscation of St. Andrew's Church from the UOC-KP, and the UOC-KP's petition for partial or full ownership of the St. Sophia Cathedral complex, the Kyivan Cave Monastery, the Vydubychi Monastery, and the Church of the Transfiguration at Berestove are discussed in the UOC-KP's appeal to the president and the prime minister of Ukraine. See *Pravoslavnyi visnyk*, 1995, no. 10: (October): 3–4.

barricades to prevent the funeral participants from entering the cathedral's grounds. After drawn-out negotiations between the Supreme Rada deputies in attendance and government officials failed, the funeral participants began digging a grave for the patriarch on St. Sophia Square near the entrance to the cathedral's grounds. To this the government responded by ordering the police to disperse the crowd and not permit the interment of the patriarch on the square. However, by the time the police had entered the square in force and began beating up and violently dispersing the assembled funeral participants, singling out UNA-UNSO members in particular, it was too late: the patriarch's casket had already been lowered into a hastily dug grave by the entrance to the cathedral's grounds.[29]

The clash on St. Sophia Square ended in tragedy and a resounding scandal that undermined prestige of the government and of the presidential administration. For the first time in Ukraine, which had attained independence without violence and was justly proud of its tolerant practices, blood had been shed and brute force applied. Metropolitan Filaret and the UOC-KP, on the other hand, could congratulate themselves on a triumph. In a single day, Filaret had been transformed from a figure suspected of arranging the patriarch's murder into a symbol of the national-democratic camp, into the sole individual who could unite the assorted national-democratic forces, which were at odds with one another. Confrontation with the government lay ahead for Filaret, but he now had the political support of the national-democrats, which was particularly important for winning election as patriarch at the future sobor of the UOC-KP.[30]

Despite the obvious efforts of the government to prevent Filaret's election as patriarch of the UOC-KP, he was elected to that post at the sobor held in October 1995. The parliamentary deputies who supported Filaret openly accused government officials of backing Filaret's competitors and of seeking to split the UOC-KP during the

---

29. Almost all Kyiv newspapers carried detailed descriptions of the events of "Black Tuesday." See especially Liudmyla Shevchuk's pro–UOC-KP, "Prostit' nas vladyko," *Molod' Ukraïny*, 20 July 1995; and Ol'ga Musafirova's pro-UOC-MP account, "Bog prostit? Kak khoronili sviateishego patriarkha Kievskogo i vsei Ukrainy-Rusi Vladimira (Romaniuka)," *Nezavisimost'*, 21 July 1995. Two full pages of *Nezavisimost'* were devoted to interviews with eyewitnesses.

30. On the launch of a criminal investigation of Patriarch Volodymyr's mysterious death, see *Nezavisimost'*, 28 July 1995. For the national-democrats' reaction to "Black Tuesday," see the letters and information about the beatings of funeral participants in *Molod' Ukraïny*, 21, 25, and 27 July 1995.

sobor. Having lost their confrontation with Filaret, the hierarchs of the largest western eparchies of the UOC-KP, led by the metropolitan of Ivano-Frankivsk, Andrii (Horak), announced they were quitting the UOC-KP and joining a weak rival, the UAOC. Some also suspected the state of being behind efforts at linking the UAOC with the UOC-MP in an anti-Filaret front. Government-supported negotiations between the latter two churches began immediately after the western Ukrainian hierarchs deserted the UOC-KP.[31]

Nonetheless, Filaret managed to stay in power, secure his election as patriarch, prevent the exodus of more western Ukrainian parishes from his church, and strengthen and deepen his alliances with national-democratic politicians. The investigation into the circumstances of Patriarch Volodymyr's death, which was potentially dangerous to Filaret, ended inconclusively. In short order the government found itself obliged to admit the pointlessness of the confrontation and its de facto defeat.

Toward the end of 1995 the Ministry for Nationalities, Migration, and Cults was dissolved, and in October the State Committee for Religious Affairs became a separate entity. Anatolii Koval' was appointed head of the new committee. Vasyl' Sereda, whose activity had been closely associated with the policy of the Kuchma administration and the events of 18 July in Saint Sophia Square, had been the likeliest candidate for that position, but he was demoted for the sake of normalizing relations between the state and the UOC-KP.[32]

---

31.   On the proceedings and results of the UOC-KP sobor, see *Ukraïna i svit* (Toronto), 25–31 October and 1–7 November 1995. Differing assessments of the sobor's proceedings are presented by Liudmyla Shevchuk's "Sviate mistse pustym ne buvaie," *Molod' Ukraïny*, 24 October 1995, and in her interview with the newly elected Patriarch Filaret, "Hotovi na diialoh liubovi," *Molod' Ukraïny*, 26 October 1995; and in Vasilii Anisimov's "No chto-to angely poiut takimi zlymi golosami," *Nezavisimost'*, 25 October 1995, in the newspaper's "scandal" section. The authorities made a show of ignoring Filaret's election as patriarch. He was greeted by the American ambassador to Ukraine, but not by President Kuchma or by the speaker of the Supreme Rada, Oleksandr Moroz. On Moroz's refusal to send congratulations to Filaret, see the interview with Moroz in *Holos Ukraïny*, 1 November 1995, where, without naming names, he condemned those national-democratic deputies who supported the UOC-KP and expressed the hope that the new deputies' association "For the Establishment of a Native Ukrainian Orthodox Church" would not support the creation of a state church (for which the national-democrats were calling).

32.   Koval' presented the committee's agenda in an interview published in *Uriadovyi kur'ier*, 8 February 1996.

A further sign of change in government policy toward the UOC-KP was the visit that Dmytro Tabachnyk, the head of the presidential administration, paid Patriarch Filaret in early 1996. Soon afterwards interviews with Filaret and articles signed by him began appearing in the government media, including the armed-forces magazine *Viis'ko Ukraïny*. The tone of Filaret's pronouncements also changed from being confrontational vis-à-vis the government to irenic, in the spirit of civil peace and religious tolerance.[33] The apogee of the new politics of reconciliation became President Kuchma's patronage of a project to give Patriarch Volodymyr's burial site a proper, permanent appearance and a gravestone. Filaret responded by cancelling plans for a mass commemoration of the anniversary of the Volodymyr's death.

Thus, for the first time in the initial five post-Soviet years of Ukrainian independence, the government renounced a policy of confrontation and entered into a dialogue with the two largest Ukrainian Orthodox Churches.

Kuchma vs. Kravchuk: The Events of "Black Tuesday"

The events of "Black Tuesday"—the police beatings of participants in the funeral of Patriarch Volodymyr on 18 July 1995—demonstrated the level of the church's engagement in Ukrainian politics and of the Ukrainian state in relations among the churches. With the election of President Kuchma, the UOC-KP became a rallying point more than ever for the national-democrats, who wanted a linguistically, culturally, and politically "Ukrainian Ukraine." Meanwhile the UOC-MP was supported by those forces striving to maintain Russian dominance in Ukraine's religious sphere and of those who simply considered Ukrainian independence a transient aberration. Patriarch Volodymyr's death and burial served as an occasion for the UOC-KP and the national-democrats to demonstrate their opposition to the new president's policy in no uncertain terms. The government, which then lent tacit support to the UOC-MP, pretended to pay little attention to the death of the patriarch, who had been a long-time Soviet political prisoner and later closely associated with national-democratic politicians.

The administration's attempt at treating the death of Volodymyr, the patriarch of a church in conflict with the government, as a matter

---

33.   See Filaret's article "Hospody, kudy nam ity?" *Viis'ko Ukraïny*, 1996, nos. 3–4: 20.

of secondary importance is particularly apparent when one compares it with the official reaction to the death of another eminent figure—the "patriarch of Ukrainian literature" Oles' Honchar. Honchar's funeral, which took place on the day before Patriarch Volodymyr's, was treated by the government with the greatest attention. The president, the prime minister, and the speaker of the Supreme Rada stood in the guard of honor beside the casket of the deceased writer, while Patriarch Volodymyr's funeral took place without the participation of the leading representatives of the state. At the time that the patriarch's funeral procession was attacked by the forces of law and order on St. Sophia Square, President Kuchma was officially visiting Belarus, Prime Minister Ievhen Marchuk was out of town as a guest at a collective farm in the Kyiv region (he was represented at the funeral by his deputy), and the speaker of the Supreme Rada, Oleksandr Moroz, was visiting the editorial office of a Kyiv newspaper.

A number of reasons may be advanced for this disparate treatment of the two funerals by the government. One reason was that Honchar was, to some extent, a figure universally respected by all groups in Ukrainian society, starting with the national-democrats and ending with the Communists. He was a symbol of vintage 1991 Ukrainian independence. Despite his earlier political conformism and membership in the CPU and its Central Committee, Honchar's undeniable patriotism and sincere concern for Ukraine's fate made him a hero and a symbol of the new Ukraine that had emerged from the cocoon of the Ukrainian SSR.

Unlike Honchar, the figure of Patriarch Volodymyr was extraordinarily controversial. A virtual saint in the eyes of the national-democrats, he was seen as the incarnation of militant nationalism by eastern Ukrainian politicians. Born in western Ukraine, long imprisoned in Soviet forced-labour camps, and a former political refugee in Canada, he was tolerated, but not permitted to join the "new" Ukrainian (ex-Soviet republican) elite. The national-independence movement, which Volodymyr's life and work embodied, had attained its goal, but had lost the struggle with the former Soviet nomenklatura over who was to determine the nature and politics of the newly sovereign country.[34]

---

34.   Various social groupings' and political circles' attitudes to Honchar's and Patriarch Volodymyr's deaths were reflected in the reactions of three newspapers—the pro–UOC-MP *Nezavisimost'*, the pro–UOC-KP *Molod' Ukraïny*, and the Supreme Rada's organ, *Holos Ukraïny*. On 19 July 1995 *Nezavisimost'* carried the news of Honchar's death on its front page (Halyna Datsiuk's article "Svet uma. Svet liubvi. Svet nadezhdy") without

The reasons for "Black Tuesday" should, of course, be sought not only in the government's actions and attitudes, but also in the plans and goals of the UOC-KP and its national-democratic allies. Deprived of the previous administration's attention and support and split by internal strife between the late patriarch and his deputy, Metropolitan Filaret, the UOC-KP was, in fact, seeking a confrontation with the government. Open conflict, as opposed to an undeclared cold war, could (and, as subsequent events were to show, did) achieve several aims: first, to force the government to reckon with the UOC-KP and end the policy of favouritism toward the UOC-MP; second, to consolidate the UOC-KP's position and its support by national-democratic politicians (mainly parliamentary deputies); and third, to erase from the memories of the faithful the long, drawn-out conflict between the late patriarch and Metropolitan Filaret, which had come to an end only with Volodymyr's death.

The national-democrats, represented at the funeral by parliamentary deputies and members of the UNA-UNSO, had their own view of the situation and their own program of action. Many Ukrainian politicians undoubtedly considered the patriarch's funeral an occasion to lend support to the national church in its conflict with "Muscovite priests," and they believed they were "entitled" to a serious concession from the government—in this particular case, permission to bury the patriarch on the grounds of the St. Sophia Cathedral. In June 1995 the national-democrats in Parliament had unwaveringly supported President Kuchma in his battle with the left, making possible a constitutional agreement between him and Parliament. It was now time for Kuchma to pay his debt to his allies.

The radical UNA-UNSO had its own agenda. The presence of its paramilitary units at Volodymyr's funeral was an expression of the

---

mentioning Volodymyr's death. On 18 July 1995 *Molod' Ukraïny* printed the news of Volodymyr's death at the top of its front page ("Pam'iati velykoho patriarkha") and of Honchar's death at the bottom ("Orlyna vysota Olesia Honchara"). On 18 July 1995) *Holos Ukraïny* carried the official announcement of Honchar's death at the top of p. 3; it was signed not only by the president and the ruling elite, but also by V'iacheslav Chornovil, a national-democratic leader in Parliament. A short announcement of Patriarch Volodymyr's death signed by the Holy Synod and the Supreme Church Council of the UOC-KP appeared at the bottom of the same page. Subsequently *Holos Ukraïny* devoted considerable attention to Honchar but, compared with other publications, rather little to what happened at Volodymyr's funeral. On 19 July it ran an article about Honchar's funeral under the title "Proshchavaite, bat'ku!" and published another memorial piece nine days after his death.

well-established partnership between the UNA-UNSO and the UOC-KP; and the important role the UNA-UNSO played in the funeral raised its status among the other national-democratic groups. It must be noted that the UNA-UNSO was the only participant in "Black Tuesday" that managed to achieve the goal it had set for itself. If both the government and the national-democratic parliamentary opposition had fallen into a serious quarrel that undermined their authority to the delight of the left, the UNA-UNSO emerged from the confrontation at St. Sophia Square as martyrs and the unofficial leaders of the national-democratic bloc. This was soon demonstrated by the formal presentation to the UNA-UNSO of the blue-and-yellow flag that had first been carried into the Supreme Rada building after the Moscow coup of August 1991. The flag, which until then had been in the possession of the Ukrainian popular front, Rukh, was bestowed upon the members of the UNA-UNSO by Patriarch Filaret during a formal prayer service held on St. Sophia Square on the ninth day after Volodymyr's death.

During the period of intense conflict between Leonid Kravchuk and President Kuchma and his administration that followed "Black Tuesday," both politicians made public their perceptions of the events of that tragic day and their views of the model of church-state relations required for the good of Ukraine. Kravchuk was the first to do so. He blamed the government for the tragedy, asserting that the reason for the conflict was the authorities' refusal to work together with the national church–an institution that was important factor in the rise of Ukrainian national consciousness and nation building. Kuchma, on the other hand, identified the provocative actions of those nationalists and church officials who had tried to drive the government into an impasse as the factor primarily responsible for the tragedy. He stressed that granting permission to inter Patriarch Volodymyr on the grounds of the St. Sophia Cathedral would have worsened the government's relations with the other churches and contravened the policy of official non-interference in church affairs.[35]

Thus the principal burden of Leonid Kravchuk's statement was a defence of official intervention in church affairs for the purpose of state building and supporting the national cause. President Kuchma, on the other hand, stressed the principle of the separation of church and state. Their statements reflected opposing views of the problem

---

35. See Kuchma's comments about "Black Tuesday" in *Holos Ukraïny*, 27 July 1995.

and were more in the nature of political declarations than practical suggestions for resolving the complex questions of church-state relations. After all, it is public knowledge that in the last months of his presidency Kravchuk established good relations with Filaret's most powerful competitor, the UOC-MP. And the Kuchma administration, for its part, initiated virtually open warfare with the UOC-KP after "Black Tuesday" and declaring its non-interference.

Clearly, it was this "flexibility" in resolving practical questions of church-state relations that allowed both political forces to achieve a compromise in the first half of 1996 in order to attain their common goal—the adoption of a new Ukrainian constitution.[36] The government ceased its pressure on the UOC-KP, while the latter, in the person of Patriarch Filaret and his political allies, renounced its anti-government propaganda and withdrew its demand for the establishment of a state Orthodox Church (which the UOC-KP was to have become under a new patriotic government). The grave of Patriarch Volodymyr was put in decent order as a result of the reconciliation of these former enemies, the reanimation of old political alliances, and a change in presidential policy on questions of culture, nationality, and religion.

The Constitutional Compromise

The adoption of the Constitution of Ukraine on 28 June 1996 signalled a political truce between the warring parliamentary factions and created the constitutional framework, long awaited by

---

36. On developments in government circles during Patriarch Volodymyr's funeral, see the explanations offered by Vice-Prime Minister for Economic Affairs Roman Shpek (during Honchar's funeral the prime minister assigned Shpek to oversee the funeral of the patriarch on the grounds that Shpek was Orthodox): Oleksii Trotsenko, "Pro podiï dovkola pokhoronu patriarkha Volodymyra (Romaniuka)," *Holos Ukraïny,* 22 July 1995. See also Ivan Bezsmertnyi, "Kryvavyi vivtorok mozhe vprovadyty 'pryntsyp domino' u velyku ukraïns'ku polityku," *Chas,* 8 September 1995, which was apparently written at the behest of persons close to Prime Minister Ievhen Marchuk. On 21 July 1995 *Nezavisimost'* reported that the former head of President Kravchuk's personal security service, Viktor Palyvoda, had been arrested in Hungary at the request of the Ukrainian authorities; that Palyvoda had opened secret accounts abroad on Kravchuk's instructions; and that a resounding political scandal was expected. Developments in the spring of 1996 made it apparent that an accommodation had been reached between the two presidents: they appeared together at a soccer match, and subsequently Anatolii Matviienko, a protégé of Kravchuk, was appointed acting presidential representative in Vinnytsia oblast.

Ukraine's citizens and foreign observers alike, within which the nation of 49 million is to develop.

Aside from establishing a constitutional framework—defining the powers of government, entrenching the principle of private property, establishing the foundations for future legislation, and so on—the constitution took a step toward the "nationalization" of the Ukrainian state. It endowed Ukrainian national symbols and the Ukrainian language with official status while providing guarantees for the protection of the Russian language and other languages of Ukraine's national minorities. In practice, the constitution set a course for the "re-Ukrainianization" of Ukraine, i.e., the creation of a new nation on the basis of the political, cultural, and linguistic traditions of the Ukrainian people.

Already in 1917 and 1918, while creating the Ukrainian People's Republic, the leaders of the Central Rada experienced problems in identifying Ukraine's population with the Ukrainian people, which they eventually came to designate as ethnic Ukrainians. This problem remained and even intensified somewhat with the renewal of Ukrainian independence after 1991, when debates concerning symbols of statehood and the official status of the Russian language posed a threat to the integrity of Ukraine's territory. The borders of the Ukrainian SSR largely coincided with the boundaries of ethnic Ukrainian settlement at the beginning of the twentieth century. But massive waves of Russian in-migration into Soviet Ukraine, as well as Moscow's nationality and cultural policies, contributed to a situation wherein, at the proclamation of Ukrainian independence in 1991, approximately twenty percent of Ukraine's population consisted of ethnic Russians and most ethnic Ukrainians in the country's east and south were linguistically and culturally Russified.[37]

---

37. For discussions of the political symbolism and status of the Ukrainian and Russian languages in Ukraine, see Bohdan Krawchenko, "People's Memory in Ukraine: The Role of the Blue and Yellow Flag," *Journal of Ukrainian Studies* 15, no. 1 (Summer 1990): 1–21; and Dominique Arel, "Language Politics in Independent Ukraine: Towards One or Two State Languages?," *Nationalities Papers* 23, no. 3 (September 1995): 597–622. On the history of the boundaries of Ukraine, see Vasyl' Boiechko, Oksana Hanzha, and Borys Zakharchuk, *Kordony Ukraïny: Istorychna perspektyva ta suchasnyi stan* (Kyiv, 1994). Questions pertaining to Ukraine's territorial integrity are discussed in my essay "Historical Debates and Territorial Claims: Cossack Mythology in the Russian-Ukrainian Border Dispute," in *The Legacy of History in Russia and the New States of Eurasia*, The International Politics of Eurasia, vol. 1, ed. S. Frederick Starr (Armonk, N.Y. and London, 1994), 147–70; and in Dominique Arel and Valeri Khmelko, "The Russian Factor

In the complex matter of defining the new nation, the constitution sought to overcome the dichotomy that had preoccupied the Ukrainian political leaders of the first decades of the twentieth century: that of "the Ukrainian people" as the Ukrainian ethnos, and "the people of Ukraine" as the entire population of the country. In the constitution's preamble "the Ukrainian people" is defined as the citizens of Ukraine in their entirety regardless of ethnic origin (i.e., the "people of Ukraine" as defined by the Central Rada's leaders), while the term "Ukrainian nation" designates the Ukrainians as an ethnic group (the "Ukrainian people" as defined by the Central Rada's leaders). Despite this obvious terminological confusion, which resulted from the compromises and feverish haste with which the basic law was adopted in the Supreme Rada, the preamble clearly testifies to an attempt at overcoming an outworn terminological and conceptual conflict in order to create a Ukrainian political nation (called "the Ukrainian people" in the constitution) on the basis of the political and cultural traditions of the Ukrainian ethnos ("the Ukrainian nation" in the preamble), potentially incorporating the "citizens of Ukraine of all nationalities."[38]

In essence, of the three possible models of nation building— exclusive nationalism, inclusive nationalism, and the multiethnic

and Territorial Polarization in Ukraine," *Harriman Review*, 9, nos. 1–2 (Spring 1996): 81–91. Oles' Honchar became the one "infallible" hero of Lytvyn's *Politychna arena Ukraïny*. For attempts by Ukrainian writers at developing a cult of Honchar, see Ivan Koshelivets', "Mozhna odverto?" *Suchasnist'*, 1997, no. 10: 112–21.

38. See the text of the Constitution of Ukraine in *Holos Ukraïny*, 13 July 1996. According to press reports, the national-democrats in Parliament actively opposed the definition of the Ukrainian people as comprising the citizens of Ukraine of all nationalities. The constitutional draft presented earlier by the Communist faction in the Supreme Rada used the formula "the people of Ukraine," understood as all the citizens of all ethnic origins residing on the territory of Ukraine ("Proekt 'Konstytutsiï (Osnovnoho zakonu) Ukraïns'koï Radians'koï Sotsialistychnoï Respubliky,'" *Holos Ukraïny*, 25 July 1995). The First Universal of the Ukrainian Central Rada appealed to "all Ukrainian people, whether residing in Ukraine or beyond its borders"; the Second Universal, to "citizens of the Ukrainian land"; the Third Universal, to "the Ukrainian people and all the peoples of Ukraine"; and, finally, the Fourth Universal, which proclaimed Ukrainian independence, to "the people of Ukraine." See the translated texts of the universals in *The Ukraine, 1917–1921: A Study in Revolution*, ed. Taras Hunczak wit the assistance of John T. von der Heide (Cambridge, Mass., 1977), 382–95.

political nation—Ukrainian lawmakers had chosen the second.[39] In the spirit of inclusive nationalism, the authors of the Constitution of Ukraine granted legal equality to citizens of all ethnic origins and religious creeds. Article 35 of the constitution guarantees all citizens of Ukraine "freedom to profess any religion or to profess none," and it makes provision for non-military service as an alternative to service in the armed forces. Religious freedom may be restricted only "in the interest of preserving social order, the population's health and morality, or the defence of the rights and freedoms of others."

According to article 35, the church and the state are separate from one another, as are the school and the church, and "no religion may be designated as obligatory by the state." Other articles, notably article 24, guarantee foreigners who are legally in Ukraine the same rights as those enjoyed by Ukraine's citizens.[40] The principles of religious legislation embodied in the Constitution of Ukraine conform to the most stringent norms of international law and are intended as a break with the Soviet atheistic tradition of crass state interference in the affairs of religious associations, as well as with the post-Soviet practice of supporting one denomination at the expense of another.

The actions of the Ukrainian authorities, most notably those of President Kuchma, during the debate on the constitution and after its adoption by the Supreme Rada testified to the government's desire to adhere to the principles of church-state relations enunciated in the constitution; these actions discontinue the practice of active intervention in interdenominational conflicts on the side of any church. On the one hand, as noted earlier, the grave of Patriarch Volodymyr of the UOC-KP on St. Sophia Square in Kyiv was put in order under the president's patronage. On the other hand, almost immediately after the adoption of the constitution President Kuchma visited his native village in the Chernihiv region, where he took part in the consecration of a new church of the UOC-MP. His actions

39. For a discussion of the politics of inclusive nationalism in Ukraine, see Motyl, *Dilemmas of Independence,* 70–5 and 79–80.

40. See *Holos Ukraïny,* 13 July 1996. The draft Constitution of the Ukrainian SSR did not include a number of guarantees of church-state separation later provided in the Constitution of Ukraine, but guaranteed freedom of atheist activity; see *Holos Ukraïny,* 25 July 1995. Similar to this was the article on freedom of religion in the draft constitution submitted for general discussion by the Supreme Rada in July 1992.

with respect to the competing UOC-KP and UOC-MP were thus intended to make apparent the authorities' desire to avoid showing partiality in their treatment of religious denominations that are in conflict with one another. In practice, this was a hiatus in President Kuchma's religious policy following two years that had been neither easy nor free of problems in church-state relations.

On the Threshold of the Third Millennium

The new government policy toward religious denominations was manifested in a number of official initiatives and declarations. One was the creation, under the auspices of the State Committee for Religious Affairs, of the All-Ukrainian Council of Churches and Religious Organizations, an advisory board composed of the heads of Ukraine's leading denominations. In the summer of 1997 the government tried to defuse tensions between the faithful of the UOC-MP and UOC-KP and to improve relations among other denominations by initiating the signing of a declaration by religious leaders on mutual respect and the peaceful resolution of existing conflicts. In the summer of 1999, a few months before the new presidential elections, Leonid Kuchma issued a statement in which he admitted the injustice of the state's persecution of religious institutions during the Communist era. He called for the speediest return of places of worship confiscated by the Soviet authorities to their original religious communities. In fact, his statement was an apology for decades of government persecution of religion. But it did little to heal the inter-Orthodox schism.[41]

Overall, the policy of non-interference in the inter-Orthodox conflict, which the government officially proclaimed and largely followed, failed to bring positive results. The UOC-KP and its more powerful counterpart, the UOC-MP, did not cease hostilities and continued to fight one another for control of major cathedrals and monasteries. The most acute conflict developed over the rights to the Kyivan Cave Monastery, the cradle of Rus' monasticism and one of

41. See Mariia Horiacha, "Suchasna derzhavna relihiina polityka Ukraïny," *Working Papers in Ukrainian Studies*, at <www.unl.ac.uk/ukrainecentre>. On the importance the government attributed to President Kuchma's 1999 statement, see his speech at the formal observance of the beginning of the second millennium of Christianity on 21 January 2000, published in *Holos pravoslav'ia*, 2000, no. 3 (February). For the UOC-MP's reaction to his 1999 statement, see Sviatoslav Rechinskii, "Itogi i nadezhdy velikogo iubileia," at <www.orthodox.org.ua>.

the most venerated Orthodox holy places. Since the summer of 1992, one part of the monastery—the Far Caves, which the government had turned over to the Orthodox Church at the time of the celebrations of the millennium of East Slavic Christianity—was under the control of the UOC-MP, while the main territory of the former monastery complex, including the Near Caves, remained under government control and housed several museums. Following the principle of equal treatment of the two major Ukrainian Orthodox jurisdictions and taking into account the UOC-MP's occupation of part of the monastery complex, the government tried to transfer another part to the UOC-KP. But it was forced to rescind its decision in the face of strenuous protests from the UOC-MP. The head of the UOC-KP, Patriarch Filaret, had never abandoned his claims to the Kyivan Cave Monastery. Having been forced to tolerate his rival's control over the oldest and most famous Rus' shrine, Filaret reached a tacit understanding with Kyiv's municipal authorities regarding the fate of the newly rebuilt St. Michael's Cathedral in central Kyiv. The cathedral, whose original edifice dated back to the times of Kyivan Rus', had been completely demolished by the Soviets in the 1930s, but was reconstructed by the city in the late 1990s. Subsequently it was turned over to the UOC-KP.[42] In turn, the Dormition Cathedral of the Kyivan Cave Monastery was also rebuilt by the city authorities, and it was turned over to the UOC-MP during the celebrations of Ukrainian independence in August 2000.[43]

Property issues were not the only problematic area in relations between the two churches. During the years 1996–99 the local and national media reported a number of violent conflicts between the

---

42.   In 1997 the Ukrainian government has awarded the UOC-KP the Vydubychi Monastery complex on the outskirts of Kyiv, the Pyrohoshcha Church of the Dormition, and St. Michael's Golden-Domed Monastery. These historic sites all date from the Kyivan Rus' era. See the letter of the deputy chairman of the State Committee for Religious Affairs, M. Novychenko, to the president of the World Congress of Ukrainians, Askold Lozynskyj, published in *Visnyk* (Winnipeg), 15–29 February 2000. On the UOC-KP's efforts to persuade the Kyiv City Council to grant official recognition of the UOC-KP's rights to the rebuilt St. Michael's Cathedral in Kyiv, see Inna Zolotukhina, "Viruiuchi i natsional-demokraty piketuiut' stolychnu administratsiiu," *Den'*, 4 February 1999.

43.   For coverage of the event and the protests by UOC-KP supporters, see Evgenia Mussuri, "Protests Mark Church Opening," *The Kyiv Post*, 31 August 2000.

adherents of the two jurisdictions. Most of the coverage concerned the person of Patriarch Filaret. On 30 April 1999 he and a group of clergymen accompanying him were attacked by members of the UOC-MP in the eastern Ukrainian city of Mariupol while Filaret was trying to consecrate a plot of land a where a new church was to be built. Filaret was hospitalized with minor bruises, while some of his supporters suffered more serious injuries.[44] The incident may be viewed as one of the most obvious results of the continuing hate campaign conducted by bishops and priests of the Moscow Patriarchate and directed personally against Filaret.

The main instrument of that campaign was the anathema, the strongest possible church condemnation, issued against Filaret by the Holy Synod of the Moscow Patriarchate in February 1997. Filaret, who was first excommunicated and later anathemized by his former colleagues in the Holy Synod, found himself in the same unpleasant situation that had befallen the eighteenth-century hetman Ivan Mazepa: after Mazepa had led a Cossack insurrection against Peter I, the tsar ordered the Orthodox Church to pronounce an anathema against the hetman. The anathema against Filaret predictably raised his profile among Ukrainian patriots, but it also contributed to heightening the atmosphere of fanaticism and religious intolerance that already existed in relations between the faithful of the Moscow and Kyiv Patriarchates.[45]

While the UOC-MP's attacks on the UOC-KP were based chiefly on the perception of Filaret and his clergy as non-canonical and thus non-Orthodox,[46] the UOC-KP adopted different tactics in its fight against its Moscow rival. On the whole, Filaret eschewed personal attacks on his enemies. His main argument against his opponents had remained the same since 1992, when he decided to abandon Russian Orthodoxy. Filaret maintained that, in accordance with Orthodox tradition, sooner or later independent Ukraine would acquire an independent (autocephalous) Orthodox Church and, no

---

44. See "1999: The Year in Review. Religious Affairs: A Relative Calm," *The Ukrainian Weekly*, 26 December 1999.

45. On the reaction in Ukraine to the anathema against Filaret, see Viktor Ielens'kyi, "Vidlunnia podiï 1997-ho," *Liudyna i svit* (1998) no. 1: 2–12, here, 3. On the reading of the anathema in UOC-MP churches on the Feast of the Triumph of Orthodoxy (19 March 2000), see "Torzhestvo pravoslaviia," *Pravoslavna Tavriia*, 2000, no. 3 (23), at <www.orth.kherson.ua>.

46. For the arguments that the UOC-MP usually employed against Filaret and his supporters, see Rechinskii, "Itogi i nadezhdy velikogo iubileia."

matter what his opponents were saying, he was on the right side of history. Nevertheless, his campaign against the Moscow Patriarchate turned negative each time he and his supporters levelled political accusations against their competitors and claimed that the UOC-MP's affiliation with Moscow was undermining the cause of Ukrainian independence and the spiritual revival of the nation. But Filaret's line of argument proved to be the most beneficial one: it helped him to attract and keep the support of a substantial sector of Ukraine's political elite. Needless to say, his accusation caused the greatest harm to the Moscow Patriarchate.[47]

Despite all of the attempts by the head of the UOC-MP, Metropolitan Volodymyr (Sabodan), to prove Filaret wrong on that score, the UOC-MP found itself increasingly in the centre of numerous controversies regarding the political and cultural loyalties of its clergy and faithful.[48] Autocephaly was by far the most sensitive issue in the UOC-MP's relations with the government, political groupings in Parliament, and society at large. On that issue the UOC-MP authorities had travelled a long way from their original claims in 1992, according to which Patriarch Aleksii II of Moscow personally made efforts to grant canonical autocephaly to the Ukrainian church, to the UOC-MP synod's withdrawal of the official application for autocephalous status in late 1996.[49] In August 2000 the UOC-MP's hierarchs asked the Bimillennial Sobor in Moscow to grant their church autonomous status. But the Moscow Patriarchate's leadership rejected even that request.[50]

---

47.   For Filaret's views on Ukrainian autocephaly and the role of the Moscow Patriarchate in Ukraine, see his extensive interview with Tatiana Nikulenko in *Bul'var*, 1997, no. 35 (91) (September 1997): 10–13.

48.   See Nikolai Mitrokhin, "Vlast' i religiia," *Russkaia mysl'*, 8 July 1999, in the section "Spetsificheskie problemy Ukrainskoi Pravoslavnoi Tserkvi Moskovskogo Patriarkhata"; and Rechinskii, "Itogi i nadezhdy velikogo iubileia."

49.   The 1996 withdrawal of Kyiv's request for autocephaly in fact paved the way for the Russian Holy Synod's anathema against Filaret in February 1997. On the UOC-MP Synod's withdrawal of its previous request for autocephaly and the negative reaction by the UOC-KP clergy in Volhynia, see Ielens'kyi, "Vidlunnia podii 1997-ho", 5–6; and Nikolai Mitrokhin, "Vlast' i religiia na Ukraine," *Rossiisko-ukrainskii biulleten'*, no. 3 (22 December 1999): 70–3.

50.   For the Moscow Sobor's decisions, see Taras Kuzio, "The Struggle to Establish the World's Largest Orthodox Church," *RFE/RL Newsline* 4, no. 171, pt. 1 (September 2000).

The Ukrainian government's official policy, which provided for equal treatment of the UOC-MP and the UOC-KP and was strongly advocated by the UOC-MP during Leonid Kravchuk's presidency, clearly lost its appeal to that church's leaders during President Kuchma's first term in office. At that time the UOC-MP, which in no way was being discriminated against by the government, changed its tactics and demanded preferential treatment from the state. The UOC-MP's ruling circles' dissatisfaction with the government's stand on the inter-Orthodox conflict was voiced in late 1999 by Sviatoslav Rechinskii, one of the most outspoken journalists associated with the UOC-MP, on that church's official Web site. He accused the head of the State Committee for Religious Affairs, Viktor Bondarenko, of dishonesty toward UOC-MP officials and of supporting pro-Filaret non-governmental organizations. Rechinskii also reprimanded President Kuchma for taking part in liturgies at UOC-KP churches on religious holidays.[51] Such criticism of the president came to a halt only after Kuchma participated in the ceremony that officially transferred the Dormition Cathedral at the Kyivan Cave Monastery to the UOC-MP in August 2000.[52] By the end of the twentieth century, the UOC-MP was clearly seeking a status similar to the one its counterparts in Russia and Belarus had achieved. In those countries the Moscow Patriarchate functioned as the de facto state church and enjoyed preferential government treatment.

In the late 1990s, having grown increasingly tired of the constant bickering between the different Orthodox jurisdictions, the Ukrainian government began favouring the old idea of creating a single Ukrainian Orthodox Church. This time around the government tried to avoid repeating its earlier mistakes, and it made it clear from the very beginning that it was not going to interfere in the internal affairs of the various Orthodox Churches (i.e., support one church against another); instead, it would encourage any efforts by those

---

51. See Rechinskii, "Itogi i nadezhdy velikogo iubileia." Rechinskii also attacked President Kuchma for inviting Pope John Paul II to visit Ukraine without consulting the UOC-MP. Kuchma clearly refused to be intimidated by UOC-MP supporters, and on Easter Sunday of 2000 he attended services at churches of the UOC-MP, the UOC-KP, and the UGCC. See "Kuchma Sees Need for Single Orthodox Church," *RFE/RL Poland, Belarus, and Ukraine Report* 2, no. 17 (9 May 2000).

52. See "Mitropolit Vladimir (Sabodan) posetil Odesskuiu eparkhiiu i provel press-konferentsiiu dlia zhurnalistov o polozhenii Tserkvi na Ukraine" (21 September 2000), at <www.orthodox.org.ua>.

churches to engage in inter-jurisdictional dialogue. Government support for the project to create one native (independent) Orthodox Church that would unite all the Orthodox faithful and end all inter-Orthodox strife, which was destabilizing society at large, was announced in January 2000 by President Kuchma in his speech at the formal observance of the millennium of East Slavic Christianity.[53] Kuchma repeated his commitment to the idea of a united Orthodox Church in his remarks to the press on Easter Sunday, 30 April 2000, thus indicating that the position he voiced in his speech on 21 January was no accident and indeed marked a change in official policy.[54] Kuchma again demonstrated his support for the creation of one Orthodox Church in Ukraine during the ceremonial transfer of the Dormition Cathedral at the Kyivan Cave Monastery to the UOC-MP in August 2000. The government was also one of the players in the "unity" talks that same year involving the UOC-KP, the UAOC, and representatives of the Constantinople Patriarchate.[55]

For Patriarch Filaret and his supporters, the change in government policy came as a major triumph, for it echoed Filaret's views on the inevitability of the creation of one national Orthodox Church in Ukraine. In marked contrast, the UOC-MP, whose bishops reacted to President Kuchma's January 2000 address by stamping their feet, viewed the new policy as a major setback.[56] The government was, in fact, sending a strongly worded message to the UOC-MP hierarchs: begin working toward Orthodox unity, or else be marginalized by other Orthodox jurisdictions in terms of church-state partnership and co-operation. Despite the UOC-MP bishops'

53. For the text of President Kuchma's speech, see "Data voistynu planetarnoho masshtabu: Urochysta akademiia v Natsional'nomu palatsi 'Ukraïna'," *Holos pravoslav'ia*, 2000, no. 3 (27) (February).

54. See "Kuchma Sees Need for Single Orthodox Church."

55. On Viktor Bondarenko's role in the negotiations, see "Raskol'niki avtokefalisty iz t.n. 'Ukrainskoi avtokefalnoi pravoslavnoi tserkvi' izbrali novogo predstoiatelia," *Radonezh*, 18 September 2000, at <www.radonezh.orthodoxy.ru/news>; and Geraldine Fagan and Aleksandr Shchipkov, "Ukraine: Constantinople to Recognize Unified Orthodox Church?" *Keston News Service*, 9 October 2000, at <www.keston.org>.

56. See the report in the UOC-KP's *Pravoslavnyi visnyk*, 2000, nos. 1–2 (January–February 2000): 8–9. For Filaret's attempts at capitalizing on Kuchma's acceptance of his formula of "one, independent Orthodox Church," see his comments on the death of Patriarch Dymytrii (Volodymyr Iarema) of the UAOC in Ievhen Holibardov, "Komu potriben novyi rozkol?" *Ukraïna i svit*, 1–7 March 2000.

initially negative reaction toward the shift in government policy, it may be argued that it is their church, and not the UOC-KP, that would benefit most from the new course. Patriarch Filaret, anathemized and condemned by the leaders of all Orthodox patriarchates, has little chance of becoming the leader of a new, unified Orthodox Church in Ukraine. The creation of such a church would be impossible without the participation of the UOC-MP, the largest denomination in the country, and a UOC-MP hierarch would likely lead that church if it were ever established.[57]

One of the crucial factors that undoubtedly influenced and will certainly continue to influence Ukrainian government policy toward the Orthodox Churches in the future is Ukraine's relations with Russia. The importance that official Moscow attributed to the Orthodox factor in its policy toward Ukraine was demonstrated by the actions of President Vladimir Putin in the spring of 2000. His first visit to Ukraine as president-elect in April 2000 was replete with political symbolism: after his brief negotiations with President Kuchma, Putin made two symbolically significant visits—one to the Kyivan Cave Monastery and another to the Russian Black Sea Fleet in Sevastopol.[58] In early May 2000, on the eve of V-E Day, Presidents Putin, Kuchma, and Aleksandr Lukashenka of Belarus met on the Russians' initiative near the village of Prokhorovka, Belgorod oblast, the site of the largest tank battle (1943) of the Second World War, to take part in a religious commemoration of the war's casualties. The event was effectively turned into a celebration of the common, "glorious" past of the three East Slavic nations and a pitch for their future unity. Patriarch Aleksii II of Moscow played a

---

57.   Kuchma's stand on the issue of a unified Orthodox Church apparently gave additional impetus to the supporters of autocephaly within the UOC-MP. The Lviv March 2000 meeting of Archbishop Avhustyn (Markevych) of the UOC-MP, Bishop Makarii (Maletych) of the UAOC, and Metropolitan Andrii (Horak) of the UOC-KP may be considered an indication of that. The meeting was co-ordinated by Archimandrite Pankratii of the Constantinople Patriarchate, but took place on the initiative of Avhustyn, who has been generally known for his pro-Moscow stand. Another representative of the UOC-MP who was at the meeting suggested that the participants issue a statement supporting Kuchma's initiative and create a trilateral commission to study the issue of establishing a united Orthodox Church. My information about the meeting comes from an undated and unsigned report entitled "Persha lastivka?"

58.   See Roman Woronowycz, "Putin Visits Kyiv as Part of His First Tour of Foreign Capitals," The Ukrainian Weekly, 23 April 2000.

leading role in the ceremony. On his initiative a "unity bell" symbolizing the three nations' common destiny was installed in the local Russian Orthodox church and rung by the three presidents. Aleksii also openly called for the unity of Russia, Ukraine, and Belarus, which, in his words, share "one faith, one history, one culture."[59]

The celebrations of the beginning of the second millennium of Christianity in Russia, Ukraine, and Belarus also demonstrated the Moscow Patriarchate's role as an instrument of Russian policy in all three countries and the patriarchate's growing potential as an "empire-restoring" institution. Aleksii II and the Moscow Patriarchate apparently resolved to use the celebrations to strengthen their presence in Ukraine and popularize the idea of East Slavic unity in that country. In the summer of 1999, only the strong protests of Patriarch Filaret and his supporters forced Aleksii to cancel his planned trip down the Dnipro River. The Moscow patriarch's ship was supposed to traverse territories in Russia, Belarus, and Ukraine and arrive in Kyiv on 24 August, Ukrainian Independence Day.[60] The patriarchate's plans for the bimillennial celebrations in 2000 included a less ambitious, but no less symbolic, procession with the cross at the Church of the Transfiguration in Moscow on 5 September 2000. Before arriving there, the cross was supposed to travel down the rivers Volga (Russia), Dnipro (Ukraine), and Western Dzvina (Belarus), a journey symbolizing the unity of the three Orthodox nations.[61] Also quite telling was the Moscow Bimillennial Sobor's refusal to grant autonomy to the UOC-MP, despite President Kuchma's personal endorsement of the request.[62] Ukrainian Orthodoxy was supposed to remain an integral part of the ROC.

The events of the last decade of the twentieth century in the predominantly Orthodox countries of Eastern Europe and the Balkans demonstrated once again the strong link between religion and national identity in that part of the world. They also reminded

---

59. On the celebrations at Prokhorovka, see "Russia, Ukraine, Belarus Leaders Recall WW2 Unity," Reuters, 3 May 2000.

60. See "1999: The Year in Review. Religious Affairs: A Relative Calm."

61. For the Moscow Patriarchate's plans for the celebrations, see "The Second Enlarged Meeting of the Russian Organizing Committee for the 2,000th Anniversary of Christianity," press release of the ROC's Department for External Church Relations, 9 September 1999, at <www.goarch.org/worldnews>.

62. See Kuzio, "The Struggle to Establish."

observers of the importance of the international dimensions of the official religious policy in each of the countries of the *Slavia Orthodoxa*. Those events also demonstrated the importance of the Russian factor in Ukraine's domestic policies. In the first ten years of the independent Ukrainian state's existence, that factor continuously influenced the formulation and implementation of government policy toward religious denominations, and it is safe to assume that it will retain its importance in the future. It is equally safe to assume that any religious policy that the Ukrainian government adopts in the future will have a direct impact on the realization of Ukraine's nation-building project and foreign policy, including its most important elements— Ukraine's relations with Russia, her attitude toward the Russian-Belarusian Union, and her relations with the West. In turn, Ukraine's foreign-policy choices will affect the international balance of power in Europe. There is little doubt that without Ukraine as a member of the newly created union of Russia and Belarus and without Ukraine throwing its weight behind the East Slavic *Pax Orthodoxa*, the revival of Russian predominance in East-Central Europe will be difficult, if not impossible, to achieve.

Index

Balkans, 21, 67, 69, 110, 197

Baranovych, Lazar (Orthodox bishop of Chernihiv), 10, 18, 32

Bartholomew I (patriarch of Constantinople), 111 n. 49, 155

Basilian monastic order, 2

Batalden, Stephen K., 88 n. *

Belarus, 3, 4, 10, 11, 13, 14, 20, 30, 31, 33, 123, 125, 127, 156, 183, 194, 196, 197

Belavin, Tikhon. See Tikhon (Belavin)

Belgium, 154

Bercoff, Giovanna Brogi, 20 n. 21

Berestechko, 101, 101 n. 26, 114, 114 n. 55

Berezovs'kyi, Onufrii. See Onufrii (Berezovs'kyi)

Beria, Lavrentii, 59, 61, 64 n. 18, 73

Bezsmertnyi, Ivan, 186 n. 36

Bidn'ov, Vasyl', 25

Bieńkowski, Ludomir, 6 n. 7, 28 n. 7

Bila Tserkva, 100

Bilas, Ivan, 60 n. 3, 60 n. 4, 60 n. 6, 71 n. 40

Bilodid, Oles', 101 n. 26

Bird, Thomas E., 148 n. 4, 148 n. 6

Black Hundreds, 75

Black Sea Fleet, 196

Bociurkiw, Bohdan R., x, x n. 1, 27, 27 n. 6, 43 n. 5, 47 n. 16, 48 n. 17, 58, 58 n. 1, 59 n. 2, 61 n. 9, 71 n. 40, 72 n. 42, 77 n. 4, 78 n. 5, 87, 87 n. 23, 89 n. 1, 90 n. 5, 91 n. 7, 105 n. 35, 114, 114 n. 57, 147 n. 3, 148 n. 6, 156 n. 25, 161 n. 38, 168 n. 3, 169 n. 7, 171 n. 13, 175 n. 18

Bodnarchuk, Ioan. See Ioan (Bodnarchuk)

Bogoiavlenskii, Vladimir. See Vladimir (Bogoiavlenskii)

Boiechko, Vasyl', 187 n. 37

Boiko, Iurii, 102, 102 n. 29

Bolkhovitinov, Evgenii (Orthodox metropolitan of Kyiv), 25

Bologna, 12

Bolsheviks, 43, 54, 63, 74, 76

Bondarenko, Viktor, 194, 195 n. 55

Borecky, Isidore (Ukrainian Catholic bishop of Toronto), 154, 155, 156 n. 23

Borets'kyi, Iov (Orthodox metropolitan of Kyiv), 8

Bourdeaux, Michael, 86, 86 n. 22, 156 n. 25, 175 n. 18

Bozhyk, Panteleimon, 46 n. 13

Brest, Synod of, 2, 58

Brest, Union of, xv, 2, 5 n. 6, 8, 9, 15, 16, 20, 21, 29, 34, 88, 108, 147, 149

Brest-Litovsk, Peace of, 55

Brezhnev, Leonid, 80, 91

Briukhovets'kyi, Ivan, 30

Brotherhoods, Church, 14, 15, 32, 34, 36, 38, 83, 100, 100 n. 23, 101 n. 25

Budny, Szymon, 2

Bukovyna, xii, xiv, 80, 104 n. 33, 130, 131

Bulgakov, Makarii. See Makarii (Bulgakov)

Byzantium, xiv, 28

Cairo, 68, 68 n. 33

Calvinists, 4

Canada, xvi, 40–57, 85, 86, 96, 97, 100, 111, 111 n. 50, 112, 122, 151, 153, 155, 161, 164, 183

Carpathian Mountains, 163

Serafim (Orthodox archimandrite), 42 n. 3
Sereda, Ostap, 54 n. 27
Sereda, Vasyl', 178, 181
Sergeeva, Ludmilla, 86, 86 n. 22
Serhii (Hensyts'kyi) (Orthodox bishop of Ternopil), 130
Sevastopol, 196
Ševčenko, Ihor, 8 n. 10, 87 n. 23
Shcherbakivs'kyi, Vadym, 25
Shcherbatiuk, Anatolii, 96 n. 17
Shcherbyts'kyi, Volodymyr, 172
Shchipkov, Aleksandr, 195 n. 55
Shegedi, Germanos. See Germanos (Shegedi)
Sheptyts'kyi, Andrei (Greek Catholic metropolitan of Halych), 22, 70, 71, 71 n. 40, 72, 82, 83, 152, 152 n. 13, 163, 170
Sherwood, Robert E., 63 n. 14.
Shevchenko, Oles', 134
Shevchenko, Taras, 105
Shevchuk, Liudmyla, 180 n. 29, 181 n. 31
Shpek, Roman, 186 n. 36
Shukalo, Ilarion. See Ilarion (Shukalo)
Shvets', Ihor, 115 n. 58
Shvets', Lazar. See Lazar (Shvets')
Siberia, 66 n. 25, 131 n. 2
Sigismund III (king of Poland), 29
Sitka, 42
Sitsins'kyi, Iukhym, 25
Skachko, Vladimir, 176 n. 21
Skaryna, Frantsishak, 2
Skoropads'kyi, Pavlo, 48, 48 n. 18, 55, 168, 169, 174
Skoryna, Oleksandr, 176 n. 21

Skrypnyk, Stepan. See Mstyslav (Skrypnyk)
Slipyi, Iosyf (Greek Catholic metropolitan of Halych), 60, 61, 69, 71, 71 n. 40, 72–73, 73 n. 44, 142, 146, 146 n. 1, 147, 148, 148 n. 5, 160, 163, 165
Sloboda Ukraine, 20
Slobodian, Louise, 155 n. 22, 156 n. 23
Smith, Anthony D., xiii, xiii n. 3
Smolensk, 130
Smotryts'kyi, Meletii, 2, 16, 37
Society for Contacts with Ukraininians Abroad, 79
Society for the Ukrainian Language, 114, 114 n. 56
Solchanyk, Roman, 84 n. 15
Solzhenitsyn, Aleksandr, 79
South America, 96
South Bound Brook, New Jersey, 96
Soviet Union. See USSR
Spellman, Francis (Catholic archbishop of New York), 65
SS. Borys and Hlib Church (Kyiv), 84
SS. Cyril and Methodius, Brotherhood of, 174
SS. Peter and Paul Church (Lviv), 99, 110
St. Andrew, Brotherhood of, 100, 102
St. Andrew's Church (Kyiv), 101 n. 26, 179, 179 n. 28
St. Andrew's Seminary (Winnipeg), 112 n. 53
St. Basil's Church (Kyiv), 84
St. Cyril's Church (Kyiv), 179, 179 n. 28